WILLIAM OF SHERWOOD'S
Treatise on Syncategorematic Words

translated with an introduction and notes by

NORMAN KRETZMANN

UNIVERSITY OF MINNESOTA PRESS, MINNEAPOLIS

© Copyright 1968 by the University of Minnesota. All rights reserved

Printed in the United States of America at the
Lund Press, Inc., Minneapolis

Library of Congress Catalog Card Number: 68-55599

PUBLISHED IN GREAT BRITAIN, INDIA, AND PAKISTAN BY THE OXFORD
UNIVERSITY PRESS, LONDON, BOMBAY, AND KARACHI, AND IN CANADA
BY THE COPP CLARK PUBLISHING CO. LIMITED, TORONTO

William of Sherwood's *Syncategoremata* was first printed, in Latin, in
J. Reginald O'Donnell's edition published in *Mediaeval Studies*, III
(1941), 46–93, by the Pontifical Institute of Mediaeval Studies, Toronto. This translation is published with their permission.

TO MY FATHER AND MOTHER

Preface

In this volume I am presenting an advanced treatise in medieval logic in much the same format as that in which I have already presented the corresponding elementary treatise in *William of Sherwood's Introduction to Logic* (Minneapolis: University of Minnesota Press, 1966). The most natural route to an understanding of the more difficult and more rewarding material in this book is through the introduction, translated text, and notes of that earlier volume. But because many of the problems with which Sherwood deals in his treatise on syncategorematic words closely resemble problems of twentieth-century philosophical logic and philosophy of language, a reader with some background in those inquiries and very little knowledge of medieval logic may acquire as much specialized information as he needs in the notes to this translation.

In preparing the translation I made use of J. Reginald O'Donnell's edition, published as "The Syncategoremata of William of Sherwood" in *Mediaeval Studies*, III (1941), 46–93. I am grateful to Father O'Donnell and to the Pontifical Institute of Mediaeval Studies for granting permission to publish this translation. I compared Father O'Donnell's edition with a microfilm of the better of the two surviving manuscripts of the treatise, and I wish to thank the administration of the Bibliothèque Nationale for permitting the microfilming of the manuscript.

I am grateful also to Marilyn McCord Adams and to the members of my seminars in medieval logic at Cornell University, the University of Illinois, and Wayne State University for their many helpful criticisms and suggestions; and to my wife, Barbara, who again helped in countless ways with the preparation of the book; and to Professor Gareth Matthews of the University of Minnesota and the editorial staff of the University of Minnesota Press, who were, as before, unfailing in their encouragement.

This book was already in the press when the long-awaited Volume II of L. M. De Rijk's *Logica Modernorum* appeared. As its subtitle — "The Origin and Early Development of the Theory of Supposition" — indicates, De Rijk's Volume II provides historical material directly relevant to Chapter Five of *William of Sherwood's Introduction to Logic* and to the whole of the present treatise. If I had had access to it while preparing these two books on Sherwood's logic, I am sure I should have found it even more valuable than De Rijk's Volume I — "On the Twelfth Century Theories of Fallacy" — which I so frequently cite. Research in twelfth- and thirteenth-century logic will for a long time to come take the two volumes of De Rijk's *Logica Modernorum* as its point of departure. I urge the reader of this book to familiarize himself with De Rijk's work, particularly with his Volume II.

Since the publication of *William of Sherwood's Introduction to Logic*, I have received many discerning criticisms and comments on it from Professor Peter Geach. Because of the close connection between that earlier book and this one it seems appropriate and valuable to present here some of the more important corrections Professor Geach has communicated to me.

Page 64, note 30: The syllogistic reduction employed by Sherwood here is *not* mistaken. Conversion of the premisses of *Fapesmo* yields a *weaker* pair of premisses; if the conclusion follows from this pair, then *a fortiori* it follows from the original pair. This shows that since *Ferio* is acceptable, *Fapesmo* is so as well. But the converse does not hold; what follows from the (stronger) premisses of *Fapesmo* need not on that account follow from the corresponding (weaker) premisses of *Ferio*.

Page 83: A scribe's error has evidently caused a '*nisi*' to be dropped from the Latin provided in parentheses at the end of Section 3.2.6. It should be emended to read ". . . *nec fiunt plura nisi adverbialiter* . . ." The corresponding English would then read "and they become many only adverbially . . ." Some of the difficulties discussed in note 64 are thereby alleviated.

Page 101: In the example at the end of Section 5.1 the premiss "*sedens est albus*" is to be translated not as 'seated is a white man' but as 'one who is sitting is white.'

Page 118: A printer's error has caused the correct second line of Rule V (on page 119) to appear incorrectly as the second line of Rule IV. The second line of Rule IV should read "*supposition does not follow, but* [*only*] *to merely confused supposition.*"

Page 119: The Latin provided in parentheses at the end of Section 13.4 — "*ut si videat unum solum*" — is to be translated not as 'as if there is only one he might see' but as 'e.g., if Socrates sees one man only.'

Page 128: The final sentence of Section 16.3 is misinterpreted and most of the attempted explanation in note 94 is on the wrong track. The sentence should read "A common term standing before [a future-tense verb] supposits for either present or future things as a consequence of composition and division, but when standing after [the verb] it supposits only for future things." 'Socrates will see something white' is an example of the second (*ex parte post*) case; in it 'something white' supposits only for such white things as there will be at that future time. 'Something white will be seen by Socrates' is an example of the first (*ex parte ante*) case; in it 'something white' may supposit, in the compounded sense, for such white things as there will be at that future time or, in the divided sense, for such white things as there are now, at least one of which (although it may then no longer be white) will be seen by Socrates at that future time.

Page 130, note 102: The compounded sense is misstated. It should be 'it is, or it is possible for it to be, the case that there is at least one individual such that it is a man and it is running.'

Pages 141–142: The translation beginning with the last two lines of text on page 141 should be revised in the following way. "For in that case 'a white thing' is divided from the predicate 'is' (an omnitemporal verb) by the word 'possible.' As a result, 'a white thing' does not derive its supposition from the 'is,' so as to supposit for white things belonging to the time [consignified by the omnitemporal verb — i.e., any and every time]; instead it supposits for those things that are white now. Consequently, the minor premiss [taken as] divided is true; and since the premiss [taken as] compounded is one and the same with respect to the substance [of discourse], people believe that it is one and the same absolutely and that it signifies the same [whether taken as divided or as compounded]. And just as it would be a good syllogism if it were taken as compounded, they believe that it is good taken as divided."

NORMAN KRETZMANN

Cornell University
July 1968

Table of Contents

TRANSLATOR'S INTRODUCTION ... 3

WILLIAM OF SHERWOOD'S INTRODUCTION ... 13

CHAPTER I. 'EVERY' OR 'ALL' (*OMNIS*) ... 17
  1. The Signification of 'Every' or 'All' ... 17
  2. Specific and Numerical Parts ... 18
  3. 'Every' or 'All' Taken Properly and Taken Commonly ... 20
  4. Proximate and Remote Parts ... 22
  5. The Rule of Three ... 23
  6. A Doubt Regarding the Rule of Three ... 24
  7. 'Every' or 'All' Attached to a Discrete Term ... 25
  8. 'Every' or 'All' Added to a Common Term Known to Have Exactly One Appellatum ... 26
  9. 'Every' or 'All' Added to a Predicate ... 27
  10. 'Every' or 'All' Added to a Term Involving a Clause or Phrase ... 28
  11. 'Another' within the Scope of 'Every' or 'All' ... 29
  12. 'When' within the Scope of 'Every' or 'All' ... 30
  13. The Effect of the Location of 'Every' or 'All' on Supposition ... 31
  14. An Illicit Transformation of a *Quale Quid* into a *Hoc Aliquid* ... 32
  15. Another Example of Such Illicit Transformation ... 33
  16. 'Himself' within the Scope of 'Every' or 'All' ... 34

17. The Immobilization of One Distribution by Another	35
18. A Second Example of Such Immobilization	36
19. A Third Example of Such Immobilization	37
20. 'Only One' within the Scope of 'Every' or 'All'	38
21. 'Every' or 'All' Taken Collectively and Taken Distributively	39
22. Other Universal Affirmative Signs	40

CHAPTER II. 'WHOLE' (*TOTUM*)   40

CHAPTER III. NUMBER WORDS (*DICTIONES NUMERALES*)   41

CHAPTER IV. 'INFINITELY MANY' (*INFINITA IN PLURALI*)   41

1. 'Infinitely Many' and Number Words	41
2. 'Infinitely Many' and 'Finitely Many'	42

CHAPTER V. 'BOTH' (*UTERQUE*)   43

CHAPTER VI. 'OF EVERY SORT' (*QUALELIBET*)   44

1. Signs Distributive of Copulata	44
2. 'Of Every Sort' Used Categorematically and Syncategorematically	44
3. 'Of Every Sort' in Combination with Other Distributive Signs	46
4. Logical Descent in Connection with a Sign Distributive of Copulata	47

CHAPTER VII. 'NO' (*NULLUS*)   48

1. Specific and Numerical Parts	48
2. Proximate and Remote Parts	49
3. The Scope of the Negation Belonging to 'No'	49
4. Another Example Regarding the Scope of Such Negation	50
5. A Term Involving a Clause or Phrase within the Scope of 'No'	52
6. Whether Attaching 'No' to a Term Causes It to Stand for Nonexistents	52
7. A Third Example Regarding the Scope of the Negation Belonging to 'No'	53

CHAPTER VIII. 'NOTHING' (*NIHIL*)   54

1. The Scope of the Negation Belonging to 'Nothing'	54

    2. The Immobilization of One Negative Word by Another   55
    3. The Illicit Use of 'Nothing' as a Name   56

CHAPTER IX. 'NEITHER' (*NEUTRUM*)   57

CHAPTER X. 'BUT' (*PRAETER*)   58
    1. Reasons for Discussing 'But' at This Point   58
    2. 'But' Taken Diminutionally and Taken Counter-instantively   58
    3. A Doubt Regarding the Additive and Exceptive Uses of 'But'   59
    4. A Confusion of the Diminutional and Counter-instantive Uses of 'But'   59
    5. A Second Example of Such Confusion   60
    6. 'But' Used Exceptively on 'Whole'   60
    7. Immobilization by Means of 'But'   61
    8. Excepting as Many Things as Are Supposited   63
    9. A Second Example of Excepting as Many Things as Are Supposited   63
    10. A Third Example of Excepting as Many Things as Are Supposited   64
    11. The Absence of Confused Supposition from a Term Designating Something Excepted   64
    12. Immobilization of a Term in Respect of Which an Exception Is Made   65
    13. The Misuse of Exception as a Means of Rendering a Wholly False Statement True   66
    14. Contrasting Truth-values in Exceptive Statements and Their Non-exceptive Originals   66
    15. Immobilization by Means of Exception in Cases Involving More than One Division   66
    16. Ambiguity in Cases Involving Exception and More than One Division   67
    17. The Exceptive 'But' Together with the Copulative 'And'   68
    18. Exception in Cases Involving More than One Time   68

CHAPTER XI. 'ALONE' (*SOLUS*)   69
    1. Reasons for Discussing 'Alone' at This Point   69
    2. 'Alone' Used Categorematically and Syncategorematically   69

3. Why 'Alone' Is Better Added to a Discrete than to a Common Term	70
4. A Supposed Pluralizing Effect of 'Alone'	71
5. A Supposed Negating Effect of 'Alone'	71
6. A Supposed Including Effect of 'Alone'	71
7. 'Alone' Excluding Generally and Specifically	72
8. Immobilization as a Result of Exclusion in the Subject	73
9. Immobilization of a Division by Means of a Preceding Exclusion	74
10. Exclusion in the Subject with One of the Terms Involving a Clause or Phrase	75
11. The Exclusive 'Alone' Together with the Copulative 'And'	76
12. Two Ways in Which a Clause or Phrase Involved in the Subject Term Can Fall under an Exclusion	77
13. The Effect of One Exclusion upon Another	77
14. A Second Example of the Effect of One Exclusion upon Another	78
15. 'Alone' Together with Number Words	78
16. The Effect of the Relative Location of Words Indicating Exclusion and Division	79
17. A Second Example of the Exclusive 'Alone' Together with the Copulative 'And'	80
18. A Third Example of the Exclusive 'Alone' Together with the Copulative 'And'	80
CHAPTER XII. 'ONLY' (*TANTUM*)	81
1. 'Only' Used Categorematically and Syncategorematically	81
2. A Doubt Regarding the Determination of a Subject by Means of an Adverb	81
3. A Comparison of 'Only' and 'Alone'	82
4. 'Only' Adjoined to a Number Term	82
5. 'Only' Added to a Copulated Term	82
6. 'Only' Adjoined to a Disjoined Term	83
7. 'Only' Adjoined to a Concrete Term	84
8. Another Example of 'Only' Adjoined to a Concrete Term	85
9. Systematic Ambiguity in Connection with 'Only'	86

10. That around Which and That in Respect
of Which Exclusion Occurs 86

11. A Second Example Having to Do with That Distinction 87

12. A Third Example Having to Do with That Distinction 88

13. An Example Having to Do with That Distinction
in Connection with 'Alone' 88

14. An Example Having to Do with That Distinction in Connection
with 'Alone' and 'And' 89

15. An Explanation of the Occurrence of Exclusion
in Respect of Different Things 89

CHAPTER XIII. 'IS' (*EST*) 90

1. Whether 'Is' Is a Syncategorematic Word 90

2. The Status of 'Is' Occurring as a Third Ingredient 91

3. 'Is' Indicating Actual Being and Conditional Being 92

CHAPTER XIV. 'NOT' (*NON*) 93

1. Whether 'Not' and 'Is' Are Opposed 93

2. Negation of a Term and Negation of a Composition 94

3. 'Not' Taken Extinctively and Otherwise 95

4. Negative Propositions with Many Causes of Truth 95

5. More Examples of Negative Propositions
with Many Causes of Truth 96

6. Negation Giving Rise to Supposition for Nonexistents 98

7. The Effect of Negation on an Inference
from an Inferior to a Superior 99

CHAPTER XV. 'NECESSARILY' (*NECESSARIO*)
AND 'CONTINGENTLY' (*CONTINGENTER*) 100

1. 'Necessarily' and 'Contingently' Used Categorematically
and Syncategorematically 100

2. 'Necessarily' as a Note of Coherence and
as a Note of Inherence 102

3. 'Necessarily' Together with the Exclusive 'Only' 103

4. 'Necessarily' Together with the Exclusive 'Alone' 103

5. 'Necessarily' Together with the Distributive Sign 'Every' 104

6. 'Of Necessity' Together with the Distributive Sign 'Every' 105

CHAPTER XVI. 'BEGINS' (*INCIPIT*) AND 'CEASES' (*DESINIT*) 106

1. 'Begins' and 'Ceases' Used Categorematically and Syncategorematically 106
2. 'Begins' a Syncategorematic Word despite Grammatical Appearances 108
3. The Expositions of 'Begins' and 'Ceases' 108
4. Immobilization Resulting from an Occurrence of 'Begins' or 'Ceases' 110
5. Confused Supposition Resulting from an Occurrence of 'Begins' or 'Ceases' 111
6. Ambiguity Resulting from the Possibility of Fixed-state or Successive-state Expositions of 'Begins' or 'Ceases' 113
7. Ambiguity Resulting from the Compounded/Divided Distinction in Connection with 'Begins' or 'Ceases' 114
8. A Second Example of Such Ambiguity 115
9. A Third Example of Such Ambiguity 115
10. An Inference from an Inferior to a Superior Acceptable under a Categorematic Use of 'Begins' or 'Ceases' 116

CHAPTER XVII. 'IF' (*SI*) 116

1. Conjunctions and Prepositions 116
2. The Difference between 'If' and 'It Follows' 117
3. Why 'If' Is Not Attached to the Consequent Although It Indicates Consequence 118
4. How 'Antecedent' and 'Consequent' Are to Be Understood in Connection with Consequence 118
5. Truth and Falsity in Conditional Propositions 118
6. Conditional Propositions and Categorical Propositions with Conditioned Predicates 120
7. Another Example Involving That Distinction 122
8. Conditional Propositions Distinguished from Categorical Propositions with Conditioned Subjects 122
9. Ambiguity Resulting from the Occurrence of a Relative Clause in the Antecedent 122
10. 'If' Noting Consequences Absolutely and under the Prevailing Circumstances 123
11. Necessary and Merely True Consequences 123

12. Natural and Nonnatural Consequences	123
13. Ambiguity Resulting from Multiple Occurrences of 'If'	124
14. Ambiguity Resulting from Exclusion or Negation in Conditionals	124
15. Ambiguity Resulting from Modes in Conditionals	125
16. Immobilization in the Antecedent but Not in the Consequent	125
17. Ascent and Descent in Undistributed Antecedents and Consequents	125
18. A Paradoxical Chain of Consequences	126
19. A Second Paradoxical Chain of Consequences	126
20. A Third Paradoxical Chain of Consequences	127
21. A Fourth Paradoxical Chain of Consequences	128
CHAPTER XVIII. 'UNLESS' (*NISI*)	**129**
1. The Logical and Grammatical Character of 'Unless'	129
2. 'Unless' Taken as a Consecutive Conjunction	129
3. 'Unless' Taken as an Exceptive Word	130
4. Ambiguity Resulting from Taking 'Unless' as a Consecutive or as an Exceptive	131
CHAPTER XIX. 'BUT THAT' (*QUIN*)	**133**
CHAPTER XX. 'AND' (*ET*)	**134**
1. The Signification and Function of 'And'	134
2. Copulating between Terms or between Propositions in a Single Sentence Involving Exclusion	134
3. A Second Example of Such Copulating	135
4. A Third Example of Such Copulating	136
5. A Distinction Giving Rise to Different Analyses in That Third Example	136
6. Copulating between an Affirmative Term and a Term Together with a Non-infinitating Negation	137
7. 'And' Taken Divisively and Taken Conjunctively	137
8. Copulating a Whole Expression in Indirect Discourse or Only a Part Thereof	138
9. A Second Example of Such Copulating	138

10. Whether a Copulative Proposition Can Be Negated
by a Single Negation 139

11. Whether a Copulative Proposition Is More than One Proposition 139

CHAPTER XXI. 'OR' (*VEL*) 140

1. 'Or' Taken as a Disjunctive and as a Subdisjunctive 140

2. Various Ways in Which 'Or' Disjoins 141

3. Ambiguity Resulting from a Disjunction Together
with a Division 142

4. A Second Difficulty in Connection with Such Ambiguity 143

5. A Third Difficulty in Connection with Such Ambiguity 143

6. A Fourth Difficulty in Connection with Such Ambiguity 144

7. A Fifth Difficulty in Connection with Such Ambiguity 144

8. A Sixth Difficulty in Connection with Such Ambiguity 145

9. A Second Example of Ambiguity Resulting from a Disjunction
Together with a Division 145

10. A Third Example of Such Ambiguity 145

11. Special Difficulties for Inductive Proofs in Connection
with Disjunction 146

12. Ambiguity Resulting from the Occurrence of a Modal Word
Together with a Disjunction 147

13. Whether a Disjunctive Proposition Is More than
One Proposition 148

CHAPTER XXII. 'WHETHER' OR 'OR' (*AN*) 148

1. The Signification and Function of '*An*' 148

2. The Difference between '*An*' and '*Vel*' 149

3. '*An*' Disjoining Differently Depending on Its Occurring Once
Only or Twice 150

4. The Effect of '*An*' on Inferences Involving Contraries,
Privatives, Relatives, or Contradictories 150

5. The Effect on Inferences of the Location of '*An*' Relative to a
Universal Sign 151

6. A Second Example of That Effect 151

7. A Third Example of That Effect 152

8. The Effect of '*An*' on Inferences in Which a Relative Pronoun
Is Permuted from the Predicate into the Subject 154

9. The Effect of '*An*' on Inferences from an Inferior to a Superior 154

10. A Second Example of the Effect of '*An*' on Inferences Involving Contraries 155

CHAPTER XXIII. THE PARTICLE '*NE*' 156

CHAPTER XXIV. 'WHETHER . . . OR . . .' (*SIVE*) 157

1. The Combination of a Disjunction and a Condition in '*Sive*' 157

2. A Second Example of That Combination 157

BIBLIOGRAPHY 161

INDEX 163

TRANSLATOR'S INTRODUCTION

Translator's Introduction

This book may be studied independently, but in several respects it is a companion volume to my *William of Sherwood's Introduction to Logic* (hereafter cited as *WSIL*).[1] Some of what Sherwood says in that elementary textbook is presupposed by what he has to say in this advanced treatise, and the notes to the present translation frequently refer to specific passages in the earlier translation.

Since I discuss Sherwood's life and writings at some length in the Introduction to *WSIL*, I shall provide only a brief survey here.[2]

William of Sherwood (or Shyreswood) was an English logician of the thirteenth century. Almost all that is definitely known of his life is that in 1252 he was a master at Oxford, that he became treasurer of the cathedral church of Lincoln soon after 1254, that he was rector of Aylesbury (in Buckinghamshire) and of Attleborough (in Norfolk), that he was still living in 1266, and that he was dead by 1272. From references in his works, however, and from the fact that his logic almost certainly had a direct influence on the logical writings of Peter of Spain, Lambert of Auxerre, Albert the Great, and Thomas Aquinas, all of whom were at Paris around the same time, it seems undeniable that Sherwood taught logic there from about 1235 to about 1250.

Sherwood's impact on his contemporaries went unacknowledged except by Roger Bacon, who, in his *Opus tertium* (1267), described him as "much wiser than Albert [the Great]; for in *philosophia communis* no one

---

[1] See Bibliography.
[2] The two paragraphs following are adopted with a few changes from my article "William of Sherwood" in *The Encyclopedia of Philosophy*, Vol. VIII, pp. 317–318. A more detailed account appears in *WSIL*, pp. 3–12.

is greater than he." Bacon's phrase *'philosophia communis'* must refer to logic; no other kind of work can be definitely attributed to Sherwood, and his logical works do seem to have been influential. They consist of an *Introductiones in logicam*,[3] a *Syncategoremata*,[4] a *De insolubilibus* (on paradoxes of self-reference), an *Obligationes* (on rules of argument for formal disputation),[5] and a *Petitiones contrariorum* (on logical puzzles arising from hidden contrariety in the premisses of an inference). Only the first two have ever been printed; they are longer and far more important than the last three. A commentary on the *Sentences* of Peter Lombard, a *Distinctiones theologicae*, and a *Conciones* (a collection of sermons) have also been attributed to Sherwood, but the only surviving works definitely by him are the five logical treatises.

The historical importance of Sherwood's work in logic has yet to be fully assessed, but some appreciation of it may be gained by viewing it against the background of the development of medieval logic.[6]

Until about the middle of the twelfth century, the subject matter of medieval logic was drawn from Aristotle's *Categories* and *De interpretatione*, together with a set of books by Porphyry and Boethius that were centered more or less closely around those two books of Aristotle. Later in the middle ages this collection of books, or the kind of logic these books contained, became known as *logica vetus*, the old logic. When the remaining four books of Aristotle's Organon began to circulate in western Europe during the twelfth century, they, or their contents, became known as *logica nova*, the new logic. The only completely new kind of material in the *logica nova* was the treatment of fallacy in Aristotle's *Sophistical Refutations*, which excited a tremendous interest in sophismata, arguments turning on the misuse of or natural ambiguities in various devices of ordinary discourse.[7] Largely because of this lasting interest, logicians of the

---

[3] Printed for the first time in 1937 in an edition by Martin Grabmann (see Bibliography); translated and annotated in *WSIL*.

[4] Printed for the first time in 1941 in an edition by J. Reginald O'Donnell (see Bibliography); translated and annotated in the present volume.

[5] Professor C. L. Hamblin of The University of New South Wales, Kensington, Australia, has very kindly informed me that a critical text of the *Obligationes*, together with the *Obligationes* of Walter Burleigh, was prepared in 1963 by Fr. Romuald Green (now of the Franciscan Seminary at Mornington, Victoria, Australia) for a doctorate at Louvain. My efforts to obtain a copy of this text have so far been unsuccessful.

[6] The two paragraphs following are adopted with a few changes from the section entitled "The Properties of Terms" (pp. 371–373) in my article "Semantics, History of" in *The Encyclopedia of Philosophy*, Vol. VII, pp. 358–406.

[7] Sophismata are discussed in more detail in Chapter I, n. 18 below.

late twelfth and early thirteenth centuries gradually developed an original logico-semantic inquiry. In order to distinguish this genuinely medieval contribution from Aristotle's contributions to logic, thirteenth-century philosophers began to speak of it as the *logica moderna*, lumping the *logica vetus* and *logica nova* together as the *logica antiqua*. Perhaps the *logica moderna* aimed originally at nothing more than providing *ad hoc* rules regarding inferences that involve problematic locutions of ordinary discourse; in any case it certainly retained that aim throughout its three-hundred–year history. But its principal aim soon became the development of a more or less general account of the various ways in which words are used to stand for things or to operate on other words so as to affect the way in which those other words stand for things.

William of Sherwood, Peter of Spain (d. 1277), and Lambert of Auxerre (fl. 1250) are among the earliest full-fledged "modernist" or "terminist" logicians. At Sherwood's time the *logica moderna* seems to have been thought of as having two branches, an account of "the properties of terms" (*proprietates terminorum*) and an account of the signification and function of "syncategorematic words" (*syncategoremata*). The two branches naturally differed in detail, and to a considerable extent the second depended on the first, but both accounts employed the same principles of explanation and had the same general aims. Most nouns, pronouns, verbs, participles, and adjectives were considered to be categorematic words, words capable of serving as subject terms or as predicate terms. The syncategorematic words were those that can occur in a statement only together with categorematic words. The two branches of the *logica moderna* were thus theoretically exhaustive of the kinds of words occurring in various roles in statements.

Sherwood deals with the first branch of the *logica moderna* — the properties of terms — in the fifth chapter of his *Introductiones* (*WSIL*, pp. 105–131). He recognizes four properties of terms: signification, supposition, copulation, and appellation. Some understanding of these notions and their interrelations is essential for a thorough understanding of Sherwood's treatment of syncategorematic words. I have tried to provide enough information about them at appropriate points in the notes to the translation below, but the reader would do well to acquire at least a general knowledge of them before studying this treatise.[8]

---

[8] See, e.g., Kneale's *Development of Logic* (hereafter cited as *Development*), pp. 246–274; or the much briefer survey cited in n. 6 above. The notes to the translation

There can be no serious doubt that Sherwood wrote his treatise on syncategorematic words after he had written the *Introductiones*. The *Syncategoremata* is an advanced treatise that draws on doctrines developed in the elementary text, particularly on those developed in Chapter Five, "Properties of Terms," and in Chapter Six, "Sophistical Reasoning." But, although Sherwood exhibits a higher level of logical sophistication in applying those doctrines in this treatise, he regularly omits details and ignores technical distinctions he had laid down in the earlier book (as the notes to the translation below will indicate). These features of the two books lead me to think that considerable time elapsed between the completion of the *Introductiones* and the writing of this treatise.

There are obviously close relations between Sherwood's logic and that of Peter of Spain, and the received view is that Sherwood's work antedates and influences Peter's. As regards Sherwood's *Introductiones* and Peter's elementary text, the *Summulae logicales*,[9] that is virtually certain. Many of the features of the *Summulae* that made it far and away the most popular logic textbook in the middle ages seem quite plainly to have developed as modifications of more difficult discussions and less felicitous mnemonic devices in the *Introductiones*.[10] But Peter also wrote a *Tractatus syncategorematum*,[11] and though I do not have evidence for more than a conjecture on this point, there are features of his two logic books and of Sherwood's that suggest that Peter's books may have been written in the interval between Sherwood's *Introductiones* and his *Syncategoremata*. Tractatus VII, the last in Peter's *Summulae*, is devoted expressly to the properties of terms. But its last two sections include material, on "distributions" and on "exponible propositions," that Sherwood considered in detail only in his *Syncategoremata*. Some of this material Peter discusses again in his *Tractatus syncategorematum*, and some of it is discussed only in those concluding sections of his *Summulae*. Both in its looser organization and in the character of much of its discussion, Peter's work on syncategorematic words appears to be earlier than Sherwood's. Moreover, there are passages

---

below provide a good deal of information about the background and development of inquiries into syncategorematic words, the second branch of the *logica moderna*, but a general introductory discussion may be found in the section entitled "Syncategoremata" (pp. 373–374) in my article "Semantics, History of" (see n. 6 above).

[9] See Bibliography below for Bocheński's edition and Mullally's partial edition and translation of this text.
[10] See, e.g., *WSIL*, p. 38, n. 54, and p. 39, n. 56.
[11] See Bibliography for Mullally's translation of this treatise.

in Sherwood's treatise that can be read as allusions to positions taken by Peter, as the notes to the translation below will show.[12] Whatever the actual historical relation of these writings to one another may be,[13] the study of either man's work on syncategorematic words is greatly aided by a close comparison with the work of the other. The following list indicates the passages in Peter of Spain that parallel the chapters of Sherwood's treatise on syncategorematic words.[14]

Sherwood's		Peter of Spain's
Introduction		TS 17
Ch. I	'Every' or 'all'	SL (Tr. Dis.) 63–81
Ch. II	'Whole'	SL (Tr. Dis.) 91–95; (Tr. Exp.) 127–129
Ch. III	Number words	. . .
Ch. IV	'Infinitely many'	SL (Tr. Dis.) 99–103; (Tr. Exp.) 119–123
Ch. V	'Both'	SL (Tr. Dis.) 83–87
Ch. VI	'Of every sort'	SL (Tr. Dis.) 95–97; (Tr. Exp.) 129
Ch. VII	'No'	SL (Tr. Dis.) 79–81; TS 25–26
Ch. VIII	'Nothing'	SL (Tr. Dis.) 81–83; TS 27
Ch. IX	'Neither'	SL (Tr. Dis.) 87
Ch. X	'But'	SL (Tr. Exp.) 109–111; TS 41–50
Ch. XI	'Alone'	TS 29–41
Ch. XII	'Only'	SL (Tr. Exp.) 105–109; TS 29–41
Ch. XIII	'Is'	TS 20–21
Ch. XIV	'Not'	SL (Tr. Dis.) 87–89; TS 21–29
Ch. XV	'Necessarily' and 'Contingently'	TS 65–73
Ch. XVI	'Begins' and 'Ceases'	SL (Tr. Exp.) 115–119; TS 58–65
Ch. XVII	'If'	TS 50–58
Ch. XVIII	'Unless'	TS 83–90
Ch. XIX	'But that'	TS 93–104

---

[12] The difficult question of the historical relations among these four treatises is further complicated by such passages as the one quoted from *Summulae logicales* in Chapter VII, n. 11 below, in which Peter of Spain *may* be referring to Sherwood's *Syncategoremata* and alluding to Sherwood himself as one of the "*antiqui.*"

[13] In all probability neither Peter nor Sherwood was the first logician to write systematically on syncategorematic words. Regarding the many thirteenth- and fourteenth-century treatises on syncategorematic words see Prantl's *Geschichte der Logik im Abendlande*, especially Vol. III, and Grabmann's "Bearbeitungen und Auslegungen der aristotelischen Logik aus der Zeit von Peter Abaelard bis Petrus Hispanus . . . ," p. 7.

[14] *TS*: Mullally's translation of Peter's *Tractatus syncategorematum*; *SL*: Mullally's translation of Tractatus VII of Peter's *Summulae logicales*; Tr. Dis.: "*Tractatus distributionum*"; Tr. Exp.: "*Tractatus exponibilium.*"

> Ch. XX   'And'   *TS* 80–83
> Ch. XXI   'Or'   *TS* 77–79
> Ch. XXII 'Whether' or 'or'   *TS* 73–77
> Ch. XXIII The particle '*ne*'   . . .
> Ch. XXIV 'Whether . . . or   . . .
> . . .'

Much of the organization of Sherwood's treatise as presented in the Table of Contents above is not to be found in the manuscripts or in O'Donnell's edition. Most of the chapter headings are supplied in the Latin text, but the chapters are not designated as such or numbered or divided into sections.[15]

From transitional passages in the treatise it is apparent that Sherwood thought of its contents as organized in a schema that groups the present chapters in the following way.

> Syncategorematic words associated with the subject
> > Distributive signs
> > > Affirmative
> > > > Distributive of supposita (Chs. I–V)
> > > > Distributive of copulata (Ch. VI)
> > > Negative (Chs. VII–IX)
> > Exceptive and exclusive signs (Chs. X–XII)
> Syncategorematic words pertaining to the composition of the predicate with the subject (Chs. XIII–XV)
> Syncategorematic words associated with the predicate (Ch. XVI)
> Syncategorematic words pertaining to one subject in respect of another, or to one predicate in respect of another, or to one composition in respect of another
> > Consecutive conjunctions (Chs. XVII–XIX)
> > Copulative conjunctions (Ch. XX)
> > Disjunctive conjunctions (Chs. XXI–XXIV)

The treatise is written in a rather informal scholastic style and evidently derives fairly closely from a course conducted by Sherwood at Paris or at Oxford. The medieval style of university instruction by debate is reflected in the format,[16] which makes it reasonable to approach the treatise as if it were the edited transcript of a seminar in philosophical logic. Sherwood's

---

[15] Further information on this organization and the basis for it in the Latin text will be found in the notes to the translation.

[16] See Chapter I, n. 9 below.

statements of his own position can often be picked out by the scholastic prefatory formula "it must be said that" (*dicendum quod*).[17]

Two manuscripts of the treatise survive, one at Paris and the other at Oxford.[18] In the Paris manuscript the *Syncategoremata* occurs immediately after Sherwood's *Introductiones* and immediately before his other three treatises. No other works by him occur in the Oxford manuscript. In his edition of the *Syncategoremata* J. R. O'Donnell says, "The two manuscripts are evidently in close relationship. The Paris manuscript has been carefully corrected; the Oxford manuscript has not been touched. Time and time again the Paris manuscript has deletions with marginal or superscript corrections, where Oxford has the reading which was deleted in the Paris manuscript. . . . I have followed the manuscript of Paris as being the better, especially since it has been so carefully corrected. In a few cases I have chosen the reading of Oxford as the more suitable and have noted it in the footnotes." [19] My translation is based on O'Donnell's edition and on the Paris manuscript, to which I have had access in a microfilm supplied by the Bibliothèque Nationale through the Library of the University of Illinois. I have not seen the Oxford manuscript. The notes to the translation cite discrepancies between the edition and the Paris manuscript only when they are not merely variants noted by O'Donnell between the Paris and the Oxford manuscripts and only when they are relatively obtrusive (e.g., not discrepancies in punctuation).

The translation is rather heavily annotated, and the density of notes is especially high in Chapter I, where so many technical notions are introduced for the first time. Nevertheless, I have tried to provide only as much explanatory material as seemed necessary for working one's way into a thirteenth-century discussion, and to avoid using the notes to develop a full commentary on the logical and semantic issues presented in the treatise. If I have succeeded in making this medieval presentation of those issues accessible to twentieth-century students of philosophy, they will, I believe, readily see the relevance of them to contemporary philosophical discussions.

---

[17] See Sherwood's Introduction, n. 14 below.
[18] Paris: Bibliothèque Nationale MS. Lat. 16,617; formerly Sorbonne 1797. Oxford: Bodleian MS. Digby 55, ff. 206–225.
[19] P. 46 of his edition.

WILLIAM OF SHERWOOD'S
Treatise on Syncategorematic Words

Syncategorematic Words

INTRODUCTION

In order to understand anything one must understand its parts; thus in order that the statement (*enuntiatio*) [1] may be fully understood one must understand the parts of it. Its parts are of two kinds: principal and secondary. The principal parts are the substantival name and the verb, for they are necessary for an understanding of the statement. The secondary parts are the adjectival name, the adverb, and conjunctions and prepositions,[2] for they are not necessary for the statement's being.[3]

---

[1] Near the beginning of his *Introductiones in logicam* (hereafter cited as *Introductiones*) Sherwood distinguishes between a statement (*enuntiatio*) and a proposition (*propositio*), saying that "what is a statement considered in itself is a proposition considered as it is [a premiss] in a syllogism" (*WSIL*, p. 22). Both in *Introductiones* and in this treatise, however, Sherwood tends to use 'statement' and 'proposition' interchangeably.

[2] Except for adjectives (adjectival names) the secondary parts listed here are traditionally classified as "indeclinables." In his *Introductiones* Sherwood says of indeclinables that "speaking strictly, they do not signify but consignify; that is, they signify together with another [word]. For what they signify they signify insofar as they are dispositions of something else" (*WSIL*, p. 24), and also that "none of these three [properties of terms] – supposition, copulation, appellation – is in the indeclinable parts of speech (since no indeclinable part signifies a substance or anything in a substance)" (*WSIL*, p. 106). Some of these earlier views of Sherwood's conflict with what he has to say about indeclinables in this treatise, as we shall see.

[3] This paragraph presents a confusion of two distinct principles of division for "principal" and "secondary" parts: principal parts are necessary and secondary parts are not necessary for (I) *the understanding*, (II) *the being* of the statement. But there are several good reasons for thinking that Principle II is the one intended throughout and that the apparent confusion is the result of a scribe's error: (1) Sherwood has begun by announcing that for an understanding of the statement an understanding of the parts of the statement is necessary. Thus it will not do to try now to distinguish one *kind* of part as necessary for an understanding of the statement,

[13]

Some secondary parts are determinations [4] of principal parts in respect
of the things belonging to them; [5] these [secondary parts] are not syncate-

---

more especially because this entire treatise is devoted to providing an understanding
of the *other* kind of part, the kind that on Principle I would evidently be *un*necessary
for an understanding of the statement. (2) Principle II is the one suggested by the
passage in Priscian that introduced the medievals to the notion of *syncategoremata*:
"According to the dialecticians, therefore, there are two [principal(?)] parts of the
sentence (*orationis*) — the noun and the verb — since they alone and of themselves
make a sentence; but they called the other parts *syncategoremata* — i.e., consignif-
icants" (II, 54, 5). (3) Principle II is the one employed by Sherwood himself in his
Introductiones: "Now, since we are to consider the statement, the first thing we have
to consider is its parts, the noun and the verb. These are called the parts of the statement because it is possible for a statement to be made up of them and of nothing
else" (*WSIL*, p. 22). This sort of observation about substantival names and verbs
dates back at least to Plato, who notes that "the simplest and shortest possible kind"
of statement is exemplified in 'Theaetetus sits.' Such a combination "gives information about facts or events; . . . it does not merely name something but gets you
somewhere by weaving together verbs and names. Hence we say it *states* something"
(*Sophist* 262A–D). (4) Correcting the confusion in this opening paragraph requires
the following emendation: for "*necessaria sunt ad hoc ut cognoscatur enuntiatio*"
read "*necessaria sunt ad esse enuntiationis*" and revise the translation to read "for
they are necessary for the being of the statement." (The grossness of the error is
perhaps explained by the occurrence of the similar phrase "*ut plene cognoscatur
enuntiatio*" three lines earlier in the Paris manuscript.)

[4] *Determinatio* is a technical notion in medieval logic, evidently deriving originally
from Aristotle, *Categories* 3b10ff: "Every substance seems to signify a certain 'this.'
As regards the primary substances, it is indisputably true that each of them signifies
a certain 'this'; for the thing revealed is individual and numerically one. But as regards the secondary substances, though it appears from the form of the name — when
one speaks of man or animal — that a secondary substance likewise signifies a certain
'this,' this is not really true; rather it signifies a certain qualification, for the subject
is not, as the primary substance is, one, but man and animal are said of many things.
However, *it does not signify simply a certain qualification*, as white does. White signifies nothing but a qualification, whereas the species and the genus *mark off* [i.e., de-
terminate] *the qualification of substance — they signify substance of a certain qualification*" (J. L. Ackrill translation). Cf. Abelard, *Dialectica*, ed. De Rijk, pp. 111–112:
"The *signification* of words, with which we intend to deal, is taken in several ways.
In one way it occurs as a result of *imposition*; thus for example the word 'man' signifies mortal rational animal, to which the name has been given through imposition.
In another way signification occurs as a result of *determination*; thus for example
when 'rational' or 'man' are subjects *they name substances about which they also
determinate rationality*. Thus Aristotle says in the *Categories*, "*genus et species
qualitatem circa substantiam determinant*" — i.e., the genus and the species are im-
posed on it in accordance with that which is formed by the quality and they show of
what sort it is." In his discussion of the effects of "adverbial modes" in *Introductiones* (*WSIL*, pp. 41–42) Sherwood introduces a distinction between kinds of determination very much like the distinction between nonsyncategorematic and syncategorematic determination offered in this and the next paragraph.

[5] The "things belonging to" a substantival name or a verb are the individual entities of which the name or verb can be truly predicated. If 'Socrates is a man' and
'Socrates is running' are true, then Socrates is one of the things belonging to 'man'
and to 'run.' Thus "in case 'some man is an animal' is false, that predicate cannot be
in any singular belonging to that subject" (*WSIL*, p. 32).

gorematic words (*syncategoremata*). For example, when I say 'white man' the word 'white' [6] signifies that some thing belonging to 'man' is white.[7] Other [secondary parts] are determinations of principal parts insofar as they are subjects or predicates.[8] For example, when I say 'every man is running' the word 'every,' which is a universal sign,[9] does not signify that some thing belonging to 'man' is universal,[10] but rather that 'man' is a universal subject.[11] [Secondary parts] of this kind are called syncategorematic

---

[6] The phrase translated as "the word 'white'" is "*ly albus.*" On the logicians' use of this medieval particle (also spelled 'li') see *WSIL*, p. 117, n. 48.

[7] There are at least two respects in which this example and its treatment are unexpected or mistaken. (1) To talk of the word 'white' *signifying* in this way deviates widely from the theory of signification Sherwood presents in *Introductiones*, Chapter Five. He seems, however, even in *Introductiones*, to have found that strict theory inconvenient, and he surely does not use it in this treatise. (2) More important is the fact that the expression 'white man' by itself surely does not signify, even in a broad sense of 'signify,' that some man is white. But since 'principal' and 'secondary' were introduced as designations for *parts of statement* rather than merely for *kinds of words* (or "parts of speech"), perhaps we are to understand 'white man' as occurring as a subject or predicate term — e.g., as in 'a white man is running.' Filling out and repairing the last sentence of the second paragraph along these lines we obtain something of this sort: for example, when I say 'a white man is running' the word 'white' determinates the word 'man' in respect of the things belonging to it in such a way as to restrict its supposition to *white* things belonging to it.

[8] To determinate a principal part insofar as it is a subject is to determinate it in respect of the predicate, and to determinate a principal part insofar as it is a predicate is to determinate it in respect of the subject. The first, nonsyncategorematic kind of determination of principal parts by secondary parts is also (or may also be) a determination of subjects and predicates, but not *as* subjects and predicates. The elucidation of this vague way of speaking is perhaps the main theoretical aim of this treatise, but we may say for now that the distinction is one regarding the scope of secondary parts considered as logico-semantic operators within a statement. Again Sherwood's discussion of the effects of adverbial modes (*WSIL*, pp. 41–42) provides a good introductory example of this scope-difference. (See also the section headed "Syncategoremata" in my article, "Semantics, History of.") Thus even when Sherwood is considering syncategorematic words that "pertain to the *subject*" (for example), he is considering secondary parts that determinate in some way *the relation of predication* by their grammatical connection with the subject-term.

[9] *WSIL*, pp. 28–29: "A universal sign is that which signifies that the predicate is said of or separated from the subject universally, that is, for any and every part. Such are 'every,' 'all,' 'no,' 'each,' 'both,' 'however many,' 'any,' and the like." On the notion of parts of the subject, see Chapter I, Sections 2–4 below.

[10] The point here is, of course, to contrast this syncategorematic determination of 'man' with the nonsyncategorematic determination of 'man' in 'a white man is running.' The distinction is less marked in Latin: '*albus homo currit*,' '*omnis homo currit*.' Moreover, '*omnis*' has the sense of 'whole,' as in "*Gallia est omnis divisa in partes tres*," so that it is at least thinkable that '*omnis homo currit*' should have the sense of 'a whole man is running' — in which case, of course, '*omnis*' would be no more a syncategorematic word than is '*albus*' in the preceding case.

[11] To say that 'man' is a universal subject may seem unenlightening. It looks as if something such as 'is universally a subject' would have come closer to what Sherwood wants here. But to say that it is a universal *subject* is to say that it is universal

words.[12] They cause a great deal of difficulty in discourse, and for that reason they are to be investigated.[13]

The name 'syncategorema' comes from 'sin-' — i.e., 'con-' — and 'categoreuma' — i.e., 'significative' or 'predicative' — as if to say 'conpredicative,' for a syncategorematic word is always joined with something else in discourse.

But, it is asked, since some of them are determinations of the subject, why do they all derive their name from the predicate?

It must be said that [14] the predicate is the completive part of the statement, but every syncategorematic word pertains in some way to both the subject and the predicate, and so the syncategorematic words derive their name from the predicate as from the completing and more important part.

The first to be investigated, however, are those associated with the subject — i.e., [distributive] signs and certain others.

---

in respect of its predicate, that the universality is *a characteristic of the predication* and not just of "some thing belonging to 'man.'"

[12] A definition of a syncategorematic word has now been built up. A syncategorematic word is a secondary word, a kind of word not required for the occurrence of any and every statement — i.e., an adjective, adverb, conjunction, or preposition — determining a principal word, a kind of word required for the occurrence of any and every statement — i.e., a substantival name or a verb — used as subject or predicate of a statement, not in respect of the things belonging to those principal words but in respect of the relation of predication. This is helpful as a starting point, but its details will not hold up throughout the treatise. For one thing, none of the last group of syncategorematic words treated (in Chapters XVII–XXIV) can be strictly described as affecting the relation of predication (with the possible and odd exception of the interrogative particle '*ne*' in Chapter XXIII). For another thing, of the twenty-four chapters in the treatise, seven deal with adjectives (I, II, III, IV, VII, IX, XI), four deal with adverbs (X, XII, XIV, XV), seven deal with conjunctions (XVII, XVIII, XIX, XX, XXI, XXII, XXIV), and *none* with prepositions. ('*Praeter*,' the subject of Chapter X, sometimes occurs as a preposition, but it is not in that use that it is discussed in this treatise.) That leaves six chapters, of which one deals with a noun (VIII), two with verbs (XIII, XVI), two with pronouns (V, VI), and one with the enclitic interrogative particle (XXIII). While the particle surely is a secondary part, nouns, verbs, and pronouns are principal parts (on the relevant "noun-character" of pronouns, see *WSIL*, p. 22). Thus it looks as if the classification of syncategorematic words under secondary parts is faulty in one or more respects.

[13] The difficulty caused by syncategorematic words is *not* in *discourse*, but in the *analysis* of discourse, in logic conceived of as *scientia sermocinalis* (see section with that heading in my article "Semantics, History of," pp. 370–371). If Sherwood had meant just what is said here, he would have been embarking on a treatise in rhetoric, or possibly in grammar, rather than in dialectic.

[14] The scholastic formula 'it must be said that' (*dicendum quod*) is regularly used to introduce the author's own position or the master's attempt to resolve a formal disputation. The frequent occurrence of the formula in this treatise is an aid in discerning its dialectical organization.

CHAPTER I. *'Every'* or *'All' (Omnis)*

1. THE SIGNIFICATION OF 'EVERY' OR 'ALL'

The first [to be investigated] is the word 'every' or 'all' — first with regard to its signification and then with regard to its function.[1]
It must be known that [2] 'every' or 'all' signifies universality. Sometimes, however, it signifies universality as the disposition [3] of a thing; in that case it is not a syncategorematic word but is equipollent [4] to 'whole' (*totum*) or 'complete' (*perfectum*), as in 'the world is all.'[5] At other times it signifies universality as a disposition of a subject insofar as it is a subject; in that case it is a syncategorematic word. For example, when I say 'every man is running' the word 'every' signifies that the word 'man' is universal in respect of serving as a subject — i.e., that it is universally subjected to the predicate.[6] Thus the *substance* belonging to the [adjectival] name 'every'

---

[1] The distinction between the word's signification (*significatio*) and its function (*officium*) is roughly parallel to the modern distinction between the semantic and the syntactic aspects of a word's use. The distinction is, understandably, not absolute. Thus the second sort of signification considered by Sherwood in this section closely approximates what he describes as function; or perhaps function and the second sort of signification are simply two designations for the same property of *'omnis'* from different points of view.
[2] The scholastic formula 'it must be known that' (*sciendum quod*) is regularly used to introduce a portion of doctrine or theory accepted or promulgated by the author, generally treated as beyond question for the purposes of the disputation or treatise. See p. 16 above, n. 14.
[3] 'Disposition' (*dispositio*) is an extremely broad term in Sherwood's use of it both in *Introductiones* and in this treatise. Often, as here, it might be considered on a par with 'characteristic'; but sometimes, as in the next sentence, it operates more nearly as does the technical term 'determination.' See p. 14 above, n. 2.
[4] Equipollence, as Sherwood treats it in *Introductiones* (*WSIL*, pp. 35-38), is a relation between "signs," such as 'every,' 'no,' 'some,' and 'not.' Two signs are equipollent if and only if they have the same distributive effects; thus 'not some . . .' is equipollent to 'no . . .' Moreover, the etymology of 'equipollence' (*'aequus'* + *'polleo'*) suggests such an equivalence of function rather than of signification. Nevertheless, in this passage and throughout this treatise Sherwood uses a broader notion of equipollence, approximating synonymy or interchangeability of words more nearly than equivalence of sign-function.
[5] Sherwood is evidently alluding to Aristotle's doctrine in *De Caelo* I, 1 (268a20–22): "Furthermore, 'all,' 'whole,' and 'complete' do not differ from one another in form, but only, if at all, in their matter, and in the subjects of which they are predicated." And the example, *'mundus est omne,'* is at least strongly suggested by Aristotle's last sentence in that same chapter: "The whole of which these [bodies] are parts [— i.e., the world —], on the other hand, is complete of necessity and, as its name signifies, wholly so — not complete in one respect and incomplete in another" (268b8–10).
[6] Grammarians recognized only pronominal and adjectival occurrences of *'omnis.'* The pronominal occurrences are not, although perhaps they ought to have been,

or 'all' is infinite substance spoken of finitely through its subject, but the *quality* belonging to it is universality.⁷

2. SPECIFIC AND NUMERICAL PARTS

The function of the word 'every' or 'all' is to divide the subject in respect of the predicate.⁸

---

of interest to Sherwood here. His attempt to account for the two kinds of use of *'omnis'* he wants to distinguish is therefore expressed in terms of the roles open to an adjective signifying universality. In (a) 'the world is all' 'all' signifies universality as a disposition of the thing supposited by the subject term. In (b) 'all men are running' 'all' signifies universality as a disposition of the subject in its relation to the predicate. (Notice that Sherwood provides at least three different formulations of his account of the role of 'all' (or 'every') in (b).) But only in (a) is there a regular (or categorematic) adjectival occurrence of 'all,' as may be seen by contrasting (a) and (b) with (a') 'the world is large' and (b') 'large men are running,' in which both occurrences of 'large' *are* regular adjectival occurrences. To say that the occurrence of 'all' in (b) is a quantifier-occurrence would be simply to mark the difference without explaining it. Sherwood's account is a praiseworthy attempt to make sense of the grammarians' notion that 'all' occurs as an adjective in both (a) and (b), despite its special, syncategorematic effect in (b). In his *Introductiones*, where his purposes are somewhat different from those he has here, Sherwood gives various other accounts of the universality of a universal sign. For example, "The sign 'every' signifies that the predicate (together with its dispositions) belongs to each part of the subject" (*WSIL*, p. 35); cf. p. 15 above, n. 9. The distinction between categorematic and syncategorematic uses of 'every' or 'all' may be viewed as a working out of observations made by Aristotle in *De interpretatione* (around 17b12), where he says, among other pertinent things, that in 'every man is white' 'man' signifies not a particular but a universal and that " 'every' does not signify the universal [signified by 'man,' or the universality of the common term 'man'], but that it ['man'] is taken universally."

⁷ The brevity of this observation suggests that there was some regular practice of alluding to the "substance" and "quality" of a substantival or adjectival name. I know of no such practice, but I suspect that something like the following lies behind this remark. We have been discussing the *signification* of 'every' or 'all,' and when we do this in the case of a substantival name such as 'man' we can summarize our results in terms of the substance and quality signified. We can say, that is, that 'man' signifies (indirectly) the primary substance known as a human being and that it does so in virtue of signifying (directly) the quality (or form) humanity, which characterizes such a substance. Thus, if we really have given an account of signification here, we should be able to do the same for 'every' or 'all.' To take the latter and easier part first, the quality (directly) signified by it is universality, as we have shown. But there is no substance (except perhaps the world) characterized absolutely by that form, and in any case it is not a substance characterized by that form in which we are now interested. Instead we must say that as a syncategorematic word, 'every' or 'all' signifies (indirectly) infinite substance, which is not made finite, or definite, until 'every' or 'all' is attached to some subject term. Thus we might say that the *substance* of 'every' or 'all' is best exhibited in some such expression as this: 'for every x such that x is . . .,' which is infinite, or perfectly indefinite, until the blank is properly filled, in which event the *quality* of 'every' or 'all' is exhibited in that we are now set to affirm (or deny) something of entities of a given sort with *universality* — 'for every x such that x is a man, x is running.'

⁸ To divide the subject in respect of the predicate is to warrant attaching the predi-

Some say [9] that the word 'every' or 'all' divides differently from the expression 'each single' (*unusquisque*) or the expression 'any and every' (*quilibet*), because 'every' or 'all' properly divides for specific parts and 'each single' [and 'any and every'] for numerical parts. As Aristotle says, "whoever knows every triangle knows specifically; whoever knows each single one knows numerically." [10] They also say that specific parts are species and numerical parts are individuals.

But on the contrary, Aristotle designates an isosceles, which is a *species* of triangle, a numerical part. Again, if they were right the word 'every' or 'all' could not be attached to a species term such as the word 'man,' since it has no species under it.[11]

---

cate separately either (a) to at least one thing of each *kind* ranged under the subject or (b) to each *individual* thing belonging to the subject. These kinds (or individuals representative of them) and individuals are, respectively, the specific parts (*partes secundum speciem*) and the numerical parts (*partes secundum numerum*) of the subject. Thus the specific parts of 'dog' might be exhibited in a series of true statements beginning as follows: 'a collie is a dog,' 'a poodle is a dog,' . . .; and the numerical parts of 'dog' in a series of true statements beginning as follows: 'Fido is a dog,' 'Spot is a dog,' . . . Thus the issue in Section 2 is between two distinct analyses available for at least some universal affirmatives. For example, 'every dog is depicted in the mural' analyzes into the exhaustive conjunction beginning 'a collie is depicted in the mural, and a poodle . . .' or (less plausibly) into the exhaustive conjunction beginning 'Fido is depicted in the mural, and Spot . . .'

[9] This is the first occurrence in the treatise of a frequently recurring pattern of exposition, broadly typical of scholasticism. Sherwood began by stating (in the first sentence of the section) what was generally agreed on regarding the function of 'every' or 'all.' Now he will bring out the details of his own position in replies to other positions on the same question. The "some" here and elsewhere in the treatise may be students or colleagues engaged in the typical debate form of teaching in the medieval universities, and sometimes they may be published philosophers. (The only authorities regularly cited by name in Sherwood's treatises are Aristotle, Boethius, and Priscian.)

[10] O'Donnell supplies a reference to Aristotle's *Posterior Analytics* I, 5 (74a25): "Hence, even if a man proves separately — whether by the same demonstration or not — of *each kind* of triangle, equilateral, scalene, or isosceles, that it contains angles equal to the sum of two right angles, he still does not know, except in the sophistical sense, that a triangle has its angles equal to the sum of two right angles, or that this is a universal property of triangles, even if there is no other kind of triangle besides these; for he does not know that this property belongs to a triangle *qua* triangle, nor that it belongs to *every* triangle, except *numerically;* for he does not know that it belongs to every triangle *specifically*, even if there is no triangle which he does not know to possess it." Note that the actual wording given in Sherwood's treatise does not appear in the passage from Aristotle.

[11] The opinion advanced in the preceding paragraph consists of two theses: (1) '*omnis*' divides the subject for its specific parts while '*unusquisque*' and '*quilibet*' divide the subject for its numerical parts; (2) specific parts of the subject are species under the subject term and numerical parts of the subject are individuals under the subject term. This rejoinder attacks thesis (1) by citing the same passage in such a way as to discredit Aristotle's authority on this point. It attacks thesis (2) by reducing it to an absurdity — if '*omnis*' divides for specific parts and specific parts are species,

Others say that a specific part is something inferior taken together with the reduplication of the superior [12] [48] [13] — e.g., 'this man insofar as he is man' is a specific part of man — and that a numerical part is 'this man' by itself. They also say that the sign 'every' or 'all' divides for that sort of specific part.

But on the contrary, if they were right there would be no difference between saying 'every man' and 'every man insofar as he is man.' [14]

It must be said, therefore, that a specific part is a part that is due to (*debetur*) a universal insofar as it is a universal — i.e., a part in the sense that it is a conditionally extant [part]. A numerical part, on the other hand, is an actually extant part, not due to a universal as such.[15] A part of man in the first sense is man conditionally in Socrates; [16] likewise man conditionally in Plato. Even if no man actually exists, these parts are. A part of man in the second sense is man actually in Socrates, or Socrates; likewise man actually in Plato. Unless there is an actually existing man, these parts are not.

3. 'EVERY' OR 'ALL' TAKEN PROPERLY AND TAKEN COMMONLY

It must be known, therefore, that the word 'every' or 'all' is sometimes taken properly and divides for specific parts, and at other times taken commonly and divides for numerical parts.[17]

---

then, since there are no species under '*homo*,' '*omnis homo currit*' is not well-formed, which is absurd.

[12] The reduplication is a phrase attached to the subject and containing a "reduplicative expression" such as 'insofar as' or 'to the extent that' (see *WSIL*, p. 91, n. 103, and p. 112, n. 31). The superior in this case is the species, superior to the individual in the "predicamental line" (see *WSIL*, p. 75, n. 32; p. 108, n. 20; and p. 119, n. 58). O'Donnell supplies a reference to Aristotle's *Prior Analytics* I, 36 (49a23-27), a passage that may be the source of the notion of reduplication.

[13] The numbers in brackets throughout the text are the numbers of the corresponding pages in O'Donnell's edition and appear at points corresponding to the *conclusions* of the pages in the edition.

[14] This rejoinder alludes to the difference pointed out in Sherwood's analysis of 'man is the noblest of creatures' (*WSIL*, pp. 111–112).

[15] Sherwood's own distinction between specific and numerical parts raises the question of whether or not the universal affirmative carries an existential implication. Evidently the statement 'a unicorn is a quadruped' concerns a Sherwoodian *specific* part of unicorn, whereas 'a unicorn is grazing on the lawn' concerns a Sherwoodian *numerical* part of unicorn.

[16] O'Donnell's edition has ". . . *in Sorte sive Sortes et* . . ."; ". . . *in Sorte et* . . ." in the Paris manuscript (hereafter cited as P).

[17] This sentence might be read as expressing a rule like those introduced in Sections 4 and 5 below. "Taken properly" and "taken commonly" may be read as "taken in the strict sense" and "taken in the broad sense." Sherwood's view then seems to

On this basis the following sophisma [18] is solved. Suppose there are only asses. Then [a] every animal is an ass, but [b] every man is an animal; therefore every man is an ass. [Proof:] [a] is true by hypothesis; [b] is necessary, because in it the genus is predicated of a species.[19]

Solution: If the word 'every' is taken properly in [a], [a] is false, for it means that the animal conditionally in Socrates and in Plato and in all the others conditionally is the ass, which is false.[20] If, however, it is taken commonly, [a] is true and [b] is false, since a distribution occurs for the actually extant parts of man, and by hypothesis there are none. If, however, the minor [b] is taken in the sense in which it is true, there will be a *figura dictionis* in the argument, for the word 'animal' is taken for numerical parts

---

be that no existential implication attaches to the universal affirmative when 'every' or 'all' is used strictly and that there is a broad sense of 'every' or 'all' in which an existential implication is involved. (See Chapter XIII, Section 3 below.) Cf. Philotheus Boehner, *Medieval Logic*, p. 30: "The scholastics, then, insisted on the existential import of a categorical, non-modal affirmative, universal proposition about the present." Cf. also Kneale, *Development*, p. 264.

[18] A fallacious inference (an inference dependent for its apparent acceptability on a fallacy or paralogism) can be employed in support of a perfectly acceptable conclusion. But for pedagogical purposes it is more effective to employ fallacious inferences that lead to obviously unacceptable conclusions (either outrageously false or nonsensical) from premises that are true or acceptable under special assumptions. In the present example, for instance, it is not surprising that the conclusion is *false*, since the first premiss, although "true by hypothesis," is based on a false hypothesis and is false in fact. But the conclusion is *analytically* false, and the first premiss is *possible* though false while the second premiss is *analytically* true (or "necessary"). A sophisma, in the strict sense, is the unacceptable conclusion of such an inference — e.g., 'every man is an ass.' (In the broad sense the sophisma is the entire fallacious inference.) Part of what accounts for the historical continuity of medieval logic is the continuous discussion of the same sophismata. In Appendix A (pp. 153–163) of his *William Heytesbury: Medieval Logic and the Rise of Mathematical Physics* (hereafter cited as *Heytesbury*), Curtis Wilson lists thirty-two sophismata treated by Heytesbury in the middle of the fourteenth century, fourteen of which Wilson identifies as having been treated by Sherwood in this treatise, which Wilson misleadingly refers to as "*Introductiones in logicam.*" (Compare the position occupied in recent philosophical literature by such twentieth-century sophismata as 'George IV wished to know whether Scott was Scott' and 'the number of the planets is necessarily greater than 7.') The most valuable recent source in English for the study of the extensive medieval sophismata literature is T. K. Scott's annotated translation of John Buridan's *Sophisms on Meaning and Truth*.

[19] The most prevalent pattern in Sherwood's treatment of sophismata is (1) the *hypothesis* ("there are only asses"); (2) the *inference*, leading to the sophisma proper; (3) the *proof*, offered in support of one or more of the premises in the inference; (4) the "on the contrary," or *disproof* (lacking in this first example); (5) the *solution*, dissolving the sophisma by exposing the fallacy (or paralogism) that made it look as if that unacceptable conclusion followed from those premises.

[20] There are four possible cases, depending on the ways in which 'every' is taken: (I) properly in [a] and in [b]; (II) properly in [a] and commonly in [b]; (III) commonly in [a] and in [b]; (IV) commonly in [a] and properly in [b]. This first sentence

in [a] and for specific parts in [b].[21] From another point of view there will be a paralogism of accident, for 'animal' is not predicated of 'man' in the way in which 'ass' is predicated of 'animal.'[22]

4. PROXIMATE AND REMOTE PARTS

Rule [I]: *The word 'every' or 'all' sometimes distributes [a subject] for the single things belonging to the genera [under the subject] and at other times for the genera of the single things [under the subject], or [in other words,] sometimes for the remote parts [of the subject] and at other times for the proximate parts [of the subject].*

On this basis the following sophisma is solved. Suppose that exactly one individual of each species of animal is running. Then [a] every animal is running. Proof: A man is running, a lion . . ., a goat . . ., and so on with respect to single things; therefore every animal is running. But [b] every man is an animal; therefore every man is running.[23]

[Solution:] [a] is ambiguous, since the word 'every' can distribute [the subject] either for the remote parts (or the single things belonging to genera), in which case it is false, since then 'animal' is distributed for all its individuals; or for the genera of single things (or the proximate parts), and the minor [b] is not taken in that way, as is clear. Thus if the propositions are taken in the senses in which they are true there will be a *figura*

---

of the solution constitutes a rejection of cases (I) and (II), and the remaining two cases are considered in that order.

[21] Case (IV) is the strongest case in the sense that it is the only one in which both premisses are true. Since both premisses are true and the conclusion is false, the inference is of an invalid form. But medieval logicians look for specific errors in reasoning — fallacies or paralogisms — as the sources of invalidity rather than contenting themselves with rejecting the inference on formal grounds. The fallacy here, Sherwood says, is *figura dictionis*. This designation has a precise technical sense in his *Introductiones*, where it is possible to translate it as 'figure of a word' (*WSIL*, pp. 146–150), but in this treatise he evidently uses '*figura dictionis*' as a general designation for fallacies of ambiguity.

[22] The designation 'paralogism of accident' has its technical sense (see *WSIL*, pp. 150–153) stretched in this treatise, too, though not so broadly as that of '*figura dictionis*.'

[23] This 'But . . .' claim functions just as do the "on the contraries" or disproofs in most of the treatise (see n. 19, this chapter). In sophismata of this pattern, the most common in the treatise, the sophisma proper is often not stated explicitly. It can, however, usually be brought out easily by extending the "on the contrary," as in this case: ". . . therefore every man is running. But, by the hypothesis, only one man is running. Therefore every man is running and only one man is running, which is absurd." The sophisma proper in this case might also be expressed as 'every animal is running but not every man is running.'

[22

dictionis in the argument, for the word 'animal' stood for [24] proximate parts in [*a*] and for remote parts in [*b*]. From another point of view there will be a paralogism of accident, for the word 'animal' is not predicated of the minor extremity [25] in the way in which the major is predicated of it.

5. THE RULE OF THREE

Rule [II]: *The sign 'every' or 'all' requires that there be at least three appellata.*[26]

This is proved in the following way. The sign 'every' or 'all' distributes for the whole and complete plurality belonging to the term to which it is attached, but every totality and completion consists in at least three; therefore it requires a trio of appellata. As Aristotle says, "Of two men we say that they are two, or both, and not that they are all."[27] Understand, however, that when it distributes for numerical parts it requires three actually extant appellata, and when it distributes for specific parts it requires three (or more) conditionally extant.

---

[24] Sherwood uses the verb *'stare'* with the preposition *'pro,'* especially in this treatise but sometimes also in *Introductiones*, in place of the more technically precise *'supponere'* or *'supponere pro'* (see *Introductiones*, Chapter Five). Thus various ways of "standing for" are so many varieties of supposition.

[25] The extremities of a syllogism are the terms of its conclusion, the minor and major terms or extremities. The middle term is the *means* (in the premisses) whereby these *extremes* are brought into relation with each other in the conclusion.

[26] On appellata see *WSIL*, especially pp. 106 and 121–122. "Notice that sometimes a suppositum of a term is something that exists and at other times something that does not exist. An appellatum, on the other hand, is simply something that exists" (p. 123). A more precise definition can be derived from the definition of appellation (*WSIL*, p. 106): the appellata of a term are the things to which the term correctly applies at present. The fact that this more precise definition omits any claim regarding the present *existence* of those things may be important in the context of Section 5.

[27] O'Donnell supplies a reference to *De caelo* I, 1 (268a9–20): "Magnitude divisible in one direction is a line, in two directions a surface, in three directions a body. There is no magnitude not included in these; for three are all, and 'in three ways' is the same as 'in all ways.' It is just as the Pythagoreans say, the whole world and all things in it are summed up in the number 3; for end, middle, and beginning give the number of the whole, and their number is the triad. Hence it is that we have taken this number from nature, as it were one of her laws, and make use of it even for the worship of the gods. Our language too shows the same tendency, for of two things or people we say 'both,' not 'all.' This latter word we first employ when there are three in question; and in behaving thus, as I have said, we are accepting nature herself for our guide." Notice that Aristotle does not offer the Pythagorean numerology as a *proof* for the correctness of the rule of three for 'every' or 'all.' He seems instead to suggest that this usage reflects, or confirms, what the Pythagoreans say about totality and the number three. The "proof" immediately following Rule [II] is evidently just a paraphrase of what Aristotle has to say in this passage.

6. A DOUBT REGARDING THE RULE OF THREE

There is some doubt about this.[28] Suppose there are only two men. [49] Then 'every man has a color' is false by reason of the above rule;[29] therefore its contradictory — 'some man does not have a color' — is true.[30] Therefore some animal does not have a color (for an inference from an inferior to a superior with negation placed after both the inferior and the superior does follow).[31] But on the contrary, the word 'animal' does have enough appellata; therefore it stands for existents alone. But 'some animal does not have a color' is false for existents, and thus absolutely false.

It must be said that the word 'man' as it stands here is not inferior to the word 'animal,' since 'man' stands for nonexistents while 'animal' stands for existents [alone].[32] Thus the following argument does not hold: 'some man is not running; therefore some animal is not running,' etc.[33]

---

[28] *Introductiones*, Chapter Five, Section 16.2 (*WSIL*, pp. 124–126), provides an instructive parallel to this section.

[29] In the parallel passage in *Introductiones* the discussion of the otherwise unsatisfactory example 'every man exists' helps to make this point clear: "Therefore, since in the example above there are two supposita [of 'man'] existing and the sentence means that the predicate is in [at least] three, it means that it is in something that does not exist. And so 'every man exists' is false . . ." (*WSIL*, p. 125). Thus, in the present example the sentence means that the property having-a-color is in something that does not exist, and it is evidently taken to be false that a nonexistent entity has a color.

[30] Rule [II] requires the following analysis of 'every man has a color': 'no man does not have a color and there are at least three men.' To say that 'every man has a color' is false *by reason of Rule* [II] is to say that that conjunction is false by reason of the falsity of the *second* conjunct. Thus this move is inadmissible, for it infers the falsity of the *first* conjunct. Rule [II] may be understood as showing that the full contradictory of a universal affirmative is an alternation: 'either some S is not P or there are fewer than three Ss.' In ordinary circumstances the requirement of Rule [II] is fulfilled — i.e., the second alternate is false — and so ordinarily it is just the first alternate that counts as the contradictory of the universal affirmative. The trick in this sophisma consists in constructing extraordinary circumstances — the two-man hypothesis — and then continuing to employ the ordinary contradictory. (But this is evidently not the line of criticism Sherwood himself adopts in the second paragraph of this section.)

[31] What is enclosed in these parentheses is another rule, but a rule of *syllogistic* and thus simply appealed to in this advanced treatise and not separately put forward and discussed. The rule defines the syllogistic mood "Bocardo," OAO₃ (see *WSIL*, p. 66). The universal premiss — left implicit here — establishes the inferior/superior relationship — 'every man is an animal' — and the inference is described as being "from an inferior to a superior" because it moves from an O-premiss about men (through the A-premiss) to an O-conclusion about animals, predicating of the superior in the conclusion what was predicated of the inferior in the major premiss.

[32] Sherwood seems not to view Rule [II] as requiring an analysis of every universal affirmative into a conjunction of the sort introduced in n. 30 above. But he does, of course, view every universal affirmative as entailing an exhaustive conjunction of corresponding singular affirmatives, and by Rule [II] we are justified in descending

7. 'EVERY' OR 'ALL' ATTACHED TO A DISCRETE TERM

There is likewise some doubt whether the word 'every' or 'all' can be attached to a discrete term.[34] It seems that it can, since [in the first place] if Socrates is running and someone says 'every Socrates is running' I argue that nothing is subsumed under the subject of which the predicate is not affirmed and that this is therefore [a case of] *dici de omni*.[35] Therefore the

---

from any universal affirmative to at least three corresponding singular affirmatives. Thus from 'every man has a color' we are justified in descending to 'man₁ has a color and man₂ has a color and man₃ has a color.' But by the two-man hypothesis, man₃ is nonexistent and hence without a color. Therefore the entailed conjunction of corresponding singular affirmatives is false, and it is for *that* reason that 'every man has a color' is false. Thus Sherwood accepts 'some man does not have a color' as true: 'some man – viz., man₃ – does not have a color.' What he rejects is the inference from this to 'some animal does not have a color,' and the only basis on which he can reject the inference is the rejection of 'every man is an animal' as false – "the word 'man' as it stands here is *not* inferior to the word 'animal.' " Under Rule [II] and the operative two-man hypothesis, the only ways in which to establish 'every man is an animal' as true are (1) by allowing the 'every' to divide 'man' for specific rather than numerical parts, which will not suit the sophisma, or (2) by allowing the 'every' to divide 'man' for numerical and for specific parts at one and the same time, and that is what Sherwood evidently rejects.

[33] 'Etc.' is frequently used in this treatise as in other medieval works on logic to indicate the recurrence of some locution recently used, particularly in an example, or the occurrence of something readily supplied by the reader. In nearly every such case I have supplied the missing material within brackets. The 'etc.' here may indicate no more than that this is only one of countless such arguments. On the other hand, although oddly placed for the purpose, the 'etc.' may be intended to indicate the omitted minor premiss – 'every man is an animal.' In that case, the example is supplied to illustrate his rejection of the Bocardo syllogism in the sophisma, since this inference is of course acceptable as long as no difficulty about the minor premiss arises as a result of the two-man hypothesis.

[34] Although Rule [II] is not mentioned in this section, the doubt is clearly directed against it. The doubt in Section 6 centers around attaching '*omnis*' to a common term that happens to have fewer than three appellata, the doubt in Section 7 centers around attaching '*omnis*' to a discrete term, a term that by its very nature can have no more than one appellatum, and the doubt in Section 8 centers around attaching '*omnis*' to a common term that is known to have exactly one appellatum. Thus the transition from Section 7 to Section 8 is a move to a weaker kind of single-appellatum term and hence to a more plausible basis for a doubt regarding the impropriety of attaching '*omnis*' to such a term. On discrete terms see *WSIL*, p. 29: "A singular statement is one in which the subject is a discrete term, which can be either a proper name or a determinate pronoun – e.g., 'Socrates is running,' or 'that one is running.' " And, as Sherwood suggests in *Introductiones* (*WSIL*, p. 51), a common term together with a singular demonstrative pronoun would also count as a discrete term. But of all three sorts of discrete terms the least unlikely recipient of '*omnis*,' from a strictly grammatical point of view, is the proper name, employed in this section.

[35] On the logical principle *dici de omni* see *WSIL*, p. 61 and p. 61, n. 22. The formula Aristotle provides in *Prior Analytics* I, 1 (24b26), is the one operative here: "one term is predicated of all of another whenever no instance of the subject can be found of which the other term cannot be asserted." The man raising this doubt (the 'I' of 'I argue that . . . ') is arguing as follows: Socrates is running, and 'Socrates'

25]

word 'every' or 'all' is correctly attached. In the second place Aristotle says "all Aristomenes is always intelligible,"[36] and it is thus attached to a discrete term.

With respect to the first part it must be said that in order that we may infer the *dici de omni* it must be understood that the plurality bound to 'every' or 'all' can be subsumed under the negation 'nothing is subsumed,' etc., and that is not the case here.

With respect to the second part it must be said that there is a sense in which the sign 'every' or 'all' can be added to a singular term improperly,[37] for a singular is many in reason although it is one in reality. For example, white, literate, musical Aristomenes is many in reason, and the sign is attached for the sake of that plurality. And the sense of 'all Aristomenes is always intelligible' is that Aristomenes in respect of all his being [is always intelligible].

8. 'EVERY' OR 'ALL' ADDED TO A COMMON TERM KNOWN TO HAVE EXACTLY ONE APPELLATUM

It is furthermore asked whether the word 'every' or 'all' can be added truly to a term such as 'sun' that has only one appellatum. It seems that it can, since there is a demonstration regarding the sun in the first mood of the first figure, and so the sign 'every' or 'all' is added to it [i.e., to the term 'sun'].[38] [On the other hand] the opposite seems to be the case, since [the sign] demands three appellata.

---

is a discrete term, therefore *dici de omni* ("nothing is subsumed under the subject of which the predicate is not affirmed"); but if *dici de omni* obtains, then a universal affirmative is warranted; therefore every Socrates is running. The conclusion violates Rule [II] but has been proven on the basis of *dici de omni*, a far more fundamental principle than Rule [II]; therefore Rule [II] is to be discarded.

[36] O'Donnell supplies the reference to *Prior Analytics* I, 33 (47b21ff): "Let 'A' stand for always existing, 'B' for Aristomenes as an object of thought, and 'C' for Aristomenes. Then it is true that A applies to B, because Aristomenes as an object of thought always exists. But B also applies to C; because Aristomenes is Aristomenes as an object of thought. Yet A does not apply to C; because Aristomenes is perishable. For no syllogism is produced, as we saw, by the above combination of terms; to produce a syllogism the premiss AB ought to have been taken universally. But it is false to postulate that *all Aristomenes as an object of thought always exists*, since Aristomenes is perishable." Notice that Aristotle does *not* state the premiss beginning 'all Aristomenes . . .' but *rejects* it, although for a reason different from the one at issue here.

[37] 'Improperly' — i.e., metaphorically or analogically. Cf. *WSIL*, pp. 135–136. The proper signification or function of a word is its own original, literal, fundamental signification or function.

[38] Peter of Spain, whose treatment of the rule of three differs markedly from Sherwood's, uses this example in support of his claim that when 'every' "is adjoined to a

It must be said that if 'every' or 'all' is taken properly and divides for conditionally existent parts it can be added to 'sun,' and this is the way the first objection runs. If, however, it is taken commonly it cannot be added, and this is the way the second [objection] runs.[39]

9. 'EVERY' OR 'ALL' ADDED TO A PREDICATE

It is asked whether [the sign] can be added to a predicate. It seems that it can, since 'no man is every man' is true.[40] [On the other hand] the opposite seems to be the case, since Aristotle says that a universal predicated universally is not true.[41] Moreover, a predicate stands for a form, for Aristotle says that a composition is of things that are in [other things].[42] Thus

---

common term having many supposita, it requires many appellata; but when it is adjoined to a term having only one suppositum, it requires only one appellatum" (*Summulae logicales* (hereafter cited as *Sum. log.*), ed. Mullally, p. 70).

[39] Sherwood's answer is that if one is speaking not just about the one and only sun there happens to be but about any possible entity of that sort, then one can correctly say 'every sun'; but if one is speaking simply of the sun, then Rule [II] prohibits 'every sun.' (Cf. John Locke, *An Essay Concerning Human Understanding*, Bk. III, Ch. VI, Sec. 1.)

[40] Peter of Spain provides a full version of this argument in support of an affirmative answer to the question. "In connection with the matters just discussed a question is raised regarding the sophisma 'no man is every man.' It is proved in the following way: Socrates is not every man, Plato is not every man, and so on with respect to [all] the others; therefore the first [proposition] is true. Or in the following way: its contradictory — viz., 'some man is every man' — is false; therefore it itself is true. On the contrary, in that case an opposite is predicated of an opposite; therefore the locution is false. Solution: the first [proposition] is true, and one responds to the disproof by means of interemption, since an opposite is not predicated of an opposite in this case; rather, 'every man' is denied of 'every man' taken for any and every suppositum belonging to it, and that is true" (*Sum. log.*, ed. Mullally, pp. 78-80).

[41] O'Donnell supplies the reference to *De interpretatione*, 7 (17b8–17b16): "But when one states something of a universal but not universally, the statements are not contrary (though what is being revealed may be contrary). Examples of what I mean by 'stating of a universal not universally' are 'a man is white' and 'a man is not white'; man is a universal but it is not used universally in the statement (for 'every' does not signify the universal but that it is taken universally). It is not true to predicate a universal universally of a subject, for there cannot be an affirmation in which a universal is predicated universally of a subject, for instance 'every man is every animal'" (tr. J. L. Ackrill).

[42] A composition, as the term is used here, is an instance of predication. O'Donnell supplies a reference to *De interpretatione*, 7 (17a38–17b2): "Now of actual things some are universal, others particular (I call universal that which is by its nature predicated of a number of things, and particular that which is not; man, for instance, is a universal, Callias a particular)" (tr. J. L. Ackrill). A much more detailed and apparently more relevant discussion is to be found in *Categories*, 5. But in any case Aristotle seems to be saying not what is attributed to him here but rather its opposite — e.g.: "It is a characteristic common to every substance not to be in a subject. For a primary substance is neither said of a subject nor in a subject. And as

since a predicate enters into composition (*componitur*), a predicate is in [something else]; but what is in the subject is not a suppositum of the predicate but the form belonging to the predicate. Therefore what is predicated is a form or of the nature (*in ratione*) of a form. But this sign is added to something for its supposita; therefore it is not added to the predicate.

It must be said that this sign cannot be added to a term after it has become a predicate, which is what these latter arguments maintain. Nevertheless, it can be added to a term as such — e.g., to 'man' — and this [resultant] whole can be predicated, which is what the first opposition maintains.[43]

10. 'EVERY' OR 'ALL' ADDED TO A TERM INVOLVING A CLAUSE OR PHRASE

Rule [III]: *When 'every' or 'all' is added to a term involving a clause or phrase (habenti implicationem)*[44] *the [resultant] locution is ambiguous in that the distribution can be united either for the whole term together with the clause or phrase or [for the term] without it.*

On this basis the following sophisma is solved. Suppose that all the white men are running but not the black. Then every man who is white is

---

for secondary substances, it is obvious at once that they are not in a subject. For man is said of the individual man as subject but is not in a subject: man is not *in* the individual man. Similarly, animal also is said of the individual man as subject but animal is not *in* the individual man" (*Categories*, 5 (3a7ff); J. L. Ackrill translation).

[43] Take as an example the true statement 'every rational animal is a man,' the predicate of which is 'man.' What sense can be made of Sherwood's claim that 'every' *cannot* be added to the term 'man' after it has become a predicate? That cannot be done without changing the function of 'is' from predication in the strict sense (in 'every rational animal is a man') to a kind of identification (in 'every rational animal is every man'). Thus, Sherwood's point may be that adding 'every' to a term after it has become a predicate cannot be done because either (a) the truth-value of the original statement is altered (as in 'every man is an animal'/'every man is every animal') or (b) the predicate-character of the term is destroyed (as in the example just discussed). Sherwood speaks more than once in this treatise (e.g., Chapter I, Section 19; Chapter XV, Section 2) as if the *temporal order* of the construction of a statement were important, as here: ". . . after it has become a predicate." However he may have intended it, there is no reason to interpret this in a literally temporal way. We need distinguish only between a predicate considered as a predicate and a predicate considered merely as a word. Thus if we intend to deny that any individual man bears the form of Hobbes's leviathan, we may construct the predicate 'every man' in order to frame the true statement 'no man is every man.'

[44] Cf. *WSIL*, p. 124 and p. 124, nn. 77, 78, 80. In *Introductiones* and in the present section of this treatise it seems right to translate '*implicatio*' as 'relative clause.' It is translated more broadly as 'clause or phrase' here in view of the evident intention to treat Section 11 as providing a case falling under Rule [III].

running. (This is proved inductively.)⁴⁵ Then 'therefore every man is running and he is white' is inferred.⁴⁶ On the contrary, the first part of this copulative is [50] false; therefore [the copulative] itself is false too.

It must be said that if 'man' and 'who is white' are compounded, the expression is compounded and true. If they are divided, it is divided and false;⁴⁷ for the word 'man' alone is distributed. In the first way the term is distributed together with the clause or phrase, in the second way without it. In the first way it is proved; in the second way it is not proved (*improbatur*).⁴⁸

11. 'ANOTHER' WITHIN THE SCOPE OF 'EVERY' OR 'ALL'

Again, every man and another man are. Proof: Socrates and another man are, Plato [and another man are], and so on with respect to the single things [belonging to the term]; therefore every man [and another man are]. On the contrary, this locution signifies that some man is other than every man; therefore it is false.

It must be said that either [a] the distribution can include the copulation and relation of the word 'another,' in which case it is proved and true; or [b] vice versa, in which case it is not proved and false.⁴⁹ In case [a] the

---

⁴⁵ The kind of "inductive" proof Sherwood evidently has in mind here and elsewhere in this treatise is exhaustive enumeration.
⁴⁶ This inference depends, of course, on reading the relative clause intended as a *modifier* as if it were an *appositive*.
⁴⁷ On 'compounded' and 'divided' see *WSIL*, p. 127, nn. 88 and 89. The compounded/divided distinction marks more than one sort of difference in Sherwood's usage. The differences are those between intonation-patterns and those between senses of a statement. Thus if I pronounce the words with a level intonation and with no marked pause between 'man' and 'who' and between 'white' and 'is,' I give 'every man who is white is running' the *compounded pronunciation*, which conveys the *compounded sense* (often called "the sense of composition") of the statement; and likewise, *mutatis mutandis*, with respect to the *divided pronunciation* and the *divided sense*. It is helpful to read the first occurrence of 'compounded' and the first occurrence of 'divided' in the text here as having to do with intonation-patterns and the second occurrence of each as having to do with senses.
⁴⁸ The way in which this frequently used formula is usually to be read may be presented in this paraphrase: "The proof depends upon taking the statement in the first way; the 'on the contrary' or disproof depends upon taking it in the second way." In this case, however, it is not the "on the contrary" but what is inferred – 'every man is running and he is white' – from the original statement that depends upon taking the original statement in the second way.
⁴⁹ Although 'copulation' is a technical term in the doctrine of the properties of terms (see *WSIL*, pp. 105 and 120–122), it seems most likely that 'copulation and relation' here designates the function of 'another' as 'distribution' designates the function of 'every' (cf. Sherwood's characterization of the purpose of a relative pronoun, *WSIL*, p. 115). Interpretation [a] seems to be 'every man-and-another-man

phrase 'another man' must be uttered continuously with the predicate and divided from the subject, so that it will be signified that it falls together with the predicate under the respect of the distribution;[50] for [by means of the distribution] it is signified that 'man' stands for each of its supposita in respect of everything that follows [it]. In case [b] [the phrase 'another man'] must be divided from the predicate, so that it will be signified that it does not receive the respect of the distribution together with the predicate. Thus when it is not distributed it in no way falls under the distribution; instead, the distribution [falls] under the copulation and relation of the word 'another.'

Some maintain, nevertheless, that the first [i.e., 'every man and another man are'] is false, and that the fallacy of *figura dictionis* occurs in the proof, since in the singular [propositions] the word 'another' supposits for distinct entities.[51]

If, however, it is taken in sense [a] they are wrong, for in that case the word 'another' falls under the distribution in a universal proposition and is confused. Nor is it inadmissible if 'another' stands for distinct entities in the singular [propositions], provided that it is confused in the universal [proposition].[52]

12. 'WHEN' WITHIN THE SCOPE OF 'EVERY' OR 'ALL'

Again, suppose that men die successively.[53] Then every man dies when only one man dies. (Let this be proved inductively.) Therefore every man

---

are,' which is supported by the inductive proof. (The point of this sophisma would be more easily grasped, it seems, if 'are running' (*currunt*) had been used instead of 'are' (*sunt*).) Interpretation [b] is 'every-man and another-man are,' which is, of course, "disproved and false" — indeed, analytically false.

[50] The phrase 'under the respect of the distribution' (together with similar phrases elsewhere in this treatise) obviously means something very much like the modern expression 'within the scope of the quantifier.'

[51] Peter of Spain maintains this position in his discussion of this sophisma — '*omnis homo et alius homo sunt*' (*Sum. log.*, ed. Mullally, pp. 74–76).

[52] In effect Sherwood is saying that there is nothing fundamentally odd about this case. It gives the appearance of oddness only because of the difficulties inherent in the expression 'every man and another man.' But consider 'every man and his wife are dancing.' Of course there is no wife such that she is every man's wife, and so the sophismatic interpretation is possible here, too. But there is nothing odd about the fact that in the induction — 'Jones and his wife are dancing, Smith and his wife are dancing, . . .' — 'his wife' has determinate supposition, whereas in 'every man and his wife are dancing' it has merely confused supposition. This is, on the contrary, the regular pattern of generalization inferences viewed under supposition theory.

[53] I.e., all men die and no two men die at one and the same time.

dies at some time, and at that time one man alone dies. But these two are opposed; therefore they are not true together.

In response to this it must be said that either [a] the word 'when' can be taken indefinitely as if it were the same as 'whenever,' in which case the expression is always false; or [b] it can be taken relatively as if it were referred to the time consignified in the verb 'dies.' Moreover, it could then either [i] be compounded with the predicate as if the whole were one predicate receiving the respect of the distribution, in which case it is proved and true; or it can [ii] be divided from the predicate, in which case it is divided, false, and disproved. In [i] the word 'when' is confused as if it were copulating for many times because it falls under the distribution. In [ii] it copulates determinately for a particular time, and it is signified that at that time dies every man and only one man.[54]

Suppose that 'every man dies when only one man dies' has been proved and that it is inferred 'therefore when only one man dies every man dies.' But this is false.

In response to this it must be said that if [a] 'when' is taken indefinitely the inference holds but the premiss is false. If, however, [bii] it is taken relatively and divided [from the predicate], [the premiss] would still be false but the inference would hold. Finally, if [bi] it is compounded [with the predicate], the premiss would be true, but there will be a paralogism of *figura dictionis* in the inference, [as a result of the inference] from the [merely] confused copulation of the word 'when' to a determinate copulation [of it].

13. THE EFFECT OF THE LOCATION OF 'EVERY' OR 'ALL' ON SUPPOSITION

Rule [IV]: *An inference from a term placed after an affirmative distribution to the same term placed before the affirmative distribution does not hold.*

On this basis the following sophisma is solved. [a] Every man is one man alone. (Let this be proved inductively.) Therefore [b] one man alone is every man; therefore Socrates or Plato is every man.[55]

---

[54] The three senses distinguished here may be presented in the following paraphrases: [a] 'every time such that only one man dies at that time is a time at which every man dies'; [bi] 'for every man there is a time such that he dies at that time and no other man dies at that time'; [bii] 'there is a time such that every man dies at that time and no other man dies at that time.'

[55] The intended sense is surely 'Socrates is every man, or Plato is every man, and

It must be said that there is a fallacy of *figura dictionis* here, since the phrase 'one [man] alone' stands confusedly in [a] but determinately in [b] in respect of the same distribution.[56]

Yet it seems that [a] is false because an opposite is predicated of an opposite, for 'every' and 'one alone' are opposed.

It must be said that if the phrase 'one alone' were standing determinately it would be opposed to 'every'; but since it stands confusedly — i.e., stands for many, each of which is one alone — it is not opposed to 'every.' [51]

Again, suppose that someone maintains that there is a fallacy of *figura dictionis* in the induction in that the phrase 'one alone' stands for distinct entities [in the singular propositions].

It must be said that this does not impede the induction provided that 'one alone' is confused in relation to those distinct entities in the universal [proposition], as is the case here.[57]

14. AN ILLICIT TRANSFORMATION OF A QUALE QUID INTO A HOC ALIQUID

Suppose Socrates says that God exists and Plato says another true thing, and so on with respect to the others. Suppose further that everyone says that you are an ass.[58] Then [a] a thing that is stated by every man is true, but [b] whatever is a thing that is stated by every man is that you are an ass; therefore that you are an ass is true.

Solution: If [a] is taken in the sense in which it is true the fallacy of *figura dictionis* occurs in the inference because a *quale quid* is transformed into a *hoc aliquid*.[59] The phrase 'a thing that is stated' is related to the

---

so on with respect to the others.' This second conclusion guarantees that [b] will not be read as a mere rhetorical inversion of word order (anastrophe).

[56] It may be helpful to view merely confused supposition and determinate supposition in the context of modern quantification theory. In the scope of the quantifiers '$(x)(\exists y)$' ('for every individual x there is at least one individual y such that . . .') predicates attached to y will have merely confused supposition. In the scope of the quantifiers '$(\exists y)(x)$' ('there is at least one individual y such that for every individual x . . .') predicates attached to y will have determinate supposition. Thus Rule [IV] as applied in this section is analogous to a rule prohibiting the inference from '$(x)(\exists y)(. . .)$' to '$(\exists y)(x)(. . .)$.'

[57] The sophisma discussed in this section is discussed again briefly at the end of Chapter I, Section 20.

[58] The hypothesis of this sophisma may be presented in the following schema. Socrates makes statements S_1 and S_4, Plato makes statements S_2 and S_4, Cicero (satisfying the rule of three) makes statements S_3 and S_4; S_1, S_2, and S_3 are true; S_4 is false.

[59] '*Quale quid*' and '*hoc aliquid*' are medieval technical terms corresponding to

phrase 'by every [man]' in such a way that one of its supposita is related to one suppositum of 'by every [man],' and another to another, and so on successively. Thus 'a thing that is stated' is related to 'by every [man]' for many taken together, and since many taken together are just like one commonly and qualitatively, the phrase 'a thing that is stated' stands here as a *quale quid*. But in the minor [*b*] the phrase 'a thing that is stated' relates some one suppositum to the entire plurality belonging to 'every [man],' and so in respect of 'every [man],' 'a thing that is stated' is as a *hoc aliquid*.[60] It would be the same if one were to say in the minor 'but nothing is a thing that is stated by every man except that you are an ass.'

15. ANOTHER EXAMPLE OF SUCH ILLICIT TRANSFORMATION

This is of the same sort. Suppose that each man owns one ass and it is running, and that Brownie is the ass they own in common and it is not running. Then each man's ass is running. But whatever is each man's ass is Brownie; therefore Brownie is running — because the supposition of the word 'ass' is changed in a similar way.[61]

Nevertheless, some maintain that these expressions are ambiguous in that the locution can be judged either in connection with the subject of the locution or in connection with the subject of the attribution. (They call the nominative itself the subject of the attribution and the oblique case it-

---

Aristotle's 'ποιόν τι' and 'τόδε τι,' respectively. (See, e.g., *Categories*, 5 (3b10ff).) Their use in this treatise is made somewhat clearer in Chapter I, Section 17 (cf. *WSIL*, p. 148).

[60] The point of Sherwood's solution could, it seems, have been made at least as readily and perhaps more in keeping with his previous solutions if he had put it in terms of determinate and merely confused supposition rather than in the roughly corresponding terms of *hoc aliquid* and *quale quid*. The analysis in terms of supposition theory is in fact suggested at the end of the first paragraph of the next section. This sophisma is referred to again at the end of Chapter I, Section 20. Peter of Spain discusses a version of it (*Sum. log.*, ed. Mullally, pp. 84–86), offering first his own and then what seems to be Sherwood's solution, remarking in conclusion that "the first solution is the better and the more subtle."

[61] The sophisma requires that 'each man's ass is running' be taken in two senses: [*a*] 'for each man *x* there is an ass *y* such that *x* owns *y* and *y* is running'; [*b*] 'there is an ass *y* such that each man owns it and it is running.' Sense [*a*] is the one supported by the hypothesis, but sense [*b*] is the one that supports 'Brownie is running,' which is false; and in sense [*a*] 'ass' has merely confused supposition while in sense [*b*] it has determinate supposition. Thus the illicit inference ruled out by Rule [IV] may be viewed as a violation of the fifth rule regarding confused and determinate supposition in *Introductiones*, Chapter Five: "An argument from distributive confused supposition to determinate supposition does follow, but not from merely confused supposition" (*WSIL*, p. 119).

self the subject of the locution, but others name them the other way around.) [62]

But this is nothing, because when the phrase 'each man's' precedes the word 'ass' it has power over it (i.e., the nominative), and so the locution is to be judged in relation to it (i.e., the [distributive] sign).[63] It is not a function of the discourse that it is judged this way or that way, but a function of ourselves only [64] (*Item quod sic vel sic judicetur non est ex parte sermonis, sed ex parte nostra tantum*).

16. 'HIMSELF' WITHIN THE SCOPE OF 'EVERY' OR 'ALL'

Suppose that Socrates sees himself only, and Plato likewise [sees himself only], and so on with respect to the others. Then every man sees him-

---

[62] The alternate analysis presented in this paragraph is evidently intended to apply to the sophismata in Sections 14 and 15. The "expressions" at issue must be 'a thing that is stated by every man is true' (*ab omni homine enuntiatum est verum*) and 'each man's ass is running' (*cujuslibet hominis asinus currit*). The "subject of the attribution," then, is 'a thing that is stated' (*enuntiatum*) or 'ass' (*asinus*), respectively; and the "subject of the locution" is 'by every man' (*ab omni homine*) or 'each man's' (*cujuslibet hominis*), respectively. Judging the locution in connection with the subject of the locution in, for example, the second sophisma means reading it in sense [*a*] (see n. 61 above); judging it in connection with the subject of the attribution means reading it in sense [*b*]. 'Judging the locution in connection with (*penes*)' this or that seems to mean taking this or that to be *the subject of the sense* of the locution.

[63] Sherwood's fundamental objection is that the alternate analysis supposes that there are two admissible readings of these expressions. His own position is, in effect, that Rule [IV] makes only one reading admissible – the reading that would be characterized in terms of the alternate analysis as "judging the locution in connection with the subject of the locution."

[64] This concluding sentence looks as if it could be important as a statement of general policy, both for this treatise and for Chapters Five and Six of *Introductiones*. It can be read in a completely general way, as if it were a statement of Sherwood's fundamental bias in all his logico-semantic theorizing. If it is read in that way, however, it is baffling as a characterization of Sherwood's position, since his work is characteristically directed toward deciding logico-semantic questions on the basis of the structure of the discourse itself as far as possible, reverting to "the intention of the speaker" (and other such functions of ourselves only) only when the structure of the discourse itself adamantly resists all his efforts to decide the question on that basis (see, e.g., *WSIL*, p. 112). Moreover, in the immediately preceding sentence he has rejected the alternate analysis by appealing to the plain structure of the discourse, which, under Rule [IV], admits of one interpretation only. It seems clear, therefore, that this concluding remark is intended only to point out what is basically wrong with the alternate analysis just considered. It is just *because* the "judging" of discourse in this way or that is not objective, "a function of the discourse itself," but subjective, "a function of ourselves only," that this alternate analysis goes wrong. No doubt it is this feature of the analysis that inspires the severity of his rejection – "But this is *nothing*."

self. (Inductive proof.) But the word 'himself' is the same as 'every man' [nominative]; therefore every man sees every man; therefore Socrates sees every man, which is false.[65]

It must be said that although 'himself' is the same as 'every man' [accusative] with respect to supposita, nevertheless 'himself' and 'every man' [accusative] relate in different ways to 'every man' [nominative]. Thus they differ in respect of it, since 'himself' relates one of its supposita to one belonging to 'every [man]' [nominative], and another to another. On the other hand, 'every man' [accusative] relates its entire plurality to the individual supposita of 'every [man]' [nominative]. The reason for this is that 'himself' has no plurality in its own right but [acquires a plurality] from 'every [man]' [nominative], and for that reason one of its supposita corresponds to one suppositum of 'every [man]' [nominative], and another to another. On the other hand, 'every [man]' [accusative] has its own plurality, which corresponds to the individual supposita of 'every [man]' [nominative]. Thus there is a fallacy of accident here.

17. THE IMMOBILIZATION OF ONE DISTRIBUTION BY ANOTHER

Rule [V]: *When there are two distributions over the same part of a locution the first immobilizes the second.*[66]

On this basis the following sophisma is solved. Suppose there are three men who see every man and are running while all the others see Socrates [only] and are not running. Then every man who sees every man is run-

---

[65] The crux of the inference is the illicit derivation of 'every man sees every man' from 'every man sees himself.' The warrant offered for this derivation — "the word 'himself' is the same as 'every man' " — may be interpreted and generalized as follows: A reflexive personal pronoun may be replaced with its antecedent *salva veritate*. The rule of replacement may acquire some plausibility in this general version from the singular premisses in the inductive proof, for it does seem to be true that a reflexive personal pronoun *with a proper name or a definite description as its antecedent* may be replaced with its antecedent *salva veritate* (if we avoid contexts involving referential opacity, such as 'Socrates is aware that he has injured himself'). Part of what the sophisma may be said to show is that this rule of replacement does not hold at all in case the antecedent of the reflexive personal pronoun is a common name together with a distributive sign.

[66] This rule should be compared with what Sherwood has to say about his fifth rule regarding confused and determinate supposition in *Introductiones*, Chapter Five (*WSIL*, pp. 119–120). A distribution is mobile when the distributed term "supposits for many in such a way as to supposit for any" — e.g., the distribution in 'every man is running,' from which one can "descend" to 'Socrates is running.' A distribution is immobile when such a descent cannot be made. Thus the distribution in 'only every man is running' is immobile, for one cannot descend to 'only Socrates is running.' See *WSIL*, pp. 108–109.

ning. (Inductive proof.) Someone may infer 'therefore every man who sees Socrates is running,' which is false.[67]

It must be said that there is a fallacy of *figura dictionis* here [in moving] from immobile to mobile supposition, and a *quale quid* is transformed into a *hoc aliquid*.[68] When a term stands for many immobilely it stands as a *quale quid*, but when it stands for many mobilely it also stands for each [52] of them as a *hoc aliquid*. The reason for this immobility is that ascent does not hold in a distributed term.[69] Therefore, since 'man who sees every man' is in fewer than is 'man who sees Socrates'[70] — for [the former] follows from the latter and not conversely[71] — if the distribution is accepted [the inference] will not hold, and thus a fallacy of the consequent is manifest.[72]

18. A SECOND EXAMPLE OF SUCH IMMOBILIZATION

This is similar — 'every man is, and everything different from him is a non-man; therefore Socrates is, and everything different from him is a non-man'[73] — because the word 'him' in the first [proposition] is referred to

---

[67] It is worth noting that Rule [V] must be taken rather strictly. That is, it must be one *distribution*, or *universal* sign, that immobilizes a second, for a *particular* sign will not immobilize a universal sign within its scope — e.g., 'some man who sees every man is running; therefore some man who sees Socrates is running.' Moreover, the two distributions must be over the same *part* and not over the *whole* of the locution, for 'every woman' does not immobilize 'every man' in 'every woman and every man are dancing.'

[68] Cf. Chapter I, Section 14.

[69] A logical ascent is an inference from a statement containing a term T_1, lower in a predicamental line than another term T_2, to a statement like the first except that T_1 is replaced with T_2. (The account of logical ascent given in *WSIL*, p. 119, n. 58, is too narrow.) T_1 is lower than T_2 in a predicamental line just in case the things to which T_1 correctly applies (in which T_1 is) constitute a proper subset of the things to which T_2 correctly applies. Ascent is possible in an undistributed term — 'a man is running; therefore an animal is running' — but not in a distributed term — 'every man is running; therefore every animal is running.' Thus when Sherwood cites the impossibility of ascent in a distributed term as the reason for the immobility in this sophisma, despite the fact that the attempt that goes wrong is an attempt to *descend*, he is attempting to provide an analysis of the sophisma that ignores the logical operations under the second distribution and explains the error solely in terms of a misuse of the first distribution.

[70] That is, 'man who sees every man' is *below* 'man who sees Socrates' in this predicamental line, and so what looks like a descent under the second distribution (and hence has a semblance of legitimacy) can be construed as an attempt at an obviously illicit ascent in the first distribution.

[71] That is, the inference 'every man who sees Socrates is running; therefore every man who sees every man is running' is acceptable.

[72] On the fallacy of the consequent see *WSIL*, pp. 159–162.

[73] At this point O'Donnell's edition omits the following words, which occur in P: *ergo Sortes est et omne differens ab illo est non homo* — i.e., the entire conclusion.

the distributed term and thus has distribution in itself, while in the conclusion it counts as a discrete term. Thus it is the same as if one were to say 'everything different from every man . . .; therefore everything different from Socrates . . .' This must be answered as above.[74]

§ 19. A THIRD EXAMPLE OF SUCH IMMOBILIZATION

Suppose Plato sees himself and himself alone, and so on with respect to the single things. Then every man sees every man. Proof: Socrates sees Socrates, Plato sees Plato, and so on with respect to the others; therefore every man [sees every man]. Then someone may infer 'therefore Plato sees every man,' which is false.

It must be said that this 'every man [sees every man]' signifies that each suppositum of 'man' sees every man. For when the word 'every' [nominative] distributes the subject in respect of the predicate either [a] it finds there the word 'every' [accusative], in which case it signifies that the whole — seeing every man — goes together with the individual supposita of the subject, or [b] the word 'every' [accusative] comes in afterwards, and it signifies that seeing a man is given over (reddatur) to the distributed subject for each of the supposita of 'man' [accusative], as if everyone were seeing Socrates, everyone Plato, and so on with respect to the others. In [a] the [first] distribution includes the second; in [b] the reverse is true. In either case it is always signified that each suppositum of 'man' sees every man. But inductively it is said of each that he sees someone. Thus it is a paralogism of the consequent, as if one were to say, 'Socrates sees someone; therefore he sees everyone.'[75]

---

[74] Peter of Spain provides a full discussion of this sophisma, treating it in the way Sherwood seems to be suggesting here (*Sum. log.*, ed. Mullally, p. 74).

[75] The sophisma and its solution should be compared in detail with the sophisma and solution contained in Chapter I, Section 16, which might be characterized as analogous to case [b] in this section. The arrival-time distinction between the two distributions is probably to be read as a distinction between two inductions. In the [a] case the singulars comprising the steps of the induction will read 'Socrates sees every man, Plato sees every man,' and so on. In the [b] case the singulars will read 'every man sees Socrates, every man sees Plato,' and so on. But surely we are warranted in descending under either distributed term in either case, which seems to be what Sherwood is suggesting when he says "in either case it is always signified that each suppositum of 'man' sees every man." The flaw in the sophisma is that it attempts to arrive at 'every man sees every man' by neither of these two legitimate inductions but rather by *simultaneous* inductions in the subject term and the predicate term. All that occurs in *that* induction is that "it is said of each that he sees someone." Thus everything in this solution up to the final two sentences is to be taken as applying to legitimate derivations of 'every man sees every man,' while the final two sentences are to be applied to the illegitimate derivation attempted in the so-

'Every man is every man' is both proved and disproved in the same way. It is also solved in the same way.[76]

20. 'ONLY ONE' WITHIN THE SCOPE OF 'EVERY' OR 'ALL'

'Every head's possessor is only one head's possessor' (*omne caput habens est unum solum caput habens*) (where the word 'every' is taken accusatively and as attached to 'head' rather than to 'possessor') [77] is proved as follows: 'this head's possessor [is only one head's possessor]' and so on with respect to the single things.[78] But on the contrary, an opposite is here predicated of an opposite, and so the locution is false.

It must be said that the word 'possessor' in the subject can either be compounded with the predicate or divided [from it], but it is always named under one and the same construction. If it is compounded the locution signifies that the force of the distribution extends to the predicate as well as to the subject. In that case the phrase 'only one [head's possessor]' in the predicate is [merely] confused, and it is not true, as was claimed above, that an opposite is predicated of an opposite. If it is divided the division signifies that the force of the distribution does not go over to the predicate, in which case the phrase 'only one [head's possessor]' is not confused [but determinate] and the locution is false.[79]

Moreover, there is a *figura dictionis* in the proof, since 'only one head['s

---

phisma. Notice that the sophisma in Section 16 is characterized as a fallacy of accident while the flaw here is said to be the fallacy of the consequent. The latter characterization seems easier to apply in both instances. See Peter Geach's discussion of this section in his *Reference and Generality*, pp. 102–104.

[76] Like Section 18 and the penultimate paragraph of Section 11, this may be a reference to Peter of Spain, who analyzes this sophisma in two ways (*Sum. log.*, ed. Mullally, pp. 76–78). Some of what he has to say in his second analysis resembles what Sherwood says about 'every man sees every man' in this section.

[77] 'Every head's possessor' can be read either in the sense 'every possessor of a head' or in the sense 'the possessor of every head,' and the instruction in parentheses requires it to be read in the second sense. Something like this sophisma is frequently found in twelfth-century logic books (see De Rijk, *Logica modernorum*, Vol. I, Index C: *caput*).

[78] The inference is evidently intended to proceed in something like the following way: the possessor of $head_1$ is the possessor of only one head, the possessor of $head_2$ . . ., . . . of $head_3$ . . .; therefore the possessor of every head is the possessor of only one head. Perhaps this has relevance here because in the preceding section it was shown that simultaneous induction in both terms produces an illicit universal affirmative, and in this section we are presented with a case in which an illicit universal affirmative is produced on the basis of an induction in the subject term alone.

[79] The compounded and divided senses may be presented as follows. Compounded: 'of every head the possessor is the possessor of only one head.' Divided: 'there is only one head such that the possessor of every head is the possessor of it.'

possessor]' always stands for different ones in the singular [propositions] and is not confused in the universal [proposition].

'Every man is one man alone,' however, cannot be analyzed in this way, since that distribution can in no way stand in the predicate. There are not two things there (i.e., in the subject) one of which can be distributed while the other is that in respect of which the distribution is made, as the word 'head' is distributed in respect of 'possessor.' But [this analysis] works well in the sophisma 'a thing that is stated by every man is true' and in others like it.[80]

21. 'EVERY' OR 'ALL' TAKEN COLLECTIVELY AND TAKEN DISTRIBUTIVELY

It should be noted that when the word 'every' or 'all' is added to a term designating a universal whole it is always taken distributively. When, however, it is added to a term designating an integral whole or a collective whole it can be taken collectively — as if one were to say 'all the water' — i.e., the whole of the water — or 'all the people' — i.e., the whole.[81]

When it is used in the plural it is sometimes taken collectively, as in 'all the apostles are twelve,' and at other times distributively, as when one can infer 'all . . .; therefore these . . .'[82]

But the following sophisma raises a doubt. Suppose Socrates and Plato are brothers, Vergil and [53] Cicero[83] are brothers, Marcus and Cato are brothers, and there are no more men. Then all men are brothers. Proof: These are brothers (indicating the first two), and these are brothers (indicating the second two), and these are brothers (indicating the third two), and there are no more men; therefore [all men are brothers]. Then someone may infer 'therefore Socrates and Vergil are brothers,' which is false.

It must be said that the induction is insufficient because the word 'all'

---

[80] See Chapter I, Sections 13 and 14. Compare Section 20 as a whole with Chapter VII, Section 4, and with the concluding sentence of Chapter VII, Section 7.

[81] A universal whole is a genus or a species (see *WSIL*, p. 78, nn. 46 and 48). Neither 'water' nor 'people' seems to designate an integral whole as that notion is employed in *Introductiones* (*WSIL*, pp. 78–79). The notion of a collective whole does not appear in *Introductiones*; cf. the discussion of a quantitative whole (*WSIL*, pp. 79–81).

[82] Evidently 'all' can sometimes occur in such a way as to be taken either collectively or distributively, as in 'all the lead weights are heavy.'

[83] Reading '*Cicero*' for '*Plato.*' Originally in P the name 'Plato' appeared as the second in each of the three pairs of names; it was corrected to 'Cato' in the third case and it should have been corrected to some other name — 'Cicero' will do — in the second case as well.

distributes for all the combinations there can be. Thus, since there can be more combinations than the induction touches, the induction is insufficient, and there is a paralogism of the consequent in the proof.

22. OTHER UNIVERSAL AFFIRMATIVE SIGNS

Enough has been said about the word 'every' or 'all.' There is no need to say anything about the words '*quilibet*' and '*quisque*' (since they have nearly the same force as does the word '*omnis*'), or of the words '*quicumque vel quiscumque.*' The latter are of the same force as the former two except that they have in them the character of the word 'or' (*sive*). It is, of course, for that reason that they require two words.

CHAPTER II. '*Whole*' *(Totum)*

Now, however, we have to deal with the word 'whole,' regarding which it must be known that sometimes it indicates (*dicit*) the wholeness of something considered as a real thing, in which case it is equipollent to 'entire' (*integrum*) and is a categorematic word.[1] At other times it indicates the wholeness of something in respect of a predicate and is a syncategorematic word, in which case, as one says, it has the same strength as 'each and every part' and is a universal sign.

The following sophisma proceeds on this basis. The whole Socrates is less than Socrates. Proof: Each and every part of Socrates is less than Socrates; therefore the whole Socrates [is less than Socrates]. Then one may infer 'therefore Socrates is less than Socrates.' Or on the contrary, the whole Socrates is equal to Socrates; therefore not less.

It must be said that 'the whole Socrates' is not equipollent to 'each and every part of Socrates' but to 'Socrates considered in respect of each and every part' (*Sortes ita quod quaelibet pars*); for since it is a universal affirmative sign, it supposits [2] that the predicate is in the subject, and there

---
[1] On various senses of the word 'whole' recognized by Sherwood see *WSIL*, pp. 26 and 78–84.
[2] This use of the notion of supposition seems plainly mistaken; 'supposits' is no doubt a slip for 'signifies.'

[40

is a fallacy of the consequent in the proof. As to the "on the contrary," it must be known that it proceeds insofar as 'whole' is a categorematic word.³

---

³ Peter of Spain presents two fuller discussions of 'whole,' including this sophisma (*Sum. log.*, ed. Mullally, pp. 90–94 and 126–128).

CHAPTER III.¹ *Number Words (Dictiones numerales)*

It must be known that each and every number word can indicate a plurality belonging to its adjunct either in reality, in which case it is a categorematic word, or in respect of a predicate or a subject, in which case it is a syncategorematic word.

For example, if one says 'ten men are carrying a stone,' the sense in the first case is that men who are ten [in number] are carrying a stone, and it is true whether they carry it together or separately. In the second case the expression signifies that the subject 'men' relates to (*respicit*) the predicate for ten supposita, and it is signified that each one carries the stone separately.

---

¹ This short chapter is not indicated by a title or even by paragraphing in O'Donnell's edition. The beginning of a new discussion is indicated in P, however, and a title — "*De dictionibus numeralibus*" — is supplied in the margin of the manuscript, as at the beginnings of other chapters.

CHAPTER IV.¹ *'Infinitely Many' (Infinita in plurali)*

1. 'INFINITELY MANY' AND NUMBER WORDS

In the same way the phrase 'infinitely many' is both syncategorematic and categorematic, for it can indicate an infinite plurality belonging to its substance² either absolutely or in respect of a predicate. We can see its

---

¹ This chapter is not indicated by a title in O'Donnell's edition. As in the case of the chapter on the word 'whole,' however, the beginning of a new discussion is indicated in P, and a title — "*Infinita*" — is supplied in the margin of the manuscript.

² I.e., to the common name to which 'infinitely many' is attached. Thus in the

signification in the following way: 'infinitely many' strips away numerical limit and thus posits an excess in respect of any number whatever; therefore it is equipollent to 'more than however many you please' (*quotlibet plura*). Thus it is apparent that this line of argument — 'infinitely many; therefore two' — does not hold good.

On this basis the following sophisma is solved. Suppose that twenty [men] are hauling a boat in common, and twenty-one another, and so on to infinity. Then infinitely many men are hauling a boat. Proof: more than however many you please are hauling a boat; therefore infinitely many. The premiss of the proof (*prima*) is apparent as follows: more than two are hauling a boat, and [more] than three, and so on to infinity; therefore [more] than however many men you please [are hauling a boat]. Then one may infer 'therefore two [men are hauling a boat],' which is false. And it is apparent that this inference does not hold good, just as 'more than two; therefore two' [does not hold good], since 'infinitely many' does not mean that two, or that three, are hauling, but that *more than* two [are hauling], and so on with respect to the others. [54]

2. 'INFINITELY MANY' AND 'FINITELY MANY'

Another sophisma: Infinitely many are finitely many. Proof: more than two are finitely many, and more than three [are finitely many], and so on successively; therefore infinitely many [are finitely many]. But on the contrary, in this case an opposite is predicated of an opposite; therefore the locution is false.

It must be said that the phrase 'infinitely many,' as has been said, can be categorematic, in which case [the locution] is false, for [the phrase] has its substance, which it multiplies in this fashion in reality, in itself.[2] The sense [of the locution in this case] is 'the real things that in reality are infinitely many, those are finitely many.'[4] In another way it can be syncategorematic, in such a way that it indicates a plurality belonging to its substance in respect of the predicate. The sense [of the locution in this case] is that the

---

sophisma presented in the next paragraph 'men' may be said to be the "substance" of 'infinitely many.'

[3] I.e., 'infinitely many' is being used pronominally in this case and not as the modifier of a noun, as in the preceding sophisma.

[4] O'Donnell's edition has '*infinitae*'; '*finitae*' in P.

[5] It seems that the sense of this sentence would be clarified if 'subject' were to supplant 'real thing.' In any case "the real thing" (*res*) is evidently to be understood as the reality (if any) corresponding to the term in question (here, 'infinitely many').

real thing [5] relates to the predicate 'to be finitely many' for infinitely many [6] supposita, and thus it is proved. Nor is an opposite predicated of an opposite in this case, since the plurality of 'infinitely many' extends to the predicate and confuses it; [7] and ['infinitely many'] stands for infinitely many, each and every one of which is finite (as is apparent on the basis of an induction). Therefore the phrase (*hoc quod dico*) 'finitely many' taken in this way is not opposed to 'infinitely many.' (Something like this was said in connection with the sophisma 'every man is one man.') [8]

---

[6] Following the Oxford manuscript (hereafter cited as O), which has '*infinitis*' here, where P has '*multis*.'
[7] I.e., causes it to have merely confused supposition.
[8] See Chapter I, Section 13. Peter of Spain discusses 'infinite' and 'infinitely many' at considerably greater length (*Sum. log.*, ed. Mullally, pp. 98–102 and 118–122).

CHAPTER V.[1] *'Both' (Uterque)*

There is one more sign distributive of supposita — viz. 'both.' Nothing more need be said of it than [has been said] of the word 'every' or 'all,' insofar as it distributes for numerical parts [2] except that it divides only for two appellata and must be attached to a term the community of which is limited to two, as when one says 'both of them are blessed,' two but not three having been indicated.[3]

---

[1] Although this short chapter is separated from the material of the first four chapters by the intervention of the discussion of '*qualelibet*,' a sign distributive of copulata, it plainly belongs with those earlier chapters, all of which discuss signs distributive of supposita. Thus the material of Chapters V and VI appears in this translation in the reverse order of its appearance in the Latin. (The chapter on 'both' is on p. 56 in O'Donnell's edition.)
[2] See Chapter I, Section 2.
[3] This distinguishes 'both' from 'every' or 'all' in respect of the rule of three (see Chapter I, Section 5). Peter of Spain discusses 'both' in more detail, employing a version of the sophisma introduced by Sherwood in Chapter I, Section 14 (*Sum. log.*, ed. Mullally, pp. 82–86).

CHAPTER VI.[1] *'Of Every Sort' (Qualelibet)*

1. SIGNS DISTRIBUTIVE OF COPULATA

Besides the aforementioned signs there are others that are distributive of copulata, just as the signs 'every' or 'all' and 'each and every' (*quilibet*) are distributive of supposita. (A suppositum is what is signified as a *what*, a copulatum as a *what sort* or a *how much*.)[2] Signs of that kind are 'of every sort' (*qualislibet*), 'however much' (*quantumlibet*), and the like.

It must be known that [signs] of this kind signify a definite accident in an indefinite (*infinita*) substance, just as other adjectives do, and signify, besides, the distribution of that same accident in respect of that substance. Thus[3] 'of every sort' definitely signifies this accident — quality — indefinitely in whatever substance or suppositum [it is attached to], and together with this [it signifies] distribution. It is equipollent to 'things of any and every sort' (*cujuslibet qualitatis res*); the particulars that correspond to it, however, are 'white,' 'black,' 'literate' (*grammaticus*), and the like.[4]

2. 'OF EVERY SORT' USED CATEGOREMATICALLY AND SYNCATEGOREMATICALLY

It must be known, therefore, that the phrase 'of every sort' is sometimes either categorematic or syncategorematic. In the first case it means that some thing has all qualities; in the second case it means that under every sort of quality (*sub qualilibet qualitate*) the thing receives the predicate.

On this basis the following sophisma is solved. Suppose that there are [only] three qualities — whiteness, literacy, music — and that Socrates has the first and is running, that Plato has the second and is running, that Cicero has the third and is running, and that Vergil has all three and is not

---

[1] Like Chapters III and IV, this chapter is not indicated by a title in O'Donnell's edition, where, as a consequence, Chapters III, IV, and VI are presented as if they were part of the chapter on the word 'whole.' In this case as in the case of Chapters III and IV the beginning of a new discussion is indicated in P, and a title — "*Qualelibet*" — is supplied in the margin of the manuscript.

[2] Cf. Sherwood's second definitions of supposition and copulation in *Introductiones* (*WSIL*, p. 107): ". . . supposition is called a signification of something as subsisting . . ., and copulation is called a signification of something as adjoining . . ."; also *WSIL*, p. 121, n. 68.

[3] O'Donnell's edition omits the '*ut*' to be found here in P.

[4] Just as the particulars corresponding to '*omnis*' are different individuals, so the particulars corresponding to '*qualislibet*' are different sorts.

[44

running. Then [a thing] of every sort is running. Proof: A white [thing] is running, a literate [thing] is running, a musical [thing] is running, and there are no more [sorts of things]; therefore [a thing] of every sort is running. But whatever [thing] is of every sort is Vergil; therefore Vergil is running (which is false).

Solution: In the first (i.e., in the proof) [5] 'of every sort' is used syncategorematically, in the second (i.e., in the disproof) categorematically; thus there is an equivocation. Alternatively, it can be said that the subject 'thing,' which is understood in the phrase 'of every sort,' stands merely confusedly in respect of its own division or distribution in the first (i.e., in the major premiss of the disproof) and determinately in the second (i.e., in the minor premiss of the disproof).[6] It is clear that this is the case when the first is proved and one says 'a white [thing] is running,' [since] the word 'thing' understood in that case supposits for one, and in the other cases for others. Thus in the universal [proposition] the word 'thing' is confused in such a way that for one suppositum it refers to (*respiciat*) one suppositum of its distribution, and for another [it refers to] another.[7] But in the minor [premiss of the disproof] for one suppositum [of the word 'thing'] it refers to its whole plurality of distribution, and so ['thing'] stands determinately

---

[5] This and the three following explanatory phrases enclosed in parentheses occur as interlinear glosses in P.

[6] The major premiss of the disproof is 'whatever [thing] is of every sort is Vergil'; the suppressed minor premiss is '[a thing] of every sort is running.' On 'thing' standing merely confusedly in respect of its own division or distribution see Sherwood's discussion of a similar example in *Introductiones*: ". . . when I say 'a man of every sort is running' the copulation is distributed; I can therefore descend to the specific copulata (*copulata specialia*) as follows: 'a man of every sort is running; therefore a white man is running, and a black [man is running], (and so on).' But the word 'man' [in the premiss] supposits merely confusedly, since we cannot descend as follows: 'a man of every sort . . . therefore Socrates . . .' A sign such as 'of every sort' signifies some accident and distributes it in respect of its substantive" (*WSIL*, p. 121).

[7] The effect of 'a thing of every sort' can be (and usually is) to confer distributive confused copulation on 'sort' and merely confused supposition on 'thing' (this is more easily spelled out for the English phrase than for the single Latin word '*qualelibet*'). As the conclusion of the proof 'a thing of every sort is running' is a universal proposition, 'thing' falling within the scope of 'of every sort'; but as the minor premiss of the disproof 'a thing of every sort is running' is a particular proposition in which 'thing,' falling outside the scope of 'of every sort,' has determinate supposition (as is explained in the next sentence). The present sentence of the text is ambiguous and obscure; what is evidently intended could be expressed in the following way. Thus in the universal proposition 'a thing of every sort is running' occurring as the conclusion of the proof the word 'thing' is confused in such a way that for one suppositum of 'thing' the sign 'of every sort' refers to one copulatum of its distribution, and for another it refers to another.

in respect of that [plurality], as was said in connection with the sophisma '[a thing that is stated] by every man [is true].'[8]

Someone will say that the first [9] is ambiguous in that '[a thing] of every sort' could either be compounded with the predicate or divided from it. The composition signifies that [10] the distribution extends to the predicate and confuses it so that it stands for many. In that case [the predicate] can be granted to the subject 'thing' for various supposita, and so 'thing' can be confused, and [the locution] is true. The division, on the other hand, signifies that the distribution does not extend to the predicate, and so it stands determinately.

But one determinate [predicate] cannot be granted to a *hoc aliquid* [11] except for one; [55] thus the subject stands for some one [thing]. And so it does stand determinately, and the locution is false. The distribution can stay in the subject and not pass over to the predicate because whatever the distribution requires is in the subject itself, for both that which is distributed — 'quality' — and that in respect of which the division [12] stands — 'thing' — are there, as was previously explained.

3. 'OF EVERY SORT' IN COMBINATION WITH OTHER DISTRIBUTIVE SIGNS

Again, suppose that there are only the three qualities and that Socrates has them all, and Plato likewise, and Cicero likewise, and that each [of them] knows this of the other[s]. Suppose further that Vergil has only whiteness and that he knows nothing of the others nor they of him. Then everything of every sort knows of every such thing that it is such (*quodlibet qualelibet de quolibet tali scit se esse tale*). Proof: This [thing] of every sort (Socrates having been indicated) knows of every such thing [that it is such], and thus also of Plato and Cicero, for they are such. Plato likewise, and Cicero likewise, and there are no more [things] of every sort. Therefore everything [of every sort knows of every such thing that it is

---

[8] See Chapter I, Section 14.

[9] Here 'the first' must mean the *minor* premiss of the disproof — i.e., 'a thing of every sort is running' considered as a particular proposition.

[10] The phrase 'the composition signifies that . . .' is an unusual way of saying "if '[a thing] of every sort' is taken to be compounded with the predicate, then . . ."; likewise 'the division signifies that . . .' a few lines down. On composition and division see Chapter I, n. 47.

[11] I.e., an individual, a primary substance. See Chapter I, n. 59.

[12] Here 'division' is being used in the sense in which it is synonymous with 'distribution' and not in the sense in which it is contrasted wth 'composition.'

such]. Then everything [white]¹³ knows of every such thing [that it is such], which is false, since none of the others knows of Vergil, and vice versa.

Some say that 'of every sort' is categorematic in the first (i.e., in the proof),¹⁴ [since] otherwise it could not be distributed by means of 'everything,' and that it is syncategorematic in the second (i.e., in the disproof),¹⁵ since otherwise one could not descend to 'white [thing].'

But it is clear that this is false, for a thing that has every quality¹⁶ can be inferred, and so a white [thing can be inferred]. This, however, was the exposition of it in the case in which it was categorematic.

It must be said that 'such thing' in the first proposition and in the second was the same as '[thing] of every sort' and in the third¹⁷ was the same as 'white [thing].' Thus it is the same as if one were to say '. . . of everything of every sort; therefore . . . of every white thing.' Therefore, since the first distribution immobilizes the second,¹⁸ there will be a fallacy of *figura dictionis* or, alternatively, a fallacy of the consequent, as has been said.¹⁹

4. LOGICAL DESCENT IN CONNECTION WITH A SIGN DISTRIBUTIVE OF COPULATA²⁰

There is one more point that must be understood — viz. that in the division of a sign distributive for copulata it is not permissible to descend

---

[13] The text is evidently corrupt at this point. O has '*quidlibet*'; P has '*quodlibet*' with '*qualibet*' added in an interlinear gloss. O'Donnell follows P without the gloss. But the sense plainly demands the insertion of 'white' (*album*) here, as is shown by the discussion that follows as well as by the parallel sophisma in Peter of Spain (*Sum. log.*, ed. Mullally, p. 96).

[14] This and the following explanatory phrase enclosed in parentheses occur as interlinear glosses in P.

[15] 'Everything of every sort knows of every such thing that it is such' occurs as the conclusion of the proof and serves as the suppressed premiss of the disproof.

[16] The phrase 'in itself' (*secundum se*) occurs at this point in P but not in O. O'Donnell follows P, but the phrase seems better omitted.

[17] The first proposition is the occurrence of 'everything of every sort knows of every such thing that it is such' as the conclusion of the proof, and the second proposition is its implicit occurrence as the premiss of the disproof. The third proposition is the false conclusion of the disproof — 'everything white knows of every such thing that it is such.'

[18] See Chapter I, Section 17.

[19] Evidently a reference to the concluding paragraph of Chapter I, Section 17. A note in the margin of P refers to "the third folio before this, at the beginning of the second page." Peter of Spain's brief discussion of the sign 'of every sort' centers around the sophisma discussed in this section (*Sum. log.*, ed. Mullally, pp. 94–96, 129).

except to species alone.²¹ For example, '[a thing] of every sort . . .; therefore a white [thing] . . .,' and *not* 'therefore this white [thing] . . .'

But on the contrary, '[a thing] of every sort . . .; therefore [a thing] having each and every quality . . .; therefore [a thing] having this quality (Socrates's whiteness having been indicated) . . .; therefore this white [thing] (Socrates having been indicated) . . .'

It must be said, however, that 'of every sort' is taken for the genera of single things and not for the single things belonging to the genera.²² Likewise [as regards] 'each and every,' insofar as it expounded 'of every sort.' ²³ The reason for this is that accidents of the kind that are designated by means of such signs as 'of every sort' and 'however much' are divided only as such and are multiplied as far as species but not as far as individuals (except by means of substance).

---

²⁰ This section occurs as an afterthought following Chapter IX, the last of the chapters on distributive signs, rather than here at the end of Chapter VI, where it obviously belongs. (The text of the section is on p. 59 in O'Donnell's edition.)
²¹ See n. 6, this chapter.
²² I.e., 'of every sort' distributes for the proximate rather than for the remote parts. See Chapter I, Section 4.
²³ I.e., although 'each and every' (*quamlibet*) usually occurs as a sign distributive of supposita (see Chapter VI, Section 1) and hence a sign in connection with which a logical descent to individuals is permissible, it occurs here in an analysis of a sign distributive of copulata and hence is bound by the restrictions on logical descent in connection with such signs.

CHAPTER VII. *'No' (Nullus)*

1. SPECIFIC AND NUMERICAL PARTS

Next, as to negative signs, and first as to the word 'no,' of which it must be known that sometimes it divides for specific parts and at other times for numerical parts.¹

On this basis the following sophisma is solved. Suppose that there is no man. Then no man is an animal. Proof: No man is; therefore no man is an animal. Alternatively: there is nothing under man with which the predicate agrees;² therefore [no man is an animal]. But on the contrary, 'every man is an animal' is true; therefore 'no man is an animal' is false.

---

¹ See Chapter I, Section 2.
² This is the logical principle *dici de nullo*, the complement of *dici de omni* (see

It must be said that it is proved insofar as ['no'] divides for numerical parts, or for actually extant parts; for such [parts], since they are not, are not animals. It is disproved, however, insofar as ['no'] is used for specific parts, since 'every man [is an animal]' is true for such [parts].

2. PROXIMATE AND REMOTE PARTS

['No'] can also divide for proximate or for remote parts;[3] but those two senses are interchangeable as far as truth and falsity are concerned, for if no individual animal is running, then neither a man nor an ass (and so on with respect to the others) [is running], and vice versa.

3. THE SCOPE OF THE NEGATION BELONGING TO 'NO'

Sometimes an ambiguity results from the negation belonging to the word 'no,' which can be carried to various things.

On this basis the following sophisma is solved. On account of no one running there are horns growing from your forehead (*Nullo currente crescunt tibi* [56] *cornua fronte*). Proof: Not on account of this one, not on account of that one (and so on with respect to the single things); therefore on account of no one [running there are horns growing from your forehead]. Then one may infer: 'But none are running; therefore there are horns growing from your [forehead].' Or one may infer: 'Therefore *while* no one is running, or *if*, or *because* no one is running,[4] [there are horns growing from your forehead],' each of which is false.

It must be said that the first [proposition] can be compounded, and [taken] in that way it is true. The composition signifies that[5] the negation extends to the whole, and in that way it is proved. Or it can be divided; and the division signifies that [the negation] stays in the participle, and in that way it is false and disproved.[6]

Chapter I, n. 35). In *Introductiones* Sherwood puts it this way: ". . . whenever nothing is subsumed under the subject of which the predicate is asserted, that is *dici de nullo*" (*WSIL*, p. 62).

[3] See Chapter I, Section 4.

[4] These are three ordinary interpretations of the Latin ablative absolute, '*nullo currente*,' translated in the sophisma as 'on account of no one running' in an attempt to preserve the ambiguity on which the sophisma turns.

[5] See Chapter VI, n. 10.

[6] Compounded: 'there is no one such that on account of his running there are horns growing from your forehead'; divided: 'on account of the fact that no one is running there are horns growing from your forehead,' or any of the interpretations of the ablative absolute proposed in the last sentence of the preceding paragraph. Peter

4. ANOTHER EXAMPLE REGARDING THE SCOPE OF SUCH NEGATION

This is similar: No head's possessor is some head's possessor (*nullum caput habens est aliquod caput habens*). 'No head's possessor' may be used accusatively [7] and [the proposition] may be proved as follows: Not this head's possessor is some head's possessor, not that . . . (and so on with respect to the single things); therefore no [head's possessor is some head's possessor]. But on the contrary, in this case an opposite is predicated of an opposite. Or one may infer: 'Therefore what possesses no head possesses some head.'

It must be said that all the singular propositions are ambiguous in that they can be compounded (so that the negation is carried to the whole, with the result that it extends to the principal verb) or divided (so that [the negation] stays in the participle). In the first case they are false; in the second case, true.[8] Understand in addition to this that 'some head's [possessor]' stands for different things.[9]

Similarly, the universal [proposition] itself can be compounded (so that the negation belonging to 'no' extends to the whole), in which case it is false just as its singulars are. Or [it can be] divided (so that the negation stays in the participle), in which case the distribution stays there too,[10] since the distribution is caused by the negation.

---

of Spain considers a similar sophisma in his *Tractatus syncategorematum* (hereafter cited as *Tr. syn.*), tr. Mullally, pp. 25–26.

[7] This is evidently a garbled version of the same sort of instruction as was attached to the similar sophisma in Chapter I, Section 20, and probably is to be read as follows: 'No' may be used accusatively and attached to 'head' rather than to 'possessor.'

[8] Compounded: 'it is not the case that the possessor of this head is the possessor of some head'; divided: 'there is some head's possessor such that it is not the possessor of this head.'

[9] The singular propositions making up the induction must be taken in the divided sense if the proof is to have any semblance of acceptability, and in carrying out the induction completely 'some head's possessor' will have to supposit determinately for at least two different things (no matter how many different things are involved in the induction). Thus the proof might begin 'there is some head's possessor — viz., the possessor of head $_n$ — such that it is not the possessor of head $_1$, there is some head's possessor — viz., the possessor of head $_n$ — such that it is not the possessor of head $_2$, . . .,' but it would have to end with a singular proposition in which the "some head's possessor" would have to be otherwise identified: '. . . there is some head's possessor — viz., the possessor of head $_1$ — such that it is not the possessor of head $_n$.'

[10] At this point the following marginal gloss occurs in P: "since in that case the distribution, just like the negation, is carried to the 'non-possessor' (*ad non habens*), not to the principal verb, 'is.' The sense is 'the possessor of no head is some head's possessor' (*habens nullum caput est aliquod caput habens*). And [the 'no'] removes

[This sophisma can be solved] also by means of this rule. [Rule I:] *When two functions are included in a word, the one pertains to nothing to which the other does not pertain.*[11] Then 'some head's [possessor]' in the predicate is not confused, and so the inference is from many determinate [suppositions] to one determinate [supposition]. Thus it is false, and there is a fallacy of *figura dictionis* in the proof. Therefore the universal [proposition] is false in every sense.

But the following objection is raised. Those singular [propositions] are true; therefore, since the singulars correspond to the universal, it seems they will have a true [universal proposition] and only this one [corresponding to them].

It must be said that the universal [proposition] that corresponds to them[12] is this: 'every head's non-possessor [is some head's possessor]' (*omne caput non habens etc.*); so that the negation stays in the participle and the distribution passes over to the predicate. If, however, he wants to infer on the basis of the equipollence 'every . . . not; therefore no . . .,'[13] then an objection must be raised based on the following rule. [Rule II:] *'Every . . . not' and 'no' are equipollent only when the negation belonging to 'not' is carried to the same thing in respect of which the*

---

the affirmative verb, and the participle can be understood as negated, and 'head' is distributed in respect of the participle and thus in respect of the verb." The participle in question is '*habens*,' here translated as 'possessor.'

[11] After discussing the sophisma 'seeing nothing is seeing something' (*nihil videns est aliquid videns*), Peter of Spain alludes to this rule, possibly including Sherwood among the "*antiqui*" (a term used in the thirteenth century to designate not only the ancients but also those recently dead; see Introduction to *WSIL*, p. 7). "It must be known that its premisses are ambiguous since the negation can determinate either the verb or the participle, as was said earlier. Thus the *antiqui* claimed that the premisses were ambiguous as a consequence of the following rule, which they offered: Whenever negation and distribution are included in one term, to whatever the one is referred the other is also referred. Thus since the distribution posited in the oblique [accusative] case cannot affect the verb in the aforementioned sentence, neither can the negation. The judgment [of the *antiqui*] is the same as regards the sophismata 'no head's possessor is some head's possessor,' 'different from no man is different from some man,' etc." (*Sum. log.*, ed. Mullally, p. 82).

[12] An interlinear gloss at this point in P says "and is true."

[13] Sherwood introduces this equipollence in *Introductiones*, explaining it in the following way: "The sign 'every' signifies that the predicate (together with its dispositions) belongs to each part of the subject; therefore whenever the predicate follows with a negation it will signify that the negated predicate belongs to each part of the subject and thus that the predicate as such is separated from every part; therefore it is equipollent to a universal negative sign. Thus if one says 'every man is not-running,' it is clear that this is universal, on account of the sign, and negative; and therefore it is as described above" (*WSIL*, pp. 35–36).

distribution belonging to 'every' occurs, and vice versa. But that is not the case here, as has been said.

5. A TERM INVOLVING A CLAUSE OR PHRASE WITHIN THE SCOPE OF 'NO'

[Rule III:] *When there is a clause or phrase (implicatio) or an adjective associated with the subject or associated with the predicate, the locution is ambiguous in that it can be compounded, so that the negation belonging to 'no' extends to the whole, or divided, so that it does not extend to the clause or phrase itself or to the adjective.*[14]

Suppose that the white men are sitting down and the others are running. Then no man who is white is running. If this is compounded, then it is true; but if 'man' and 'who [is white]' are divided, then it is false. The division signifies that no man is running and that he is white.

Again, suppose that no one sees white men, but only the others. Then no man sees a man who is white. This is true insofar as it is compounded and false insofar as it is divided.

6. WHETHER ATTACHING 'NO' TO A TERM CAUSES IT TO STAND FOR NONEXISTENTS

There is a doubt whether the word 'no' makes a term attached to it stand for nonexistents. And it seems that it does so, for, as matters stand (*rebus enim se habentibus*), this now follows: 'no man is running; therefore Caesar is not running.'[15] Proof: Grant the opposite, that Caesar is running, and it follows that some man is running, since he cannot run unless he is and is also a man. But if one can infer thus, then 'man' supposits for nonentities, as it seems. But this is contrary to the rule of suppositions, since ['man'] has sufficient appellata.[16] [57]

Again, suppose that ['man'] stands in one and the same way in the con-

---

[14] Cf. Chapter I, Section 10.

[15] The inference proceeds on the view that Caesar *was* a man, but as matters stand at present he is nothing at all.

[16] The "rule of suppositions" invoked here is the "rule regarding supposition and appellation" introduced and discussed at length by Sherwood in *Introductiones*: "An unrestricted common term, having sufficient appellata and suppositing in connection with a present-tense verb that has no ampliating force, supposits only for those [things subordinate to it] that do exist" (*WSIL*, p. 123). Since there are at least three extant men at present, 'man' has sufficient appellata.

trary and the contradictory. In that case 'every man is running' would be false for all presently running [men].[17]

It must be said that this holds correctly: 'no man [is running]; therefore not Caesar [is running].'[18] And it is not an argument from a quantitative whole [19] in that case,[20] since Caesar is not a man. In the same way, this is not [an argument from a quantitative whole]: 'no thing having eyes sees; therefore neither does wood' (*nullum habens oculos videt; ergo nec lignum*). And just as the term 'thing having eyes' does not supposit for wood, so 'man' in this case does not supposit for Caesar.

7. A THIRD EXAMPLE REGARDING THE SCOPE OF THE NEGATION BELONGING TO 'NO'[21]

Suppose that Socrates says that a man is an ass. Then what is stated by no one is truly said by no one (*a nullo enuntiatum a nullo vere dicitur*).[22] Proof: What no one states is truly said by no one; therefore what is stated by no one [is truly said by no one]. On the contrary, what is stated by someone is truly said by no one, since what Socrates states can be truly said by no one.

Solution: It can be said that the negation belonging to [the first] 'no one' can stay in 'what is stated,' and then the principal composition [23] remains negated by the other negation. Or [the first negation] can pass over to the principal verb by falling on the other negation, with the result that the

---

[17] At this point the following marginal gloss occurs in P: "That is, 'man' would stand for a nonexistent just as in the universal negative."
[18] The sense of 'not Caesar is running' is 'it is not the case that Caesar is running.'
[19] On the (dialectical) argument from a quantitative whole see *WSIL*, pp. 79–81. As one example of such an argument Sherwood gives 'no man is running; therefore Socrates is not running.'
[20] A marginal gloss occurring at this point in P says "but rather an argument from the superior." On the (dialectical) argument from the superior see *WSIL*, pp. 95–96.
[21] This section occurs following the three sections of the chapter on 'nothing,' but those three sections are not marked off in any way in P as dealing with a distinct topic. The clearest arrangement seems to be the recognition of those three sections as a separate chapter (Chapter VIII of the translation) and the inclusion of this section in the chapter on 'no.' (The text of this section is on p. 59 of O'Donnell's edition.)
[22] Cf. the similar sophisma in Chapter I, Section 14.
[23] 'Composition' is used here in another of its technical senses, one closely approximating though somewhat broader than the sense of 'predication,' or 'subject-predicate relation.' (Cf. Peter of Spain's long discussion of the notion of composition, *Tr. syn.*, tr. Mullally, pp. 17–21.) In this sophisma the principal composition is effected in the principal verb '*dicitur*' ('is . . . said').

principal composition is affirmed. In the first sense 'what is stated' has to be divided from that which follows, in the second it has to be compounded [with that which follows]. In the first case it is proved, in the second case it is disproved.

But it seems that since [the first] 'no one' falls under the circumstances belonging to 'by,' it can be carried only to 'what is stated.' Thus some say that 'what is stated by no one [is truly said by no one]' is always negative and that '[what is stated] by someone [is truly said by no one]' does not contradict it since [the latter] is likewise negative.

It must be said, however, that [the first] 'no one' is always carried to 'what is stated,' but in two ways, since [this occurs] either before it is ordered in relation to 'is [truly] said' or after.[24] In the first case the negation stays in 'what is stated.' In the second case it passes over to the predicate. The first sense is represented by means of division, the second by means of composition.[25] (And in this way the division [26] in 'every head's possessor . . .' and the negation in 'no head's possessor . . .'[27] can extend to the predicate in the sense of composition and not extend in the sense of division, and so also in similar cases.) [28]

---

[24] On this temporal metaphor see Chapter I, n. 43.
[25] Compounded: 'no one states anything that is truly said by no one'; divided: 'everything that is stated by no one is something that is truly said by no one.'
[26] I.e., the distribution. For the sophisma in question see Chapter I, Section 20.
[27] See Chapter VII, Section 4.
[28] Besides considering the sophisma cited in n. 6, this chapter, and the rule cited in n. 11, this chapter, Peter of Spain discusses 'no' very briefly in his *Summulae logicales*, considering only the sophisma 'no man is every man' (*Sum. log.*, ed. Mullally, pp. 78–80).

CHAPTER VIII.[1] *'Nothing' (Nihil)*

1. THE SCOPE OF THE NEGATION BELONGING TO 'NOTHING'

A sophisma [can occur] in [connection with] the negative sign 'nothing' in that the negation can be carried to various things. If [*a*] nothing is, then [*b*] that nothing is is true; and if [*b*], then [*c*] something is true; and if [*c*], then [*d*] something is; therefore, by [*a*], if nothing is, something is.

---

[1] The discussion of 'nothing' occurs in P as a portion of the chapter on 'no' (see Chapter VII, n. 21), and the beginning of the discussion contains no clear indication that Sherwood considered the syncategorematic word '*nihil*' as a topic quite dis-

It must be said that [b] 'that nothing is is true' is ambiguous in that the first 'is' and the second 'is' can be either compounded or divided. The division signifies that the negation stays in the first 'is'; [taken as] compounded it signifies that the negation passes over to the second 'is.' In the first case [b] is affirmative and does not follow from [a],[2] since an affirmative never follows from a negative (for negation posits nothing and affirmation posits something). In the second case [b] is negative, the sense being 'it is not true that something is,' and does follow from [a]. But then [c], which is affirmative, does not follow from [b], for the reason given earlier. (Certain difficulties pertaining to the treatise on insolubilia [3] could be touched on here, but they are put off until another time.)

2. THE IMMOBILIZATION OF ONE NEGATIVE WORD BY ANOTHER

Rule: *If there are two negative words, even from different parts of speech, the first immobilizes the second.*

For example, 'nothing is nothing.' Proof: Its contradictory — 'something is nothing' — is false; therefore it is true. Then [someone may infer] 'therefore nothing is no substance.' On the contrary, something [4] is no substance.

This can be solved by means of the rule just stated by assigning the fallacy of *figura dictionis* or of the consequent, because the 'nothing' in the predicate is in fewer than is 'no substance.' [5]

---

tinct from '*nullus*.' Peter of Spain distinguishes between them by saying that 'nothing' "signifies the same as 'no' but includes within itself the term receiving its distribution, since 'nothing' is a universal sign with negation, and 'thing' (*res*) is the term receiving its distribution" (*Sum. log.*, ed. Mullally, p. 80). The last section of Sherwood's chapter on 'no' (*nullus*), the section *following* the discussion of 'nothing' in P, introduces a sophisma in which '*nullus*' is used as a pronoun — 'no one' — so that it too might be described as including within itself the term receiving its distribution. In Sherwood's view, evidently, the difference noted by Peter of Spain between '*nihil*' and '*nullus*' is not so marked as Peter suggests, since '*nullus*' can occur not only as an adjective but also as a pronoun.

[2] The Latin here is '*non sequitur ex priori*' — 'it does not follow from the former.' A gloss in the margin of P at this point identifies "the former" as [a]: "i.e., from 'if nothing is.' "

[3] Sherwood's treatise on insolubilia is in P (ff. 46ᵛ–54ᵛ) immediately following his treatise on syncategorematic words. Insolubilia are, generally speaking, paradoxes of self-reference — e.g., 'what I am saying is false' — which were considered not strictly insoluble but uniquely difficult. See Introduction to *WSIL*, p. 15. On insolubilia generally and Sherwood's treatment of them in particular see Kneale, *Development*, pp. 227–229.

[4] A gloss in the margin of P at this point says "viz., a quality."

[5] Peter of Spain discusses this sophisma with somewhat different results (*Tr. syn.*, tr. Mullally, p. 27).

3. THE ILLICIT USE OF 'NOTHING' AS A NAME

'Nothing and the chimera are brothers' may be proved inductively or as follows: 'Something and the chimera are brothers' is false; therefore 'nothing and the chimera [are brothers]' is true. Then someone may infer 'therefore nothing and the chimera are.' On the contrary, neither nothing nor the chimera is; therefore the first [proposition] is false.

Some say that the first [proposition] is ambiguous in that the negation can fall either under the copulation [6] or over it. If under, then the sense is 'this very nothing (*hoc ipsum nihil*) is the chimera's brother,' and it is false. If over, then it denies that something is the chimera's brother, and it is true, and 'nothing and the chimera are' does not follow. Rather, it is a paralogism of the consequent, since 'to be brothers' is in fewer than is 'to be.'

It must be understood, however, that the word 'nothing' cannot be an infinite name,[7] for the *auctores* [8] always use it in such a way that the negation is carried to something outside and does not stay in the word 'nothing.' Thus [the word 'nothing'] is not something to which one and the same actual entity [can] be assigned (*unde non est aliquid cui assignari aliquis actus idem*). And therefore it cannot be one or the other of the things copulated by the word 'and,' and the negation always falls *over* the copulation. Thus the first [proposition] is true, the second is false,[9] and there is a fallacy of the consequent in the inference,[10] as has been said. The "on the contrary" could [be true] too, since it contradicts it [11] in the sense in which it is understood that 'nothing' falls *under* the copulation. [58]

---

[6] This is copulation as the function of the word 'and' and not copulation as one of the "properties of terms" (see Chapter VI, n. 2).

[7] 'Man' is a finite name (or noun), 'non-man' an infinite name. On this finite/infinite distinction see *Introductiones*, Chapter One, Section 5 (*WSIL*, pp. 23 and 24).

[8] This may mean the classical authors available at the time or, more probably, the elementary reading books assigned in connection with the study of grammar in the twelfth and thirteenth centuries. See L. J. Paetow, *The Arts Course at Medieval Universities with Special Reference to Grammar and Rhetoric*, pp. 53–55.

[9] By 'the first' Sherwood evidently means 'nothing and the chimera are brothers,' although an interlinear gloss in P at this point says "of the disproof," which would make this a reference to 'neither nothing nor the chimera is.' It is a little less easy to say what is meant here by 'the second,' although what is said about it seems to show that the reference is to 'nothing and the chimera are' taken in the sense intended for it in its original occurrence – i.e., 'a non-thing and the chimera exist.'

[10] Another interlinear gloss in P at this point says "of the disproof," but the inference referred to is evidently the inference of 'nothing and the chimera are' from 'nothing and the chimera are brothers,' as is indicated at the end of the preceding paragraph.

[11] I.e., 'nothing and the chimera are brothers.' A second hand has inserted the word '*non*' here in P, and O'Donnell adopts this reading in his edition; but the inser-

tion is evidently mistaken, for the translation would then read 'since it does not contradict it . . .' Sherwood's point is, however, that if the original proposition is read as he claims it must be read, with the 'nothing' falling *over* the 'and,' then the "on the contrary" can be true together with the original proposition, for it contradicts the original only under the illicit interpretation of the original.

CHAPTER IX. *'Neither' (Neutrum)*

There is, in addition, a negative sign that negates for two only—viz., 'neither.' From it arises such a sophisma as the following: 'Having neither eye, you can see' (*neutrum oculum habendo potes*[1] *videre*). Proof: Not having the left eye [you can see, and not having the right eye you can see]; therefore [having] neither [eye you can see]. On the contrary, [one may infer] 'therefore *while* you have neither eye, or *because*, or *if* you have neither, you can [see],' which is false.[2]

It must be said that if the singular [propositions] are compounded, then the negation is carried to the principal verb and they are negative and false. If they are divided, then the negation stays in the participle and they are true.[3] But in the premises 'you can' copulated different capacities and 'see' [copulated] different seeings.[4] In the first case the universal [proposition] '[having] neither [eye, you can see]' follows correctly.[5] In the second case it does not; instead, there is a *figura dictionis*. One can, however, infer this universal: 'not having both eyes, [you can see]; but '[having] neither [eye, you can see]' does not follow,[6] as has been said more fully in connection with the sophisma 'no head's possessor . . .'[7]

Enough has now been said regarding signs distributive of supposita and of copulata.

---

[1] O has '*potes*'; P has '*potest*.' O'Donnell's edition follows P at this point, although P has '*potes*' rather than '*potest*' in the remainder.
[2] Cf. Chapter VII, Section 3. Peter of Spain explains this analysis by citing a grammatical rule: "gerunds ending in '. . . *do*' have to be resolved by means of 'while,' 'if,' or 'because' " (*Sum. log.*, ed. Mullally, p. 86).
[3] Compounded: 'it is not the case that having the left eye you can see'; divided: 'lacking the left eye you can see.'
[4] I.e., the capacity to see with the right eye only, the capacity to see with the left eye only; and seeing with the right eye only, seeing with the left eye only.
[5] Where the conclusion is read as 'it is not the case that having either eye you can see' and the inference, although valid, is unacceptable because of its false premisses.
[6] Peter of Spain discusses this sophisma (*Sum. log.*, ed. Mullally, p. 86), but analyzes it as an instance of the fallacy of accident.
[7] See Chapter VII, Section 4.

CHAPTER X. *'But' (Praeter)*

1. REASONS FOR DISCUSSING 'BUT' AT THIS POINT

Since enough has now been said regarding distributive signs, we must next speak of the exceptive word 'but,'[1] both because an exception always tends to fall over a division [2] and to be immediately linked to it, and because exception is opposed to division (*tum quia oppositum habet ad ipsam*). [59] This is clear in that the word 'every' or 'all' indicates a total plurality and the word 'but,' by subtracting some part from the totality, [indicates] the opposite. There might nevertheless be some reason for treating of the exclusives [3] before [the exceptives], but it need not concern us.[4]

2. 'BUT' TAKEN DIMINUTIONALLY AND TAKEN COUNTER-INSTANTIVELY

It must be known that the word 'but' is sometimes taken additively — as when one says 'there are six clerks in here but one master,' [i.e.,] 'and a master too' — sometimes exceptively, and that in two ways: sometimes diminutionally, sometimes counter-instantively. [It is taken] diminutionally when it signifies that a diminution from some whole occurs as regards the thing itself, as in 'Socrates has eleven fingers but one.' [It is taken] counter-instantively when it excepts a part from a whole in respect of a predicate, as in 'every man but Socrates is running'; [5] for it signifies that Socrates is excepted from the whole 'every man,' not as regards the thing itself, but in respect of the predicate.

[Taken counter-instantively, 'but'] is a syncategorematic word in the strict sense. And it is said to be taken counter-instantively because it sets

---

[1] The English word 'but' is not regularly listed among the words available for translating '*praeter*' ('except,' 'besides,' etc.). Nevertheless, 'but' seems to be the only English word that will do all the jobs '*praeter*' does in the examples with which Sherwood is concerned. Finding *one* such word in English is especially worthwhile in view of Sherwood's claim regarding other languages in Section 3 of this chapter.
[2] I.e., a distribution.
[3] 'Alone' and 'only' are exclusives, discussed in Chapters XI and XII, respectively.
[4] Peter of Spain discusses exclusives before discussing exceptives, both in *Summulae logicales* and in *Tractatus syncategorematum* (see n. 39, this chapter). He supplies no reason for doing so in the earlier book, but in *Tractatus syncategorematum* he takes up exclusives immediately after negation, saying that "having spoken of the negations of a proposition, we must treat of exclusive words, which have within themselves the power of negation" (*Tr. syn.*, tr. Mullally, p. 29).
[5] Cf. *Introductiones*, Chapter One, Section 15 (*WSIL*, p. 31).

[58

aside [the proposition] that Socrates is running, which counter-instantiates 'every man is running' (*derelinquit Sortem currere,*⁶ *quae instat huic: omnis homo currit*).

3. A DOUBT REGARDING THE ADDITIVE AND EXCEPTIVE USES OF 'BUT'

But there is a doubt whether ['but'] is taken in a completely equivocal way, since it is taken either exceptively or additively. It seems that it is so, since 'to except' and 'to add' are contraries, and so there is the greatest diversity on the part of their significata. [On the contrary,] the opposite seems to be the case, since we find both senses represented by one and the same utterance in other languages; it is therefore probable that there is some agreement on the part of their significata because of which they are designated by means of one and the same utterance.

It must be said that the latter [opinion] is true. For when I say 'six [clerks] but [one] master,' it signifies that the master is also separated from the others — I do not say as regards the thing itself or in respect of a predicate, but in respect of the act of counting. For the sense is 'six, not counting the master.' Thus in all its significations ['but'] denotes separation in some way or other.

4. A CONFUSION OF THE DIMINUTIONAL AND COUNTERINSTANTIVE USES OF 'BUT'

A sophisma occurs, however, in that ['but'] can be taken either diminutionally or counter-instantively,⁷ and it is the following: 'all numbers but 2 exceed unity by a number [greater than 1]' (*quotlibet praeter duo excedunt unitatem in numero*⁸). Proof: 'All numbers exceed unity by a number [greater than 1]' is false, and there is no counter-instance except for 2 (*nisi in binario*); therefore when that exception has been made it will be true; therefore the first [proposition] is true. Then someone may infer 'all

---

⁶ Another hand has inserted '*non*' after '*Sortem*' in P. O'Donnell includes the '*non*' in his edition without comment, but it is evidently mistaken.

⁷ O'Donnell's edition omits without comment the words '*vel instantive*,' although they occur in P.

⁸ '*Quotlibet*,' ordinarily translated as 'as many as you like,' 'any amount,' is translated here as 'all numbers,' which seems a smoother reading in the context of this sophisma. The '*in*' here is evidently a mistake; it does not occur in the repetition of this formula as the first proposition of the proof. I am indebted to Professor Peter Geach for suggesting this emendation.

numbers but 2 [exceed unity by a number greater than 1]; therefore 3 but 2, or 4 [but 2 exceed unity by a number greater than 1],' which is false.[9]

Solution: 'All numbers' has two kinds of totality in it, for it has a universally distributed whole the parts of which are the numbers (*speciales numeri*), and it has an integral whole in it by reason of its supposita.[10] Therefore in the first [proposition][11] 'but' is taken counter-instantively for the purpose of excepting from the former totality; in the second [proposition][12] it is taken diminutionally for the purpose of excepting from the latter totality. Thus a fallacy of equivocation occurs.[13]

5. A SECOND EXAMPLE OF SUCH CONFUSION

Suppose there are only ten men and they are running. Then ten but two are running. Proof: ten but two are eight, and eight are running; therefore ten but two [are running]. But on the contrary: either two are running or ten are running; not, therefore, ten but two [are running].

It must be said that the 'ten' in the first [conclusion] is taken collectively and categorematically and the 'but' diminutionally. In the "on the contrary" the 'ten' is taken syncategorematically and the 'but' counter-instantively.[14]

6. 'BUT' USED EXCEPTIVELY ON 'WHOLE'

Some say that the following sophisma has to be solved by always taking 'but' counter-instantively. Let the whole of Socrates be called '*a*,' the whole of Socrates but his foot '*b*.' Thus *a* is an animal, and *b* is an animal. Therefore, if *b* is part of *a*, then an animal is part of an animal. For they say that in the appellation '*b*' 'whole' must be taken distributively, since otherwise the exception cannot be made. In that case '*b* is an animal' is false in the same way as 'every part of an animal but its foot [is an animal].'

It must be known, however, that the 'whole' can be taken collectively and the 'but' not counter-instantively but diminutionally.

---

[9] '3 but 2' "taken diminutionally" is '3 minus 2'; similarly '4 but 2.'
[10] The first kind of totality in '*quotlibet*' is evidently the entire series of numbers; the second kind of totality seems to be any quantity measured numerically.
[11] A marginal gloss at this point in P says "i.e., in the proof."
[12] A marginal gloss at this point in P says "i.e., in the disproof."
[13] On the fallacy of equivocation see *Introductiones*, Chapter Six, Section 3.1.1 (*WSIL*, pp. 135–139).
[14] On categorematic and syncategorematic uses of number words such as 'ten' see Chapter III.

Others say that 'b is an animal' is false since b is a part. But on the contrary, let a foot be cut off and it will be said truly that b is an animal. But nothing is still an animal that was not earlier an animal; therefore 'b is an animal' is true.

It must be said, therefore, that b is an animal and b is a part of an animal, but in different ways. For b is a part in respect of the body itself and not in respect of the soul; for one is not to say that the whole soul completes (*perficit*) a itself [60] while a part of it completes b, but rather that the whole completes a and the same whole b. It is an animal, however, in respect of the soul. Thus it is clear that although b and the animal are one and the same, nevertheless insofar as they are considered from the standpoint of a part (*respiciuntur ab eo quod est pars*) they are not one and the same but different, since b is considered from that standpoint in respect of the body and, as has been said, it is not in respect of the body that it is an animal. Thus a paralogism of accident occurs.

7. IMMOBILIZATION BY MEANS OF 'BUT'

It must be noted, however, that when the word 'but' is taken counter-instantively it always tends to except from a division. Rule [I]: [*When 'but' is taken counter-instantively*] *it tends to take (vult reperire) a mobile division and render it immobile*. The reason for this is that it excepts some part from the division in respect of the predicate. But that part must, then, be excepted [from the division] in the same way as it previously was in the division; therefore it was in the division in respect of the predicate. But one [part] was supposited in the same way as another was; therefore all the parts were supposited divisively in respect of the predicate; thus the division was mobile.

It seems, however, that it does not render [the division] immobile, for 'every man but Socrates . . .; therefore Plato . . .' can be inferred.

It must be understood that the rule means that one cannot infer in the subject together with its determination,[15] for 'every man but Socrates is running; therefore Plato but Socrates is running' cannot be inferred.[16]

The following additional [example is raised] against the rule: 'every

---

[15] The subject term in the following example is 'man'; its determination is 'but Socrates.' On determination see Sherwood's Introduction to this treatise, n. 4.

[16] A marginal gloss at this point in P says "because Plato is not something common from which something can be excepted, and an exceptive word always excepts from a whole."

animal but Socrates is running; therefore every man but Socrates is running.'[17]

It must be said, however, that the rule does not say that the descent does not hold good in any way, but rather that it does not hold good in general. For it holds good only when the descent is made to a part that contains the excepted part as the exception touched [it] (*ut tetigit exceptio*).[18]

But on the contrary, if nothing but Socrates is running, Socrates is running; and if Socrates is running, something is running. Therefore, by the first, if nothing but [Socrates is running, something is running]. Therefore, by the destruction of the consequent, if not something is running, then not nothing but Socrates is running; and if that, then something but Socrates is running.[19] Therefore, if nothing [is running], then something [is running], which is false. And this again [seems] counter to the rule, since the 'but' in the last premiss does not except from a division.

It must be said, however, that the argument 'not nothing but Socrates is running; therefore something but Socrates [is running]' does not hold good, since 'not nothing' and 'something' are not always equipollent, but [only] when [the 'not' and the 'nothing'] fall over one and the same thing. But that is not the case here, since the 'not' arrives after the exception[20] and falls over the exception, while the 'nothing' falls under the exception.[21] For first of all there is the division belonging to 'nothing,' and after that (*et consequenter*) the exception is made from it, and after that the negation belonging to 'not' arrives.[22]

---

[17] The conclusion '*ergo omnis homo praeter Sortem currit*' appears in P but is omitted from O'Donnell's edition. The point of this second objection to the rule is that although one cannot descend from the species to an individual under it "in the subject together with its determination," one evidently can descend from the genus to a species under it.

[18] A marginal gloss at this point in P says "i.e., the aforesaid example — 'every man but Socrates.'" But it is in the present example and not in that one that the descent holds good, as Sherwood acknowledges, observing that the rule is such that this acceptable descent does not constitute an exception to it.

[19] By equipollence of signs: ". . . a universal negative [sign] with a preceding negation is equipollent to a particular affirmative [sign]" (*WSIL*, p. 37). Sherwood rejects this move in his reply.

[20] See Chapter I, n. 43.

[21] A marginal gloss at this point in P says "the sense is 'not nothing but Socrates is running' — 'no thing runs not but Socrates'; i.e., not excepting Socrates, and even Socrates is not running." Despite the obvious difficulties the writer of the gloss has in expressing the sense, his view is correct in outline. See n. 22, this chapter.

[22] Sherwood's depiction of the scope of the three syncategorematic words in terms of their arrival times may be presented in the following three stages of devel-

8. EXCEPTING AS MANY THINGS AS ARE SUPPOSITED

[Rule II:] *When as many things are excepted from a division as are supposited, the locution is false or ungrammatical (incongrua).*

In connection with this [rule], however, one paralogizes as follows: Suppose that Socrates sees everyone other than himself and does not see himself, and so on with respect to the single things. Then every man sees every man but himself. Proof: Socrates sees every man but himself, and Plato [sees every man but himself], and so on with respect to the single things; therefore every man [sees every man but himself]. But on the contrary, the 'himself' supposits for every man; therefore as many things are excepted as are supposited; therefore the locution is false.

It must be said that the rule has to be understood in the following way. If as many things are excepted [as are supposited], *and in the same way*, [then the locution is false or ungrammatical]. But that is not the case here, since the plurality belonging to [the second] 'every man' is taken many times virtually (*multotiens sumitur virtualiter*),[23] while the plurality belonging to 'himself' is excepted for one suppositum from that plurality taken once, and for another suppositum from that same plurality taken again. Thus the supposita of 'himself' taken once can correctly be excepted from themselves taken more than once (*sic bene potest esse quod supposita ejus quod est se semel sumpta excipiantur a seipsis pluries sumptis*).[24]

If, however, [the inference] were to proceed in this fashion — 'every man sees every man but himself; therefore every man sees every man but every man' — it would not hold good. The reason for this has been stated in [connection with] the sophisma 'every man sees himself; therefore every man sees every man.'[25]

9. A SECOND EXAMPLE OF EXCEPTING AS MANY THINGS AS ARE SUPPOSITED

This is similar. Suppose that Socrates is seen by every man other than himself, and Plato [is seen by every man other than himself], and so on with respect to the single things. Then with the exception of every man,

---

opment. (A) '*nothing* is running'; (B) '*with the exception of Socrates* nothing is running'; (C) '*not* with the exception of Socrates nothing is running.'

[23] On the doctrine invoked in this analysis see *Introductiones*, Chapter Five, Section 12 (*WSIL*, pp. 116–117).

[24] Peter of Spain introduces a version of Rule II and discusses this sophisma, giving a briefer solution along the same general lines (*Tr. syn.*, tr. Mullally, p. 43).

[25] See Chapter I, Section 16.

every man sees him. Proof [61] by induction;[26] thus with the exception of every man, [every man sees him]. On the contrary, as many are excepted as [are supposited].

It must be said, therefore, that the [first] 'every man' taken once is excepted from the [second] 'every [man]' taken many times. Thus they are not excepted and supposited in one and the same way.

10. A THIRD EXAMPLE OF EXCEPTING AS MANY THINGS AS ARE SUPPOSITED

Again, everything is everything with the exception of everything but itself. Proof: Socrates is everything [with the exception of everything but himself], since 'Socrates is everything' is false for everything but himself. Thus when an exception has been made for those things it will be true. But on the contrary, the 'itself' supposits for everything; therefore as many are excepted as are supposited.

It must be said, however, that they are not [supposited and excepted] in one and the same way, since the 'itself' taken once is excepted from 'everything' taken many times.

11. THE ABSENCE OF CONFUSED SUPPOSITION FROM A TERM DESIGNATING SOMETHING EXCEPTED

Rule [III]: *A term designating something excepted is not confused by the division from which the exception is made.*[27] The reason for this is that the division falls under the exception and so its force does not extend over the exception.

Suppose that every animal other than man is running but man is not [running].[28] Then every animal but man is running. Proof: 'every animal is running' is false, and there is no counter-instance except in man; there-

---

[26] I.e., 'with the exception of Socrates, every man sees him (Socrates); with the exception of Plato, every man sees him (Plato); . . .; therefore with the exception of every man, every man sees him (every man).'

[27] The point is to contrast this with the ordinary effect of distribution (or division), which is the "confusion" of the subject and predicate terms. Thus in 'every man is an animal' 'man' has "distributive confused" supposition and 'animal' has "merely confused" supposition, 'confused' having the same general sense as 'indeterminate.' See *Introductiones*, Chapter Five.

[28] In the Latin text this sentence begins with '*Sed contra*' ('But on the contrary'), but the example is not offered as an exception to the rule and there is nothing else to which it might be opposed. The insertion of the phrase here seems to be a scribe's error, probably deriving from the beginning of the next paragraph.

fore when an exception has been made for man it will be true; therefore 'every animal but man is running' is true.

But on the contrary, by the rule just stated, 'man' [29] is not confused [by the division]. Therefore one can infer 'every animal is running but Socrates' or '[every animal is running] but Plato,' and one can say that 'man' is not confused by the distribution but by the exception.

Or, better, it must be said that 'every' can divide either for the single things belonging to the genera or for the genera of the single things.[30] If [it divides] for the single things belonging to the genera, then 'man' is excepted for some designated suppositum, and the locution is false.[31] If [it divides] for the genera of the single things, then 'man' is not excepted in that way, but simply,[32] and a descent cannot be made. In this case the locution would be true and not contrary to the rule.

12. IMMOBILIZATION OF A TERM IN RESPECT OF WHICH AN EXCEPTION IS MADE

[Rule IV:] *Neither ascent nor descent holds good in a term in respect of which there is an exception.*

The reason for this is that every exceptive has the force both of affirmation and of negation. Because of the affirmation descent does not hold good; because of the negation ascent does not hold good.

Thus the following is not valid: 'every man but Socrates is white; therefore every man [but Socrates] is a colored thing' (*omnis homo etc. est coloratum*).[33] But on the contrary, this ascent holds good: 'every ten but two are eight; therefore every ten but two are some number (*aliquot*).'

It must be said that the 'but' is taken diminutionally in the latter case,

---

[29] Reading '*ly hominem*' for '*ly homine.*'
[30] This is a reference to the doctrine of division by 'every' for "remote" or for "proximate" parts. See Chapter I, Section 4.
[31] In this case the sense would be 'every individual animal with the exception of some man is running,' which is not supported by the hypothesis.
[32] For 'man' to be excepted "simply" is for it to be excepted in such a way as to acquire simple supposition, in which case it supposits not for individual men but for the species man. See *Introductiones*, Chapter Five, where the paradigm case of simple supposition is that of 'man' in 'man is a species' (*WSIL*, p. 107).
[33] In P the scribe originally wrote '*omnis homo etc. est hoc album vel coloratum*' ('every man, etc., is this white or colored thing'), but the words '*hoc album vel*' have been deleted. In O the words '*album vel*' remain. The intended conclusion surely is '*omnis homo praeter Sortem est coloratus*' ('every man but Socrates has a color'). The ascent is illicit because 'Socrates is black' is consistent with the premiss but not with the conclusion.

for the sense is that every ten diminished by two are [eight]. The rule, however, is understood with respect to the cases in which it is taken counter-instantively.

13. THE MISUSE OF EXCEPTION AS A MEANS OF RENDERING A WHOLLY FALSE STATEMENT TRUE

[Rule V:] *A universal [statement] that is false as a whole is not made true by means of an exception.*

But on the contrary, every ten but three is odd, since seven [is odd]; nevertheless 'every ten is odd' is false as a whole.

It must be said that the 'but' is taken diminutionally in this case, for the sense is that every ten diminished by three is odd. The rule is understood with respect to cases in which ['but'] is taken counter-instantively.

14. CONTRASTING TRUTH-VALUES IN EXCEPTIVE STATEMENTS AND THEIR NON-EXCEPTIVE ORIGINALS

[Rule VI:] *If the original statement (praejacens) is true as a whole, a [corresponding] exceptive statement is false, and vice versa.*

But on the contrary, every ten but two are even, since eight [is even]. Nevertheless the original statement — 'every ten are even' — is true.

The solution is as before.

15. IMMOBILIZATION BY MEANS OF EXCEPTION IN CASES INVOLVING MORE THAN ONE DIVISION

[Rule VII:] *If there is more than one division and an exception is made from one in respect of another, then the one in respect of which the exception is made is immobilized.*

For example, suppose that Socrates does not see an ass but all the other [men] see Brownie and no other [ass]. Then 'no man sees an ass' is false, and for Brownie alone; therefore when he has been excepted it will be true. [Then someone may infer] 'no man sees an ass but Brownie; therefore Socrates does not see an ass but Brownie; therefore he sees Brownie,' which is false.

It must be said that the 'but' arrives at 'ass' after it is distributed, but it is distributed by virtue of the negation belonging to 'no.' Therefore the 'no' arrives in the subject before the 'but' arrives in the predicate. Thus the 'no' falls under in respect of the exception and under the negation that lies in the exception, and a *figura dictionis* occurs.[34] Alternatively, a fallacy of the consequent occurs, since ['no one sees an ass but Brownie'] is equipollent to these two: [*a*] 'no one sees an ass other than Brownie' and [*b*] 'not no one sees Brownie.' And the other exceptive [62] [statement][35] is equipollent to these: [*c*] 'Socrates does not see an ass other than Brownie' and [*d*] 'Socrates sees Brownie.' But [*a*] entails [*c*], although [*b*] does not entail [*d*]; because while 'not no one' is equipollent to 'someone,' 'someone [sees Brownie]; therefore Socrates [sees Brownie]' does not follow but is a fallacy of the consequent.

16. AMBIGUITY IN CASES INVOLVING EXCEPTION AND MORE THAN ONE DIVISION

Sometimes, however, ambiguity occurs in that the division from which the exception is made can include the other [division], in which case that other is immobilized by means of the exception; or [the division from which the exception is made can] be included by [the other division], in which case it is not [immobilized], since it does not fall under the exception. This is also the case when neither division depends on the other.

For example, suppose that Socrates sees every ass and the other [men] see every [ass] other than Brownie. Thus 'every man sees every ass' is false, and for Brownie alone, since they see all the others. Therefore 'every man sees every ass but Brownie' is true. Therefore Socrates sees [every ass but Brownie], which is false, since he does see Brownie.

It must be said that the second division together with its exception can include the first, in which case it is equipollent to these [propositions]: 'every man sees every ass other than Brownie' and 'not every man sees Brownie.' In that case it is true and the first [division] is immobilized. Alternatively, [the second division together with its exception] can be included by [the first division], in which case it is false and disproved. In the first case it signifies that seeing every [ass] other [than Brownie] goes together with every [man], while seeing Brownie does not go together with every [man] (*sed non videre burnellum conveniat omni*). In the second case [it signifies] that this whole — seeing every other [ass] and not seeing Brownie — goes together with every [man].

---

[34] Cf. Chapter X, Section 7. The present section is discussed by Peter Geach in *Reference and Generality*, pp. 102–104.

[35] A marginal gloss at this point in P says "viz., 'Socrates does not see an ass but Brownie.'"

17. THE EXCEPTIVE 'BUT' TOGETHER WITH THE COPULATIVE 'AND'

Suppose that Socrates and Plato are carrying a rock together and everyone else [is carrying a rock] by himself. Then 'every man is carrying a rock' is false, and for Socrates and Plato only; therefore when they have been excepted it will be true. Therefore every man but Socrates and Plato [is carrying a rock].

But on the contrary, if the 'and' copulates between propositions,[36] then this is a copulative both parts of which are false, and so the whole is false. If [the 'and' copulates] between terms, then [the conclusion] signifies that Socrates and Plato are not carrying a rock, which is false.

Solution: If [the 'and'] copulates between the terms 'Socrates' and 'Plato,' then it is false, as the "on the contrary" maintains. But if [it copulates] between the terms 'but Socrates' and 'but Plato,' it is true, for in that case the exception is pluralized (*multiplicatur*) by means of the copulation and ['Socrates and Plato'] is excepted divisively. 'Socrates' and 'Plato' must be compounded in the first case, divided in the second case.[37]

18. EXCEPTION IN CASES INVOLVING MORE THAN ONE TIME

[Suppose that] in fact (*in rei veritate*) Socrates sees every man at t_1 and that he sees every man but Plato at t_2. Then at two times Socrates will see every man but Plato. Proof: 'At two times Socrates will see every man' is false, and there is no counter-instance except in Plato; therefore when he has been excepted it will be true. Then [someone may infer] 'therefore at one time he will see every man but Plato, and at another time [he will see every man but Plato].' But[38] on the contrary, only at one time – viz., at t_2 – will he see [every man but Plato].

It must be said that either the exception can include the 'at two times,' or vice versa. If the 'at two times' includes [the exception], [the proposition

---

[36] I.e., between 'every man but Socrates is carrying a rock' and 'every man but Plato is carrying a rock.'

[37] The distinction between these cases is made clearer if we replace 'man' with 'potential rock carrier.' First: 'every potential rock carrier with the exception of Socrates and Plato is carrying a rock'; second: 'every potential rock carrier with the exception of Socrates and with the exception of Plato is carrying a rock.' In this case the compounding and dividing of the terms is perhaps best seen in intonation patterns (see Chapter I, n. 47): 'every potential rock carrier but Socrates-and-Plato is carrying a rock'; 'every potential rock carrier but Socrates / and Plato / is carrying a rock.'

[38] Reading '*Sed*' for '*Vel*.'

'at two times Socrates will see every man but Plato'] signifies that seeing every man but Plato goes together with Socrates at two times, which is false. If the 'at two times' is included [by the exception], [the proposition] signifies that seeing every [man] other [than Plato] goes together with Socrates at two times while seeing Plato does not, which is true, and in that sense it is proved. In the first case this whole — seeing every man but Plato — must be compounded, so that it is signified that this whole is pluralized by means of the 'at two times.' In the second case the 'but [Plato]' must be divided from the rest, so that it is signified that the 'at two times' does not extend to the 'but,' but vice versa.[39]

---

[39] First case: 'at two times Socrates will see-every-man-but-Plato'; second case: 'at two times Socrates will see every man / but Plato.' Peter of Spain discusses exceptives, considering many of the same rules and examples as Sherwood considers, in at least two places (*Sum. log.*, ed. Mullally, pp. 108–110; *Tr. syn.*, tr. Mullally, pp. 41–50).

CHAPTER XI. *'Alone' (Solus)*

1. REASONS FOR DISCUSSING 'ALONE' AT THIS POINT

After having spoken of [distributive] signs and also of exceptive words, which attach immediately to the signs, we must speak next of the word 'alone':[1] first, because it has to do with (*cadit circa*) the subject as the signs also do; and second, because of its opposition to the word 'every' or 'all,' for 'every' or 'all' always indicates one-with-another, 'alone' one-not-with-another.

2. 'ALONE' USED CATEGOREMATICALLY AND SYNCATEGOREMATICALLY

The first question is whether or not the word 'alone' is a syncategorematic word.

It seems it is not, since if one says 'Socrates walks proud,' the word 'proud' signifies how [63] Socrates is while walking. Thus, since it indicates a quality of Socrates [and a quality] is a categorical thing (*res prae-*

---

[1] After discussing exception Sherwood turns to exclusion (see Chapter X, Section 1); he first identifies 'alone' as an exclusive word in Chapter XI, Section 6.

dicamentalis), ['proud'] is not a syncategorematic word.² Similarly, if one says 'Socrates eats alone,' [the word 'alone'] signifies how Socrates is situated (*qualiter li*³ *Sortes se habet*) while eating. Thus, since it indicates a mode of Socrates and a relation, which is a categorical thing, ['alone'] will not be a syncategorematic word.⁴ For the categories indicate real things and the dispositions of real things insofar as they are real things.

This is clear also in another way, since 'alone' signifies not-with-another and thus indicates separation, which is a relation and a categorical thing (*res praedicamenti*).

It must be said that when ['alone'] signifies separation from others as regards the thing itself it is a categorematic word, as has been shown ⁵ — as if one were to say 'Socrates is alone,' or [as] in the preceding example, where ['alone'] signifies that the others are separated from Socrates in the act of eating. When, however, it signifies the separation of one thing from another in respect of the sharing of the predicate (*in participando praedicatum*), it is a syncategorematic word — as in 'Socrates alone is running' — for it signifies that the others do not share the predicate.⁶

3. WHY 'ALONE' IS BETTER ADDED TO A DISCRETE THAN TO A COMMON TERM

It can also be asked why ['alone'] is better added to a singular or discrete term than to a common term.⁷

The reason for it is that in the understanding ⁸ of ['alone'] there occurs

---

² Evidently an allusion to a basis for the categorematic/syncategorematic distinction: categorematic words are those that indicate categorical things (substances, qualities, quantities, relations, places, times, postures, states, actions, and passions), syncategorematic words are those that do not. From Sherwood's own point of view this would be an overly simple and to some extent wrongheaded basis for the distinction, which he tends to base upon the function (*officium*) of words rather than upon what they indicate or signify. See his Introduction to this treatise.

³ The particle '*li*,' ordinarily used to indicate that the expression immediately following it is being used to refer to the expression itself (see *WSIL*, p. 117, n. 48), is evidently out of place here.

⁴ See *WSIL*, p. 43, n. 73.

⁵ See the second paragraph of Sherwood's Introduction to this treatise.

⁶ Thus while 'Socrates is eating alone' (*Sortes comedit solus*) contains a categorematic occurrence of 'alone,' 'Socrates alone is eating' (*Solus Sortes comedit*) contains a syncategorematic occurrence.

⁷ One of the reasons for considering two exclusives — 'alone' (*solus*) and 'only' (*tantum*) — seems to be the view that the former is better adapted for excluding around discrete terms and the latter around common terms. Peter of Spain gives a different account of the difference between them (*Tr. syn.*, tr. Mullally, pp. 39–40).

⁸ 'Understanding' (*intellectus*) here seems synonymous with 'signification' in

the word 'another,' which in both the masculine and the feminine signifies a difference in respect of number (in the neuter it signifies essential difference),⁹ for it indicates numerical difference — i.e., [the difference] of one single thing from another [of the same kind]. It is on that account that it is added to a singular [or discrete term].

4. A SUPPOSED PLURALIZING EFFECT OF 'ALONE'

It is also asked whether 'Socrates alone is running' is singular or plural, since it signifies just as much as 'Socrates and not another [are running].'

It must be said that it is not [plural], since it signifies what it signifies as a disposition of the subject and consequently does not produce number together with the subject in such a way that we should say [that there are] two subjects there.

5. A SUPPOSED NEGATING EFFECT OF 'ALONE'

It is also asked whether ['Socrates alone is running'] is simply affirmative. And it seems that it is not, since negation is part of the signification of 'alone.'

It must be said that it is not [negative], for ['alone'] signifies separation from others, as a consequence of which negation is understood; and this does not produce a negative expression. And if one says that Aristotle defines this word by means of negation ¹⁰ and that it therefore signifies negation, it must be said that he likewise defines the *dici de omni* ¹¹ by means of negation and it nevertheless does not signify negation.

6. A SUPPOSED INCLUDING EFFECT OF 'ALONE'

It is furthermore asked why the word 'alone' is called an exclusive rather than an inclusive [word]; for when someone says 'Socrates alone is running' Socrates is included under running but the others are excluded.¹²

Chapter XI, Section 7 (third paragraph). Cf. the contrasting analyses in Chapter XI, Section 1, of what is indicated by 'every' and by 'alone.'

⁹ See the remarks about the ambiguity of the neuter '*aliud*' in Chapter XI, Section 7.

¹⁰ O'Donnell supplies a reference to *De sophisticis elenchis*, 22 (178a39ff): "Again, it is argued that a man cannot give what he does not have, for he does not have one die alone. Is not what really happens that he does not give what he does not have but rather gives it in a way in which he does not have it — viz., as a single thing? For 'alone' does not mean a particular thing or a quality or a quantity but rather a certain relation to something — viz., that it is not with another."

¹¹ See Chapter I, n. 35.

¹² The terminological question is of no real importance, but it does have some jus-

It must be said that it is because the inclusion occurs not as a result of the force of the word 'alone' but as a result of the force of the statement as it is before the 'alone' is inserted into it (*ex virtute suae praejacentis*). The exclusion, on the other hand, is [an exclusion] of the others and does occur as a result of the force of the word ['alone'].

7. 'ALONE' EXCLUDING GENERALLY AND SPECIFICALLY

Rule [I]: *The word 'alone' sometimes excludes generally and at other times excludes specifically.*

For example, 'Socrates alone is running.' In the first case the sense is 'nothing other than Socrates is running,' since everything other than Socrates is generally excluded. In the second case it signifies specifically that nothing other than Socrates in that same genus is running.

And it is asked what the cause of this diversity is. Some say that it occurs because the word 'other' (*aliud*),[13] which occurs in the signification of ['alone'], is used ambiguously — other in respect of genus (e.g., quantity and substance), other in respect of species (e.g., man and ass), and other in respect of number (e.g., Socrates and Plato). And in the first case 'alone' produces a general exclusion, in the second a specific, and in the third a numerical (for [14] these men speak of not just two but three kinds [of exclusion]).[15]

But on the contrary, on this view when ['alone'] produces a general exclusion it excludes only those things that belong to other genera, which is false, since every other thing is excluded.

They say that this is the result of category-difference — i.e., that only those things are excluded that are suited to share the predicate. Therefore when the predicate is suited to be in all things ['alone'] excludes generally every other thing; and when it is suited to be specifically in things belonging to a certain genus ['alone'] excludes specifically the things belonging to

---

tification. The distributives and the exceptives differ from the exclusives in that they perform their functions on the terms to which they are attached. 'Every' distributes (or divides) 'man' in 'every man is running'; 'but' excepts 'Socrates' in 'every man but Socrates is running.' The exclusives, however, exclude not what they are attached to but everything else.

[13] '*Aliud*,' the neuter form referred to in Chapter XI, Section 3.

[14] Reading '*enim*' for '*autem*.'

[15] In his discussion of this rule (*Tr. syn.*, tr. Mullally, pp. 31–32), Peter of Spain explicitly rules out the possibility of numerical exclusion, understanding by numerical exclusion the exclusion of that which is numerically the same as what is included (p. 32).

[16] See n. 7, this chapter.

that genus. 'Socrates alone is' is an example of the first; 'Socrates alone is running' is an example of the second.

But on the contrary, it is correct to say 'Socrates alone is Socrates' and 'only (*tantum*) man is risible,'[16] and [64] yet there is nothing besides these subjects that is suited to receive these predicates. Thus according to them nothing is excluded [by means of the word 'alone' in those statements].

Again, since we are accustomed to distinguish in this fashion in connection with one and the same predicate — i.e., that either general or specific exclusion can be carried [to it by means of 'alone'] — [the distinction between exclusions] does not result from a difference of predicate.

It must be said that the distinction arises from the fact that the negation not-another, which lies in the word 'alone,' can negate either absolutely or within a genus. If [it negates] absolutely it universally removes every other thing and produces a general exclusion. If [it negates] within a genus it specifically removes the other things belonging to that genus and a specific exclusion is produced.

8. IMMOBILIZATION AS A RESULT OF EXCLUSION IN THE SUBJECT

Rule [II]: *An inference from an inferior to a superior does not hold when an exclusion is produced in the subject.*

For example, 'Socrates alone is running; therefore Socrates alone is moving.' The following sophisma proceeds in accordance with this. 'Socrates alone is the same as Socrates alone.' Proof: Socrates is the same as Socrates alone, and nothing other [than Socrates] is the same as Socrates alone; therefore Socrates alone [is the same as Socrates alone]. On the contrary, therefore Socrates alone is undifferent from Socrates alone; therefore non-different; therefore [Socrates alone] does not differ from Socrates alone. On the contrary, 'Plato does not differ from Socrates alone' is true; therefore 'Socrates alone [does not differ from Socrates alone]' is false.

It must be said that there is a fallacy of the consequent in the argument 'Socrates alone is non-different [from Socrates alone]; therefore Socrates alone does not differ [from Socrates alone],' since being-non-different-from-Socrates-alone is in fewer things than not-differing-from-Socrates-alone. The former goes together with Socrates alone; the latter, however, with Socrates and others.

But on the contrary, an affirmative proposition with an infinite predicate is equipollent to a negative [proposition] with the same subject and the finite predicate — these two, for example: 'Socrates is nonwhite,' 'Socrates is not white.' Therefore these two — 'Socrates is non-different,' 'therefore Socrates does not differ' — are equipollent. Therefore the two of them will be equipollent also with an exclusion added to each; therefore the argument holds.

It must be said that [two propositions] with one and the same subject are equipollent [when] the infinitation [17] and the negation fall over one and the same thing, but not when they do not do so. For example, suppose that Socrates is black. Then 'Socrates is a non-man [colored] white' is false even though 'Socrates is not a man [colored] white' is true. The cause of this is that when the infinitating negation cuts into one and the same word with that which is infinitated, it is necessary that it fall over one word alone. Thus in the first [example just above] the word 'man' alone is negated, and for that reason [the proposition] is false. In the second 'a man [colored] white' is negated. Similarly in the case proposed, since in the first [proposition] 'different' is negated, [while] in the second the whole differing-from-Socrates-alone [is negated].

9. IMMOBILIZATION OF A DIVISION BY MEANS OF A PRECEDING EXCLUSION

Rule [III]: *An exclusion preceding a division renders it immobile.*

On this basis the following sophisma is solved. From Socrates alone differs whatever is not Socrates.[18] Proof: From Socrates differs [whatever is not Socrates] and not from another, since not from Plato differs [whatever is not Socrates], since he [Plato] does not differ from himself, and so on with respect to the others; therefore the first [proposition] is true. On the contrary, therefore from Socrates alone differs Plato (who is not Socrates), which is false, since he differs from Cicero.

It must be said that the 'whatever' is immobilized by means of the negation that lies in the preceding exclusion. Thus there is a fallacy of *figura dictionis* here. Alternatively, [there is a fallacy] of the consequent, since 'whatever [is not Socrates]' is in fewer [things] than 'Plato.' [19] Therefore

---

[17] See Chapter XIV, Section 2.
[18] The clumsy word order is required if the exclusion is to precede the division in the English as in the Latin (*a solo Sorte differt quicquid non est Sortes*).
[19] This seems to be a misleading way of saying that whatever is not Socrates *dif-*

since the inference is drawn from the less common to the more common by the preceding exclusion, there is a paralogism of the consequent. This is clear if the affirmative [element] of the conclusion is compared with the affirmative [element] of the premiss and the negative with the negative, since the premiss as well as the conclusion is resolved into an affirmative and a negative.[20]

10. EXCLUSION IN THE SUBJECT WITH ONE OF THE TERMS INVOLVING A CLAUSE OR PHRASE

[Rule IV:] *When there is an exclusion in the subject and a clause or phrase involved*[21] *in the subject or the predicate the locution is ambiguous in that the clause or phrase can either [A] fall under the exclusion or [B] not.*

Example of [A]: Suppose that Socrates is white and is running and that the others are black and are running. Then Socrates alone who is white is running. Proof: Socrates who is white is running and no other who is white is running, since no other is white; therefore Socrates alone [who is white is running]. [Then someone may infer] 'therefore Socrates alone is running and he is white,' which is false.

Solution: It is proved insofar as the clause ['who is white'] falls under the exclusion; it is disproved insofar as it does not fall under the exclusion. In the first case the expression is compounded; [65] in the second case, divided.

Example of [B]: Suppose that there are only ten men. Then there are nine men alone who are not alone. Proof: There are nine men [who are not alone], and there are no more who are not alone, since the ten are those who are alone. On the contrary, therefore there are nine men alone and they are not alone.

Solution: It must be said that it is proved insofar as the clause ['who are

---

fers from fewer things than Plato differs from, an observation that would support the charge that the inference involves the fallacy of the consequent.
[20] The premiss is resolved into the affirmative 'from Socrates differs whatever is not Socrates' (true) and the negative 'not from another than Socrates differs whatever is not Socrates' (true). The conclusion is resolved into the affirmative 'from Socrates differs Plato' (true) and the negative 'not from another than Socrates differs Plato' (false). Although the affirmative element of the conclusion does follow from the affirmative element of the premiss, the negative element of the conclusion of course follows from neither element of the premiss. But since the negative element of the premiss would follow from the negative element of the conclusion, the flaw in the inference may be said to be the fallacy of the consequent.
[21] See Chapter I, n. 44.

not alone'] falls under the exclusion; it is disproved insofar as it falls outside [the exclusion]. In the first case the 'who [are not alone]' must be compounded with the preceding 'alone'; [22] in the second case, divided [from it].

11. THE EXCLUSIVE 'ALONE' TOGETHER WITH THE COPULATIVE 'AND'

Nevertheless, some say that this last — 'there are nine men alone and they are not alone' — is ambiguous in that the copulation can fall under the exclusion, so that it is signified that the 'nine' can truly be ordered together with the whole 'there are . . . and they are not alone' and not [23] more [than nine can truly be ordered together] with that same whole. In that case the expression is compounded and true.[24] Alternatively, [the copulation can]not [fall] under the exclusion, so that it is signified that there are nine men alone and they are not alone.

And on this basis the following sophisma is solved. Suppose that Socrates is white and Plato is whiter than he and [whiter] than no other. Then Socrates alone is white and Plato is whiter than he. Proof: Socrates is white [and Plato is whiter than he], and no other is white and Plato is whiter [than he]; therefore Socrates alone [is white and Plato is whiter than he]. But on the contrary, this is a copulative the first part of which is false; therefore the whole [is false].

Some say that the first is proved insofar as the copulation falls under the exclusion and the expression is compounded and true, but that it is disproved insofar as [the copulation] falls outside [the exclusion], and [the expression] is divided and false. (But whether this is well said will become apparent in the chapter on 'and.' [25])

---

[22] Since the example in Latin reads '*soli novem homines sunt qui non soli sunt*' the stipulation for the first case is that the '*qui*' ('who') must be compounded with the preceding '*sunt*' ('are'). The 'are' is changed to 'alone' to suit the English example. In both the first and the second examples in this section the compounded/divided distinction is best presented as a difference in intonation patterns. Cf. Chapter X, n. 37.
[23] The '*et non*' originally in P at this point has been deleted and '*immo*' has been put in its place. O retains the '*et non*,' which seems preferable to '*immo*' here.
[24] Compounded: 'of nine men alone is it true to say both that they are and that they are not alone.'
[25] See Chapter XX, Section 2.

❧ 12. TWO WAYS IN WHICH A CLAUSE OR PHRASE INVOLVED IN THE SUBJECT TERM CAN FALL UNDER AN EXCLUSION

Furthermore, it must be known that when there is a clause or phrase involved in the subject it can fall under the exclusion in two ways, either in connection with that (*ex parte ejus*) *around* which the exclusion occurs or in connection with that *in respect of* which the exclusion occurs, as in the aforesaid example.[26] In the first case the sense is that no one other than the white Socrates [is running]. In the second case it is disproved, and the sense is 'no one other who is white [is running].' In the first case the 'who is white' must be compounded with the 'Socrates [alone].' In the second case it must be divided from 'Socrates alone' and compounded with the predicate. And there is a third sense in which it must be divided from both — viz., according as the clause ['who is white'] falls outside [the exclusion].[27]

❧ 13. THE EFFECT OF ONE EXCLUSION UPON ANOTHER

[Rule V:] *If there is a double exclusion, the one can include the other, or vice versa.*

On this basis the following sophisma is solved. Two alone are fewer than three alone. Proof: Two alone are fewer than three and not than others, since it is not the case that two alone are fewer than four; therefore two alone are fewer than three alone. On the contrary, therefore two are fewer than three alone, which is false, since they are fewer than four.

It must be said that the first [proposition] is proved insofar as the second 'alone' includes the first 'alone.' It is disproved the other way around, however. In the first case the '[three] alone' must be divided from the 'fewer than'; in the second case, compounded [with it]. For the division signifies that the force of the first exclusion remains there and does not cross over to the second, but rather vice versa. The composition, on the other hand, signifies that the force of the first extends to the second. We can, however, recognize that in the proof the second [exclusion] includes the first by the fact that in the proof the concern was with the second (*ad secundum habebatur respectus*); and that the first [exclusion] includes the second in the

---

[26] A marginal gloss at this point in P says " 'Socrates alone who is white' " — i.e., the first example in Section 10. In 'Socrates alone who is white is running' it is 'Socrates' *around* which the exclusion occurs and 'is running' *in respect of* which the exclusion occurs.
[27] See the discussions of the examples in Section 10.

disproof is clear from the fact that in the disproof the concern is with the former.[28]

14. A SECOND EXAMPLE OF THE EFFECT OF ONE EXCLUSION UPON ANOTHER

This sophisma is similar. The nominative alone precedes the genitive alone.[29] Proof: The nominative alone precedes the genitive and none other; therefore alone. Then [someone may infer] 'therefore the nominative precedes the genitive alone,' which is false.

The solution is as before.

15. 'ALONE' TOGETHER WITH NUMBER WORDS

Suppose that Socrates knows the seven arts and Plato [knows] three of them. Then more things are known by Socrates than by Socrates alone. Proof: Seven are known by Socrates and only four by Socrates alone, since three are known by another; therefore more things [are known by Socrates than by Socrates alone]. But on the contrary, the seven are known by Socrates alone, since no other knows the seven; therefore as many are known by Socrates alone as by Socrates.

It can be said that 'seven are known by Socrates alone' signifies that the seven are known by Socrates and the seven are not known by another. If 'the seven' is taken divisively,[30] the division means (*vult*) that one [art] is not known by another, nor another [art], nor a third, and so on in succession, [66] which is false. If ['the seven' is taken] conjunctively,[31] the expression is more than one (*plures*) — in part true, in part false. In the disproof there is a fallacy of the consequent [in the inference] from the negation placed before the number term to the same [negation] placed after it. For the argument goes as follows: 'no other knows the seven; therefore the seven are not known by another.' ('No other sees every man; therefore every man is not seen by another' is similar.)

But this solution presupposes that when the 'alone' is placed after the

---

[28] The concern in the proof or in the disproof is with the portion of the first proposition that is varied in it, the other portion being held constant.

[29] That is, in the traditional order of the cases: nominative, genitive, dative, accusative, ablative, vocative.

[30] If 'men' in 'the men are too heavy for the boat' is taken divisively, the sense is 'each one of the men individually is too heavy for the boat.'

[31] If 'men' in 'the men are too heavy for the boat' is taken conjunctively, the sense is 'all the men taken together are too heavy for the boat.'

word 'seven' it cannot include it, and whether this is true will be said later.[32]

16. THE EFFECT OF THE RELATIVE LOCATION OF WORDS INDICATING EXCLUSION AND DIVISION

Suppose that Socrates is seen by every man and sees himself only.[33] Then every man sees Socrates alone. Proof: Every man sees Socrates and not every man sees another, since Socrates does not see another; therefore every man [sees Socrates alone]. [Then someone may infer] 'therefore Plato sees Socrates alone,' which is false.

Solution: The first [proposition] is proved insofar as the 'alone' includes the division, for the negation belonging to the exclusion falls over the division in the proof. The disproof, on the other hand, proceeds insofar as the division includes the 'alone.' In the first case the 'alone' must be divided from the predicate, so that it is signified that the division does not extend to it; in the second case, compounded [with the predicate].

But on the contrary, the 'alone' is placed after the division; therefore if we extract (*accipiamus*) the negation from it, [the negation] too must be placed after. Thus the sense is 'every man sees Socrates and every man does not see another,' and it will be false.

But on the contrary, Aristotle says that every animal has touch alone,[34] and if the negation belonging to 'alone' were placed after the division [in that case], it would be false.

Again, by this reasoning[35] the negation would not be placed before the 'see' [in 'every man does not see another'], since the exclusion follows [the 'sees' in 'every man sees Socrates alone'].

When the sentence 'every man sees Socrates' has been produced, if I should want to signify that the 'Socrates' stands prescinded (*cum praecisione*) in respect of the division I should apply the word 'alone'; and if the 'alone' is to signify this, the negation precedes its division, and this is true. Consequently, although ['alone'] is placed after the division it can nevertheless include it.

---

[32] See Chapter XI, Section 16, especially the last two paragraphs.
[33] Reading '*et videat se tantum*' for '*et quilibet alius videat se tantum.*' I am indebted to Professor Peter Geach for suggesting this emendation.
[34] O'Donnell supplies a reference to *De anima* III, 12 (also 13), where Aristotle several times says that the sense of touch is the only one necessary to every animal, from which it might be derived that every animal has touch alone – i.e., that touch is the one sense to be found in every animal.

On this basis one can analyze (*distingui*) the proposition 'seven are known by Socrates alone' in the sophisma before last, since if the 'alone' includes the 'seven' it is true; and if ['alone'] is included [by it], it is false. Since the previous solution is more common, although this one is more true, this is of no concern (*de ista non curandum*).

🖞 17. A SECOND EXAMPLE OF THE EXCLUSIVE 'ALONE' TOGETHER WITH THE COPULATIVE 'AND'[86]

Suppose that Socrates is carrying a rock by himself and that Socrates and Plato are at the same time carrying another [rock]. Then Socrates alone is carrying a rock. Proof: No other [is carrying a rock]; therefore [Socrates] alone [is carrying a rock]. On the contrary, Socrates and another are carrying [a rock].

It must be said that in the "on the contrary" the '[Socrates] and [another]' is taken conjunctively. But there is no contradiction except insofar as it is taken divisively.[87]

🖞 18. A THIRD EXAMPLE OF THE EXCLUSIVE 'ALONE' TOGETHER WITH THE COPULATIVE 'AND'

Socrates alone and two are three. Proof: Socrates not together with another and two are three; therefore [Socrates] alone [and two are three]. On the contrary, Plato and two are three; not, therefore, [Socrates] alone [and two are three].

It must be said that the 'alone' can fall under the copulation [belonging to 'and'], in which case it is proved, or over it, in which case it is disproved; for in that case it signifies that no other [than Socrates] and two are three. But understand that in the first case ['alone'] is a categorematic word, since it is a part of a copulated subject.[88] That subject, however, is copulated before the predicate arrives there, and accordingly the 'alone' comes into this sentence before the arrival of the predicate. Thus it is not a syncategorematic word, since every syncategorematic word has the predicate in view (*habet respectum ad praedicatum*). In the second case, however, it

---

[85] I.e., the reasoning to be found in the first "on the contrary."
[86] See Chapter XI, Section 11.
[87] See nn. 30 and 31, this chapter.
[88] See Chapter XI, Section 2.

is a syncategorematic word, and so there is a paralogism of equivocation.³⁹

---

³⁹ Peter of Spain discusses this sophisma and others in his treatment of exclusives (*Tr. syn.*, tr. Mullally, pp. 29–41). His discussion of this sophisma (p. 41) omits the characteristically Sherwoodian analysis in terms of the arrival times of elements of the sentence. Sections 13 and 14 of Chapter XII are really discussions of 'alone' rather than of 'only,' but since they are part of a general discussion of "exclusion in respect of different things" I have left them there.

CHAPTER XII. *'Only' (Tantum)*

📖 1. 'ONLY' USED CATEGOREMATICALLY AND SYNCATEGOREMATICALLY

We must speak next of the word 'only,' regarding which it must be known that as regards its first signification¹ it is not a syncategorematic word. Instead it indicates a certain measure of an act, just as 'much' and 'little'² indicate uncertain measures, and it is an adverb of quantity as they are. But when this consideration (*ratio*) of measure [67] is restricted to the consideration of a subject in respect of a predicate or of a predicate in respect of a subject, then the word 'only,' denoting a measure in this way, takes on the nature (*ratio*) of a syncategorematic word, as when I say 'only Socrates is running.' For it indicates how much of the subject is under the predicate — viz., that the subject Socrates and no more is under it. In that case it is an exclusive word.

📖 2. A DOUBT REGARDING THE DETERMINATION OF A SUBJECT BY MEANS OF AN ADVERB

But the following doubt is raised. Since it is an adverb, how can it determinate a subject, seeing that every adverb means (*vult*) to be referred to a verb?

And it must be said that this is true, but [an adverb means to be referred

---

¹ The "first signification" of the Latin adverb '*tantum*' is 'so much' (as some standard, expressed or understood). There seems to be no closely parallel use of 'only,' but there are, of course, nonsyncategorematic uses of it, as in 'Napoleon's only son.'
² O'Donnell's edition has '*parum*' here, following P. The translation follows O, which has '*parvum*.'

to a verb] either immediately or mediately. When the word 'only' determinates a subject, however, it determinates it in respect of a predicate, and thus it does relate (*respicit*) to a verb mediately.

3. A COMPARISON OF 'ONLY' AND 'ALONE'

It must be known that ['only'] can, in the same way as the word 'alone,' exclude either generally or specifically,[3] since it immobilizes a division very much as does ['alone'].[4] Moreover, it impedes an inference from an inferior to a superior (and vice versa) in much the same way.[5] ['Only' and 'alone'] likewise agree in many other respects.

4. 'ONLY' ADJOINED TO A NUMBER TERM

Rule [I]: *The word 'only' adjoined to a number term excludes a greater but not a smaller number.*

For example, if one says 'only three,' one cannot infer 'therefore not two' but instead 'therefore not four or five.' But on the contrary, when such a thing is said, everything other than three is excluded. But two are other than three, since they are not three; therefore two are excluded.

And it must be said that the word 'only' excludes not everything other, but what is other in respect of the predicate. Now there is a predicate in respect of which two are other than three, and another [predicate] in respect of which [two are] not [other than three]. In the first case a smaller as well as a greater number is excluded; in the second case, only a greater. Example of the first: 'only three are three,' or 'only three are hauling the boat' (supposing ['three'] is used conjunctively).[6] Example of the second: 'only three are running.'

5. 'ONLY' ADDED TO A COPULATED TERM

Rule [II]: *When the word 'only' is added to a copulated term the expression is ambiguous in that* ['*only*'] *can exclude either around the whole or around a part, and in the latter case either around the first part or around the second.*

On this basis the following sophisma is solved. Only the true is opposed

---

[3] See Chapter XI, Section 7.
[4] See Chapter XI, Section 9.
[5] See Chapter XI, Section 8.
[6] See Chapter XI, Section 15.

to the false. Proof: The true is opposed to the false, and nothing other than the true [is opposed to the false]; therefore only the true [is opposed to the false]. Then [someone may infer] 'therefore only the true and the false are opposed.' On the contrary, the white and the black are opposed. (And suppose that the first [proposition] is taken in the sense in which the exclusion occurs around 'the true.'[7])

It must be said that 'only the true and the false [are opposed]' is ambiguous in that the exclusion can occur around the whole 'the true and the false,' in which case the sense is 'it is not the case that the white and the black [are opposed]' and so on, with the result that other copulated terms are excluded and the expression is false. Or [it can occur] around the first part, in which case the expression is true and follows from the premiss, and the sense is 'it is not the case that the white and the false are opposed, it is not the case that the black [and the false are opposed],' and so on with respect to the others. Or [it can occur] also around the other part, in which case the expression is true, although not to the original premiss, and the sense is 'it is not the case that the true and the white are opposed,' [and so on with respect to the others].[8]

6. 'ONLY' ADJOINED TO A DISJOINED TERM

Similarly also when ['only'] is adjoined to a disjoined term, as in 'only what is true or false is a proposition.' On the contrary, 'what is white or false [9] is a proposition,' or 'what is true or white [is a proposition].'

And [it must be said that] it is proved just in case the exclusion occurs around the whole disjoined term. It is disproved, however, in the first place if one excludes around the first part, in the second place if [one excludes] around the second part.[10]

---

[7] The point of this stipulation emerges only in Chapter XII, Sections 9-11. 'Only' can exclude around various elements of the sentence 'only the true is opposed to the false,' but both the proof and the disproof depend on its being taken to exclude around 'the true' rather than around 'is opposed to' or 'the false.'
[8] Peter of Spain discusses this sophisma under a different rule and provides a radically different solution for it (*Tr. syn.*, tr. Mullally, p. 33).
[9] Reading '*falsum*' for '*verum*.'
[10] On the model of the analyses in the preceding section, the occurrence of the exclusion around the whole disjoined term results in the reading 'it is not the case that anything other than what is true or false is a proposition'; around the first part, 'it is not the case that what is anything other than true or false is a proposition'; around the second part, 'it is not the case that what is true or anything other than false is a proposition.' The "on the contrary" provides counter-instances to the second and third readings.

The following is similar. Only what is rational or irrational is an animal. On the contrary, what is rational or a stone is an animal, or what is a stone or irrational is an animal.

7. 'ONLY' ADJOINED TO A CONCRETE TERM

[Rule III:] *When ['only'] is adjoined to a concrete term it can exclude either in respect of the substance or in respect of the designated quality.*

This produces diversity, strictly speaking, in such concrete terms as have qualities belonging to them that can inhere together with their opposites in one and the same thing at one and the same time. Such are 'the one' and 'the other,' 'master' and 'student,' 'one' and 'many'; for [when taken] divisively they are the subject of a unity, [while] the same ones [taken] conjunctively are the subject of a plurality.[11]

On this basis the following sophisma is solved. Suppose that only Socrates and Plato exist and that each is the master of the other. Then only a master exists. Proof: A master exists, and nothing other than a master exists; therefore only [a master exists]. On the contrary, a student exists.

[It must be said that] if the exclusion is made in respect of the substance it is true, [68] and in that case it is proved, for 'other' indicates diversity in substance. If [it is made] in respect of the [designated] quality it is false, and in that case it is disproved.[12]

[Similarly,] only one of them exists.[13] Proof: Whatever exists is one of them [and nothing other than one of them exists; therefore only one of them exists]. On the contrary, the other of them exists.

---

[11] For a pair of such concrete terms to be taken conjunctively is, evidently, to be taken as applying in one and the same respect, while to be taken divisively is to be taken as applying in different respects. Thus, while no single person can be both a master and a student at one and the same time in one and the same respect, he may, of course, be a master in one respect and a student in another. On terms taken conjunctively and divisively see also Chapter XI, Sections 15 and 17.

[12] In 'only a master exists,' if the exclusion occurs in respect of the substance, the sense is 'there is at least one substance that has the quality of being a master and there is no substance other than a substance that has the quality of being a master.' If the exclusion occurs in respect of the designated quality, the sense is 'there is at least one substance that has the quality of being a master and there is no substance that has a quality other than the quality of being a master.'

[13] An interlinear gloss at this point in P says "the earlier supposition having been retained." This is a second sophisma based on the same hypothesis and evidently to be solved along the same lines.

8. ANOTHER EXAMPLE OF 'ONLY' ADJOINED TO A CONCRETE TERM

Again, only one exists. This may be proved in the same way.[14] On the contrary, many exist. The solution is the one just given.

Some draw a distinction here, [saying] that 'one' is equivocal;[15] for [taken] in one way it is the source of number (*principium numeri*), in which case it has 'many' as its opposite, and [taken] in a second way it is converted with 'being.'[16] In this second way ['only one exists'] is proved; in the other way, disproved.

But on the contrary,[17] every unity from which, together with another, a pair (*binarius*) arises is the source of number, but everything that exists as such a unity is one; therefore everything that exists is one in unity of number; therefore 'one' [in the sense in] which [it] is the source of number is converted with 'being.' Thus just as 'only being exists' is true, so 'only one exists' is true, even in the sense in which unity is the source of number.[18]

Others say that there is a fallacy of *figura dictionis* if someone says 'whatever exists is one; therefore only one exists' or 'nothing exists that is not one; therefore only [one exists].' For 'one' when it stands in the predicate stands generally for every one, but when it stands in the subject it stands for a one simply.[19] [Or] 'one exists, and nothing other than one exists; [therefore only one exists],' since when I say 'nothing other than one [exists]' it is the same as if I were to say 'nothing which is not one exists,' and thus ['other than one'] has the force of a clause or phrase [involved in the subject].[20]

---

[14] Cf. the three different versions of the proof given in the fourth paragraph of this section.
[15] This is the approach taken by Peter of Spain in his discussion of this sophisma (*Tr. syn.*, tr. Mullally, p. 31).
[16] On convertible or interchangeable terms see *Introductiones*, Chapter Four, Section 3.2.5 (*WSIL*, p. 81 and p. 81, n. 56).
[17] In this section the "on the contrary" paragraphs seem to contain Sherwood's responses to the views of others contained in the second, fourth, and sixth paragraphs.
[18] Cf. Boethius, *Commentaria in Porphyrium a se translatum*, Bk. III (*P.L.*, 64.109D–110A).
[19] 'One' stands in the predicate of the premiss and in the subject of the conclusion.
[20] The relative clause 'which is not one' can be compounded with 'nothing' — i.e., taken to modify 'nothing' — or divided from 'nothing' — i.e., taken in apposition to 'nothing.' The claim thus seems to be that there is a reading of 'nothing other than one exists' under which that premiss is inconsistent with the first ('one exists') — viz., 'nothing — [which is] other than one — exists.' On clauses or phrases involved

On the contrary, according to this an inference of the following kind does not hold—'whatever exists is a man; therefore only man exists' (*quicquid est, est homo; ergo tantum homo est*).

In response to this they say that such words as 'one' and 'the one' when they stand in the subject mean to stand for some one of their supposita, but the word 'man' stands indifferently for one and for many.[21]

But on the contrary, suppose that there is an inference such as 'one exists, and no non-one (*nullum non unum*) exists; therefore only one exists.' And if in response to this one says that 'non-one' stands virtually[22] in the predicate,[23] since it is as if I were to say 'being not one' (*non ens unum*) or 'that which is not one' (*quod non est unum*), [then] let it be said that similarly the 'one' stands [virtually] in the conclusion, since [it stands in] 'only one'—i.e., 'only being one' (*tantum ens unum*) or 'only that which is one' (*tantum hoc quod est unum*).

9. SYSTEMATIC AMBIGUITY IN CONNECTION WITH 'ONLY'

Rule [IV]: *There are as many senses as there are words in sentences of this kind.*

This is because the 'only' can exclude around one thing or around another. For example, 'Socrates only strikes Plato.' If it excludes around 'Socrates' the sense is that no one else strikes [Plato]. If around 'strikes,' the sense is that Socrates is not running, and so on for other actions.[24] If around 'Plato,' the sense is that Socrates is striking no one else.

10. THAT AROUND WHICH AND THAT IN RESPECT OF WHICH EXCLUSION OCCURS

Rule [V]: *When that around which the exclusion occurs bears a rela-*

---

in the subject term cf. Chapter I, Section 10; Chapter VII, Section 5; Chapter XI, Sections 10 and 12.

[21] The claim seems to be that words such as '*unum*' and '*alter*' can have only determinate supposition when they stand in the subject, whereas common nouns such as '*homo*' can have either determinate or confused supposition when they stand in the subject.

[22] On standing (or suppositing) "virtually" see *Introductiones*, Chapter Five, Section 12 (*WSIL*, pp. 116–117).

[23] Since 'non-one' stands in the subject rather than in the predicate and since the comparison is made with the way in which 'one' stands "in the conclusion," it seems that this should be 'premiss' (*praemissa*) rather than 'predicate' (*praedicato*).

[24] If, as the rule and the wording of this sentence suggest, the exclusion is to be around 'strikes' rather than around 'strikes Plato,' the sense should be that Socrates does not *heal* Plato, and so on for other actions of which Plato is the object.

tion (habet respectum) to different things, the exclusion can occur in respect of [any of] them.

Understand that the exclusion occurs *around* that the opposite of which is excluded, but *in respect of* that to which the negation is referred.²⁵

This is true of the word 'alone' as much as of the word 'only.' Thus 'the boat can carry one alone' is ambiguous; for if the exclusion occurs in respect of the 'can,' the sense is 'it *cannot* carry more than one,' if in respect of the 'carry,' the sense is 'it can *not carry* more than one.' ²⁶

11. A SECOND EXAMPLE HAVING TO DO WITH THAT DISTINCTION

Suppose that six men are running and that Socrates knows three of them are running and not more. Then Socrates knows only three men are running. (And suppose that 'only' excludes around 'three.' ²⁷) Proof: Socrates knows three [men are running], and he does not know more [are running]; therefore he knows only three [men are running]. On the contrary, whatever is known is true; therefore that only three men are running is true.

It must be said that according to Rule [IV] 'only' can exclude around the single words of this expression. According to Rule [V], however, in case it excludes around 'three' it can exclude either in respect of 'knows' (in which case the sense is 'he does not know more [than three are running]' and it is proved) or in respect of 'are running' (in which case the sense is 'he knows more are not running' and it is disproved).

But the senses resulting from the fact that the exclusion can occur around various things are these. If around 'Socrates,' the sense is 'no one else knows [three men are running].' If around 'knows,' the sense is 'does not doubt,' 'is not unaware,' [and so on for other cognitive states]. If around 'three,' there are two senses, [69] as has been said. If around

---

²⁵ This distinction is introduced in Chapter XI, Section 12, q.v. In the three analyses provided in the preceding section that *in respect of which* the exclusion occurs is (A) '. . . strikes Plato,' (B) 'Socrates . . .' or 'Socrates . . . Plato' (see n. 24, this chapter), (C) 'Socrates strikes . . .'; or, more fully, (A) someone other than Socrates striking Plato, (B) Socrates doing something other than striking Plato, or Socrates doing something to Plato other than striking him, (C) Socrates striking someone other than Plato.
²⁶ I.e., it need not carry more than one.
²⁷ See the third paragraph of this section for an account of the other elements of this sentence around which 'only' might be taken to exclude. See also n. 7, this chapter.

'men,' the sense is 'he does not know three asses [are running],' etc. If around the whole 'three men,' the sense is 'he does not know anything else is running.' If around 'are running,' the sense is 'he does not know more are arguing,' [etc.] If around the whole 'three men are running,' the sense is 'he does not know anything else.'

Understand, however, that in case it excludes around 'men' or around the whole 'three men' it can do so in two ways: either in respect of 'knows,' as has been said, or in respect of 'are running,' so that the negation is referred to it. Similarly, [in case it excludes] around 'are running,' [it can do so] either in respect of 'knows,' as has been said, or in respect of 'three,' so that the negation is attached to it and not to 'knows.'

⌐ 12. A THIRD EXAMPLE HAVING TO DO WITH THAT DISTINCTION

Sophisma: the first supposition having been retained,[28] it is true only six men are running (since only six men are running); therefore it is possible only six men are running. On the contrary, it is possible ten are running. (And suppose that ['only'] always excludes around 'six.')

It must be said that in the first [proposition] the exclusion can occur either in respect of 'are running' or in respect of 'it is true,' and in either case it is true. In the first case the sense is 'it is true more men are not running'; in the second case the sense is that it is not true more men are running. The conclusion is similarly ambiguous, but true in the first case and false in the second. In the first case it does follow from the first [proposition] and, as is clear, the "on the contrary" does not prevent it. In the second case it does not follow; rather, there is a paralogism of the consequent: 'this is not true; therefore it is not [29] possible.' This is clear if the affirmative is compared with the affirmative and the negative with the negative.[30]

⌐ 13. AN EXAMPLE HAVING TO DO WITH THAT DISTINCTION IN CONNECTION WITH 'ALONE' [31]

Sophisma: from Socrates's running alone (*ad solum Sortem currere*)

---

[28] The first supposition is no doubt the first half of the hypothesis for the sophisma in Section 11 — i.e., that six men are running. But as used here it has been strengthened by the implicit addition of the supposition that no other men are running.

[29] O'Donnell's edition omits the '*non*' that occurs in P at this point.

[30] I.e., if the first reading of the premiss is compared with the first reading of the conclusion and the second with the second.

[31] See Chapter XI, n. 38.

it follows that a man is running. Proof: If Socrates is running, a man is running; therefore [from Socrates's running alone it follows that a man is running]. On the contrary, from the running of someone other than Socrates it follows that a man is running; therefore not from Socrates's [running] alone [does it follow that a man is running].

It must be said that the first [proposition] is ambiguous in that the exclusion can occur either in respect of 'running' (in which case it is true and proved) or in respect of 'it follows' (in which case it is false because the "on the contrary" prevents it).

But on the contrary, the word 'Socrates's,' around which the exclusion occurs, bears no relation to 'it follows'; therefore the exclusion cannot occur in respect of it.

And it must be said that although it bears no immediate relation to it, still it does bear [a relation to it] through the medium of 'running.'

14. AN EXAMPLE HAVING TO DO WITH THAT DISTINCTION IN CONNECTION WITH 'ALONE' AND 'AND'

Again, from Socrates's running alone it follows that Socrates is running. Proof: From Socrates's running [it follows that Socrates is running], and it is not the case that from the running of someone other [than Socrates it follows that Socrates is running]; therefore from [Socrates's running] alone [it follows that Socrates is running]. On the contrary, from Socrates's [running] and from someone else's [running it follows that Socrates is running], since if Socrates and someone else are running Socrates is running.

It must be said that the first [proposition] is true in every sense, but the "on the contrary" is ambiguous in that it can be either compounded or divided.[32] If it is compounded, that proposition is true; but it does not counter-instantiate the exclusion unless it is considered as divided, as was said above.[33] If it is divided, that proposition is false, as is clear.

15. AN EXPLANATION OF THE OCCURRENCE OF EXCLUSION IN RESPECT OF DIFFERENT THINGS

The reason why an exclusion can occur in respect of different things is that in such cases that around which the exclusion occurs bears a relation

---

[32] Compounded: 'from Socrates's running and someone else's running it follows that Socrates is running'; divided: 'from Socrates's running it follows that Socrates is running and from someone else's running it follows that Socrates is running.'
[33] Apparently a reference to Chapter XI, Section 11.

first to one thing and then to another. Thus if the exclusion comes into it before that second thing is ordered [in the sentence], it excludes in respect of the first thing only; but if after, it excludes in respect of that second thing. For it always excludes in respect of that to which that around which the exclusion occurs bears a relation at the time of its arrival (*in suo adventu*) [in the sentence].[34]

---

[34] See Chapter I, n. 75. Peter of Spain discusses 'only' briefly in *Summulae logicales* (ed. Mullally, pp. 104–108). His discussion of 'only' in *Tractatus syncategorematum* (tr. Mullally, pp. 29–41) is mixed together with his discussion of the other exclusive word, 'alone.'

CHAPTER XIII. *'Is' (Est)*

¶ 1. WHETHER 'IS' IS A SYNCATEGOREMATIC WORD

Since we have now discussed or decided about syncategorematic words pertaining to the subject, we can proceed in two ways — by deciding either about those that pertain to the composition [of a predicate wtih a subject] or about those that pertain to the predicate.

Proceeding in the first way, let us first decide about the verb 'is,' not because it is a syncategorematic word but because it is supposed by many to be a syncategorematic word.[1] They [70] rely on Aristotle's remark that 'is' signifies [2] a certain composition that cannot be understood without the components;[3] for they believe that 'consignify' is [the same as] his 'signify.'[4] And in that way alone is it consignificative and conpredicative,[5] as is a syncategorematic word.

---

[1] O'Donnell supplies a reference to Abelard at this point: *Glossae super Peri ermeneias*, in *Beiträge zur Geschichte der Philosophie und Theologie des Mittelalters*, Vol. XXI, No. 3, ed. Bernhard Geyer (Münster, 1927), p. 359. Abelard does discuss the verb 'is' there (also pp. 339 and 451), but he does not describe it as a syncategorematic word. Cf. *WSIL*, p. 13, n. 50. I know of no one earlier than Sherwood who does characterize 'is' as syncategorematic.
[2] P has *'significat'*; O has *'consignificat.'* O'Donnell follows O, which seems mistaken in view of the Aristotle passage (see n. 3, this chapter) and Sherwood's comment immediately afterward.
[3] O'Donnell supplies the reference to *De interpretatione*, 3 (16b23): "For not even 'to be' or 'not to be' is a sign of the actual thing (nor if you say simply 'that which is'); for by itself it is nothing, but it additionally signifies some combination, which cannot be thought of without the components" (tr. J. L. Ackrill).
[4] Cf. Sherwood's own remarks in *Introductiones*, Chapter One, Section 11: "Some

But on the contrary, a verb is a note of that which is said of something else, but that [which is said of something else] is a predicate; therefore every verb is a note or sign of a predicate. Therefore the verb 'is' is a sign of a predicate and not of the composition of a predicate with a subject alone.

But perhaps he will say that 'is' is not a verb but the root of all verbs.[6]

But on the contrary, a proposition is made out of a name and a verb alone; therefore 'is' itself is a verb.[7] Therefore it is said to consignify, not because it signifies together with another word and is an ingredient in an expression[8] but because it signifies composition along with its principal significatum.[9] But it is not a syncategorematic word on that account.

2. THE STATUS OF 'IS' OCCURRING AS A THIRD INGREDIENT

But still it seems that when 'is' is a third ingredient (*tertium adjacens*) it is not the predicate but rather the composition alone, as in 'a man is an animal,' since in the converse of it[10] only 'animal' is the subject. Therefore, since to be converted is to make a predicate of a subject, we ought to say that all propositions have the same predicate, for if another verb [than 'is'] is predicated it is permissible to resolve it into its participle and the verb 'is.' For example, 'a man runs'[11] — i.e., 'a man is running'; 'a man walks' — '[a man] is walking'; and so on with respect to the others.

As to the first [point], it must be said that when I say 'a man is an ani-

---

say that the word 'is' is a third part [of the statement], the copula. But that is not the case; for since it is a verb it signifies that which is said of something other than itself, and thus it is a predicate. But it does *consignify* composition, which is [the function of] the copula (*que est copula*). And every other verb by its very nature consignifies in this respect" (*WSIL*, p. 27; see also p. 27, n. 25). Cf. Peter of Spain, *Tr. syn.*, tr. Mullally, p. 21.

[5] Reading '*conpraedicativum*' for '*praedicativum.*' Cf. Sherwood's explanation of the term '*syncategorema*' in his Introduction to this treatise.

[6] See the first paragraph of the next section.

[7] Because such combinations as 'Socrates is' and 'man is' are propositions.

[8] The technical sense of 'expression' (*oratio*) is more important here than elsewhere in this treatise. In Chapter One, Section 8, of *Introductiones* Sherwood offers this definition: "An expression, then, is an utterance significant by convention, parts of which do signify," distinguishing between an expression and a word (*dictio*), "the parts of which do not signify" (*WSIL*, p. 25).

[9] I.e., being.

[10] I.e., 'some animal is a man.'

[11] '*Homo currit,*' which would ordinarily be translated as 'a man is running,' is translated in this way here in order to preserve the distinction between '*homo currit*' and '*homo est currens.*' The second of these expressions might also be read as 'a man is a running thing.'

mal,' the thing belonging to the verb 'is' is specified by 'animal.'[12] But it is the nature of specification that the specificant and the specificate pass into (*cedant in*) the specificant[13] itself. Thus the thing belonging to the verb 'is' passes into what is one and the same with [the thing belonging to] 'animal,' and in predicating the real thing belonging to it [the verb 'is'] stands just as 'animal' does here. Thus although 'animal' is predicated, 'is' is no less predicated.

As to the other [point], it must be said that, as is already clear, by means of various adjuncts [the verb 'is'] passes into various predicates. Thus although the verb 'is' will be predicated in any and every proposition, still there will not be one and the same predicate in all [propositions].[14]

3. 'IS' INDICATING ACTUAL BEING AND CONDITIONAL BEING

It must be known that the verb 'is' is sometimes taken equivocally, for sometimes it indicates actual being (*esse actuale*), which is due to (*debetur*) something actually existing, and sometimes conditional being (*esse habituale*), which is due to that which is in itself some nature and is suited (*natus*) to be conditionally in some singular although it is not actually.[15]

---

[12] Being is "the thing belonging to the verb 'is,'" and the combination of 'is' and 'animal' is here said to pick out one special sort of being.

[13] Reading '*specificantem*' for '*specificatum*.' When being is specified by 'animal,' it is thought of not as being, specified in a certain way, but as animal; and when animal is specified by 'man,' it is thought of not as animal, specified in a certain way, but as man; and so on. Thus the specificant and the specificate pass into the *specificant*, not into the specificate. This is borne out by what Sherwood has to say about this example in the next sentence. It is possible also to suppose that this is a garbled version of a more complicated doctrine, according to which the thing belonging to the verb 'is' would be the *specificandum*, 'animal' the *specificant*, and the thing belonging to 'animal' the *specificate* (the result of the specification of being by 'animal'). On this interpretation the sentence in question would read "But it is the nature of specification that the specificant and the specificandum pass into the specificate itself," allowing the second '*specificatum*' to stand and reading 'specificandum' for the first '*specificatum*.'

[14] Thus Sherwood's view is that the so-called third-ingredient occurrences of 'is' (as distinct from its second-ingredient or predicative occurrences, as in 'Socrates is') are not occurrences of 'is' as an entity (the "copula") distinct both from the subject and from the predicate, but as an indispensable ingredient in the predicate itself. In his response to the first point he states this view with respect to propositions in which a name (substantival or adjectival) is the predicate term — e.g., 'a man is an animal,' 'a man is rational.' In his response to the second point he states this view with respect to propositions in which a verb is the predicate term — e.g., 'a man runs' — every such case (ignoring tense and number) being analyzable into 'is' plus the present participle of the original verb — 'a man is running.'

[15] Cf. a parallel discussion in *Introductiones*, Chapter Five, Section 16.2 (*WSIL*, pp. 125–126).

[If 'is' is taken] in the first way 'every man is an animal' is false when no man exists. [If 'is' is taken] in the second way it is true; and ['is'] is used in this way according as 'every' divides for specific parts.[16]

Some say also that when no man exists 'man is' is ambiguous with the same ambiguity, for they say that it is false [if 'is' is taken] in the first way, true [if 'is' is taken] in the second way.

But others say that in this and in other [propositions] in which 'is' is not a third ingredient it indicates actual being alone, but where it is a third ingredient and a superior is predicated of an inferior it is taken equivocally, as in 'man is an animal,' for it indicates animal being in man (*dicit enim esse animal in homine*). Therefore when animal has being in the second way described, ['is'] can indicate that kind of being; and when also occasionally it has being in the first way described, ['is'] can also indicate that kind of being.

This is well enough said, since, as it seems, if one were thus to say 'man is,' ['is'] would indicate being simply and complete, which indeed is not in man if not actually. And in this case there is not anything (as there was in the other example) that leads it to indicate being in the second way described — i.e., diminutional being.[17]

---

[16] See Chapter I, Section 2.

[17] The other example is 'a man is an animal,' and in it the specificant, 'animal,' leads the 'is' to indicate a specific sort of being, which constitutes a diminution of the notion of "being simply and complete." See n. 13, this chapter.

CHAPTER XIV. *'Not' (Non)*

1. WHETHER 'NOT' AND 'IS' ARE OPPOSED

Next, as to the word 'not.' It seems that it ought to be a verb, because it signifies division, which, it seems, is opposed to the composition denoted by the verb 'is.' Thus ['not'] ought to be a verb just as ['is'] itself [is a verb], for contraries belong to one and the same genus.

It must be said that this reasoning errs in two ways. First, because [71] although the word 'not' does signify division only, the word 'is,' as was said before,[1] does not signify composition only; and so they do not signify

---

[1] Chapter XIII, Section 1.

contraries. Second, also because the composition denoted or consignified by means of the verb 'is' is not opposed to 'not,' because the composition is a mode of signifying² dependently, by reason of which it requires the nominative for itself, and this is the reason the proposition is one of its parts (*et hoc est illud quo propositio est unum ex suis partibus*).³ When, on the one hand, the mind consents to [the composition], it asserts, and there is an affirmation; when, on the other hand, [the mind] dissents, it disasserts (*deasserit*), and there is a negation. Therefore the composition belonging to the verb 'is' is, as it were, a subject for affirmation and for negation, and the negation belonging to 'not' is opposed to affirmation and not to the composition (unless affirmation is called "composition"; but that [composition] is different from the composition belonging to the verb ['is'], as has been said).

2. NEGATION OF A TERM AND NEGATION OF A COMPOSITION

It must be known, moreover, that [the negation belonging to 'not'] sometimes stays in one term, in which case it produces infinitation. At

---

² O'Donnell has a note at this point referring to the *Summa modorum significandi* of Siger of Courtrai (d. 1341), edited by G. Wallerand in *Les Oeuvres de Siger de Courtrai* (Vol. VIII of *Les Philosophes Belges*, Louvain, 1913). But Siger's treatise represents an advanced stage in the development of the medieval grammatico-metaphysical inquiry known generally as "speculative grammar" and is not likely to contain material directly relevant to this passage (see section on speculative grammar in my article, "Semantics, History of"). The term '*modus significandi*' antedates the development of speculative grammar and can be found in the work of such twelfth-century philosophers and grammarians as Peter Abelard and Peter Helias, deriving from passages in the logical works of Boethius (see Charles Thurot, *Notices et extraits de divers manuscrits latins pour servir à l'histoire des doctrines grammaticales au moyen âge* (Paris, 1869), pp. 150–154; also Martin Grabmann, "Die Entwicklung der mittelalterlichen Sprachlogik," pp. 104–146 in his *Mittelalterliches Geistesleben*, Vol. I, Munich, 1926). More directly relevant to Sherwood's use of the term here is the fact that Peter of Spain uses it in the same general context: "As regards logical composition, some are signified in a word; others, however, in a proposition. Certainly that which belongs to a word is a composition of the essential and accidental modes of signifying (*modorum significandi*) of the eight parts of speech, to treat of which at length belongs to the grammarian" (*Tr. syn.*, tr. Mullally, p. 18).

³ The main line of Sherwood's rejection of the view that 'is' (or composition) is opposed to 'not' (or negation) is spelled out fairly clearly in the remainder of this section. A composition (of subject and predicate) is what gets "asserted" (affirmed) or "disasserted" (denied), and so negation is opposed to affirmation rather than to composition. But his first remarks in explanation of his own position, in the last three clauses of this sentence, are very difficult to understand. Apparently a considerable amount of theory is being presupposed in this passage. One aspect of it, the claim that the proposition is one of the parts of composition, may be clarified by a passage in Peter of Spain's *Tractatus syncategorematum* in which five "modes" of composition are distinguished, only the fifth of which is the sort of composition

other times it is referred to the composition of one [term] with another,[4] and this in two ways — by producing negation either in a genus or outside a genus. This, however, results not from its own force, but from the fact that speakers sometimes confine their discourse (*suos sermones*) to determinate matter.[5] For example, if it is one's intention to speak of animal and one says 'nothing other than man . . .,' 'no other animal . . .' is understood. (This has already been said about the word 'alone.'[6] Insofar as it is [considered] in itself, however, [the negation belonging to 'not'] negates for all.

3. 'NOT' TAKEN EXTINCTIVELY AND OTHERWISE

Sometimes ['not'] is taken extinctively, at other times not. For example, 'not in case Socrates is running (*non Sorte currente*) you are an ass.' If [the negation belonging to 'not'] is referred to the whole, ['not'] is taken extinctively and [the proposition] is true. If it stays in the participle, [the proposition] is false.

Similarly, 'you are not a man who is an ass.' But it is better that we should say that expressions can be compounded or divided, as has been said in preceding [discussions].[7]

4. NEGATIVE PROPOSITIONS WITH MANY CAUSES OF TRUTH

It frequently happens that a negative [proposition] has many causes of truth, and in that case if some one of them is inferred from that [proposition] there will be a fallacy of the consequent. (And it must be known that a negative can be verified for the same cause for which the [corresponding] affirmative can be falsified.)

On this basis the following sophisma is solved. 'Only you are an ass' is false; therefore 'not only you are an ass' is true; therefore you and someone else are asses.

It must be said that the first [proposition] could be falsified either because you are not an ass or because although you are an ass someone else

---

Sherwood is concerned with here, "the composition of a perfect proposition" (tr. Mullally, p. 21; cf. p. 20).

[4] Peter of Spain labels these "infinitating negation" and "negating negation," respectively, and discusses them at some length (*Tr. syn.*, tr. Mullally, pp. 22–25).

[5] A prefiguring of the notion of a "universe of discourse" or a "limited universe" to be found in logicians of the nineteenth and twentieth centuries.

[6] Chapter X, Section 7.

[7] See Chapter VII, Sections 3 and 5.

is an ass too. And the negative 'not only you [are an ass]' can be verified for [either of] those two [causes]. Therefore, since only the second mode, or second cause, of the truth of [the negative] is inferred from it, there will be a fallacy of the consequent.

But on the contrary, one negation lies in the 'only,' and another [negation] is expressly placed before it. Those two, it seems, must count as one affirmation.[8] Therefore the aforesaid conclusion does follow.

Understand, however, that in 'not only you [are an ass]' there are two propositions virtually, and the negation that lies virtually there [in the 'only'] pertains to one of them alone. The first negation, on the other hand, pertains to the whole. Thus since they do not pertain to one and the same thing, they will not count as one affirmation.

5. MORE EXAMPLES OF NEGATIVE PROPOSITIONS WITH MANY CAUSES OF TRUTH

The following sophisma is likewise solved on that basis. More things are true of just that many things than are true of fewer than that many (*plura sunt vera de sibi totidem quam sunt vera de paucioribus se*).[9] Proof: As many things as are true (*quaecumque sunt vera*) of fewer than that many things are true of just that many things, since three stateables (*enuntiabilia*) [10] are true of fewer than that many things because they are true of two things. For example, these three [stateables] — viz., that Socrates is a man, that Socrates is an animal, that Plato has a color — are true of two things — viz., Socrates and Plato — and thus of fewer than that many [stateables]. And similarly three [stateables] are true of three things and

---

[8] Sherwood discusses the affirmative or negative character of various combinations of affirmative and negative signs in *Introductiones*, Chapter One, Section 19, "Equipollent Signs," and Section 20, "Statements Containing Two Signs" (*WSIL*, pp. 35–39).

[9] The awkwardness of the English here reflects the awkwardness of the Latin, which is needed to give the sophisma as much plausibility as it has. The meaning of this proposition, the sophisma proper, is made clear by the examples introduced in the proof.

[10] The notion of a stateable bears a strong resemblance to the twentieth-century philosophical notion of a proposition as that which admits of being expressed in a statement. I know of no instance of its occurrence earlier than in Sherwood and in Peter of Spain. The latter says that the second of the two sorts of form that can be said to belong to a common term is a form "that is preserved both in existent and in non-existent things. Take for example stateability, which is the form of a stateable. For there are some existent stateables, such as that God is and that all things are true, and other non-existent stateables, such as that a man is an ass and that all things are false . . ." (*Sum. log.*, ed. Mullally, p. 60). (Mullally's translation of this passage, on p. 61, obscures its sense.)

thus are true of just that many things. For example, these three [stateables] — viz., that Socrates is a man, that Cicero is a man, that Plato is a man — are true of three things — viz., Socrates, Cicero, and Plato. And in the same way four [stateables] are true of fewer than that many, and four are true of just that many things, and so on with respect to the other [numbers]. Therefore however many [stateables] are true [of fewer than that many are true of just that many things]. And this does not convert, for two [stateables] are true of just that many things and two are not true of fewer than that many things, since there are no fewer (*pauciora*), but less (*paucius*) [than two]. Therefore not vice versa; therefore more [things are true of just that many things than are true of fewer than that many].

But on the contrary, infinitely many things are true of just that many things, and infinitely many are true of fewer than that many things, [72] and infinitely many are not more than infinitely many; therefore 'more [things are true of just that many things than are true of fewer than that many]' is false.

It must be said that this is true, and that a fallacy of the consequent occurs in the proof. This is either because the proposition 'however many [stateables] are true of just that many things are true of fewer than that many' can be falsified, or because there are some (*sit sumere aliquot*) that are true of just that many things that (*quot*) are not true of fewer than that many, whether in the larger numbers or in the smaller.[11] Thus 'not however many are true of just that many [are true of fewer than that many]' is verified by these two causes, and he means (*intelligit*) this when he says "and not vice versa." But 'more things are true [of just that many things than are true of fewer than that many]' has only one of those causes, for he says that in the larger numbers [12] there are some (*sit sumere aliquot*) that are true of just that many and not of fewer than that many. Thus there is a paralogism of the consequent.

An example of the same thing: Suppose that there are only six men and that they are white, and that three are hauling a boat together, and that those three together with a fourth are hauling another boat, and those four together with a fifth another, and those five together with a sixth another. Then however many are hauling a boat are white. And this does not con-

---

[11] I.e., in the infinitely many/infinitely many case or in the two/one case.

[12] A marginal gloss at this point in P says "and in another way in the smaller numbers." O'Donnell incorrectly connects it with the preceding occurrence of the phrase 'larger numbers.'

vert, since two are white and are not hauling a boat. Therefore more are white than are hauling a boat.[13] On the contrary, only six are white, and that many are hauling a boat. Thus there is a paralogism of the consequent,[14] as is clear enough.

Nevertheless, some say that 'infinitely many are not more than infinitely many' is false if we are speaking of infinitely many that are infinitely many in only one of those two ways (*ex altera parte tantum*),[15] and that is the case in what is proposed. For that reason they solve [the sophisma] by negating that proposition. There are many reasons against this, but we may let them go for now.

6. NEGATION GIVING RISE TO SUPPOSITION FOR NONEXISTENTS

Negation takes more than affirmation puts. For example, 'a man is running' means (*vult*) only that someone is running, but the negation 'no man is running' extends itself to all.

But if it is understood in this way one can by the same reasoning give *these* contraries, since if one says 'every man is running' this affirmation extends itself to all, but the negation ['some man is not running'] only to someone.

For that reason let us say that in a non-ampliating [affirmative] proposition about the present there is reference to (*habetur respectus ad*) present things alone, while in a negative to nonexistents as well.[16] If no man is

---

[13] An interlinear gloss at this point in P says "this is the sophisma."
[14] An interlinear gloss at this point in P says "i.e., in the proof."
[15] This difficult passage refers back to the first "on the contrary" in this section and seems to be making something like the following point. It is true that infinitely many stateables are true of infinitely many things, where stateables and things are in a one-to-one correspondence. This may be described as infinitely many stateables in the first way. It is likewise true that infinitely many stateables are true of fewer than infinitely many things, where stateables and things are in a many-to-one correspondence, and this is infinitely many stateables in the second way. But it is furthermore true that infinitely many stateables in the *second* way, in a many-to-one correspondence, are true of *infinitely* many things, and these infinitely many stateables are more than those infinitely many stateables that were originally said to be true of infinitely many things. Thus it is not true in general that infinitely many are not more than infinitely many. Sherwood's concluding remark suggests that he rejects the notion of unequal infinities.
[16] In *Introductiones*, Chapter Five, Section 16 (*WSIL*, pp. 123–131), Sherwood discusses at length a rule regarding supposition and appellation: "An unrestricted common term, having sufficient appellata and suppositing in connection with a present-tense verb that has no ampliating force, supposits only for those [things subordi-

running, then neither is Caesar; for if Caesar were running, Caesar would be, and thus would be a man; therefore a man would be running. Therefore, by the first, if Caesar is running, a man is running; therefore if no man is running, neither is Caesar.

But on the contrary, if this argument holds, then it seems there is an argument from a quantitative whole here,[17] and in that case 'man' will stand for Caesar and thus for a nonexistent.

But it must be said that this is not true, as is clear in the following example. No man who actually exists is running; therefore neither is Caesar. For this follows: if Caesar is running, Caesar actually exists and likewise is a man; therefore if no man who actually exists [is running], neither is Caesar. Although this argument holds, it is clear that the whole term 'man who actually exists' does not supposit for Caesar. Nor is there an argument from a quantitative whole here or in the preceding [argument]. Instead there is an argument from opposites,[18] since the affirmative, that Caesar is running, conflicts with (*repugnat*) the premiss in both terms — not because Caesar is a man, but because if he were running he would be a man. And because the affirmative conflicts with [the premiss], the negative follows.

7. THE EFFECT OF NEGATION ON AN INFERENCE FROM AN INFERIOR TO A SUPERIOR

Rule: *Negation impedes an inference from an inferior to a superior.*

But on the contrary, from where does this follow: 'a man is not running; therefore an animal is not running'? For if every animal [is running], then every man [is running].[19]

But it must be said that the rule must be understood [to apply] when the negation extends both to that inferior and to that superior, which is

---

nate to it] that do exist" (*WSIL*, p. 123). Many portions of that discussion are relevant to an understanding of this passage.

[17] Sherwood discusses arguments from a quantitative whole in *Introductiones*, Chapter Four, Section 3.2.4 (*WSIL*, pp. 79–81). One of the examples used there is 'no man is running; therefore Socrates is not running.'

[18] Sherwood discusses arguments from several different sorts of opposites in *Introductiones*, Chapter Four, Section 4.2 (*WSIL*, pp. 97–99).

[19] I.e., since man is indeed inferior to animal in a predicamental line, as the second sentence of this "on the contrary" observes, and since the inference in question is evidently an inference from an inferior to a superior involving negation, why is it not impeded (as it surely is not)?

not the case here. Thus this does not follow: 'not a man is running; therefore not an animal is running.' [20]

---

[20] The inference in question in the "on the contrary" may be read as 'there is a man that is not running; therefore there is an animal that is not running.' Sherwood's point is that the kind of negation mentioned in the rule is the kind to be found either in 'it is not the case that a man is running; therefore it is not the case that an animal is running' or in 'there is a non-man that is running; therefore there is a non-animal that is running.' (The Latin '*non homo currit; ergo non animal currit*' admits of either of these interpretations.)

CHAPTER XV. '*Necessarily*' *(Necessario) and* '*Contingently*' *(Contingenter)*

1. 'NECESSARILY' AND 'CONTINGENTLY' USED CATEGOREMATICALLY AND SYNCATEGOREMATICALLY

Next, as to the words 'necessarily' and 'contingently.' [1] And it must be known that the word 'necessarily' can be either a categorematic or a syncategorematic word. If it is categorematic it is a determination of a predicate; if it is syncategorematic [it is a determination] of a composition. (Similarly with respect to 'contingently.' [2])

But on the contrary, the composition is nothing except what is in the extremes or in an extreme [of the proposition]; therefore [73] if 'necessarily' determinates the composition it determinates one or the other of the extremes. But not the subject; therefore the predicate.

Again, if 'necessarily' is an adverb, then it determinates something that is an act and is in the manner of an act (*est actus et ut actus*). But the composition belonging to the verb in a sentence is not consignified [3] in the manner of an act; therefore an adverb does not determinate it. The assumption is clear, for the thing belonging to the verb to which the composition

---

[1] This chapter should be compared with Sherwood's treatment of modal statements in *Introductiones*, Chapter One, Sections 21–28 (*WSIL*, pp. 39–50).
[2] Although the title '*Necessario, Contingenter*' is supplied in the margin of P, the modal adverb 'contingently' is not explicitly discussed in this chapter. What is said of the syncategorematic functions of 'necessarily' is evidently supposed to apply also to 'contingently' and perhaps to the other modal adverbs – 'possibly,' 'impossibly' – as well. See *WSIL*, pp. 40–41.
[3] Reading '*consignificatur*' for '*consignificat*.'

belongs per se is signified not[4] in the manner of a substance but in the manner of an act proceeding from the subject, while that to which the act belongs is always signified in the manner of a substance.[5] And thus it seems that 'necessarily' determinates the predicate in the second case just as in the first.

It must be granted [that it does so], but in a different way; for in the first case it determinates the verb in respect of the thing belonging to it, in the second case in respect of the composition belonging to it, or insofar as it is a predicate. For example, if one says 'the heaven moves necessarily,' it signifies in the first case that the motion of the heaven is necessary, in the second case that the composition of the verb with the subject is necessary.

On this basis the following sophisma is solved. The soul of Antichrist will be necessarily. Proof: The soul of Antichrist will have necessary being because at some time it will have unceasing, incorruptible being. On the contrary, [the soul of Antichrist] will be contingently because it is possible that it will not be.

It is clear that it is proved in case ['necessarily'] is categorematic and disproved in case it is syncategorematic and [there is] a determination of the predicate in respect of the composition, for in that case 'the soul of Antichrist contingently will be'[6] is true, but in the other case false.[7]

---

[4] O'Donnell's edition omits the '*non*' that occurs in P at this point.
[5] The analysis provided in this paragraph evidently takes something like the following line. An adverb determinates what a verb signifies, and what a verb signifies — the thing belonging to a verb — is generally describable as an act and in the manner of an act. A verb occurring in a sentence may also consignify the composition of the subject with the predicate, but that composition is not to be confused with the act the verb *signifies*. Thus in 'Socrates runs' 'runs' signifies the act of running and consignifies the composition of that act with the substance signified by 'Socrates,' that to which the act belongs. If 'necessarily' is an adverb, it ought to operate as do other adverbs, such as 'swiftly' or 'erratically,' which would in no way determinate the composition but only the act if they were attached to the verb in 'Socrates runs.' Cf. Sherwood's discussion of this peculiarity of modal adverbs in *Introductiones* (*WSIL*, pp. 41–42).
[6] Here as elsewhere in this chapter the position of the modal word in the translation corresponds to its position in the original. Thus the similar phrase in the preceding paragraph is '*erit contingenter*' and in this paragraph the phrase is '*contingenter erit*.' The position of the modal word sometimes affects its operation, but this change was evidently considered to be without relevant effect.
[7] Peter of Spain also discusses this sophisma (*Tr. syn.*, tr. Mullally, pp. 68–69). Cf. Sherwood's earlier discussion of it in *Introductiones*, and see the notes accompanying that discussion (*WSIL*, p. 42). In those notes I suggested that one reason for the interest shown by medieval logicians in examples dealing with Antichrist was that it was an "open question whether Antichrist would be a man (and thus have a soul) or a supernatural being." In a letter to me (January 15, 1968) Professor Peter Geach has suggested a much more plausible explanation, which I gratefully adopt:

2. 'NECESSARILY' AS A NOTE OF COHERENCE AND AS A NOTE OF INHERENCE

Rule [I]: *The word 'necessarily' can sometimes be a note of coherence and at other times a note of inherence.*

For example, contingents necessarily are true. Proof: 'Contingents are true' is necessary; therefore it will be true when it has been modified by the mode of necessity; therefore 'contingents necessarily are true' is true. On the contrary, no contingents necessarily are true.

It must be said that it is proved insofar as 'necessarily' is a note of coherence and disproved insofar as it is a note of inherence. When it is a note of coherence it signifies that the form belonging to the predicate and the form belonging to the subject are at one and the same time and [necessarily] cohere in some suppositum.[8] And in that case the subject stands simply in some way or other, and not for this or for that [individual].[9] It is clear that it is in this way that [the proposition] is proved. When ['necessarily'] is a note of inherence it signifies that the form belonging to the predicate necessarily inheres in some suppositum of the subject.[10] And [in that case] the subject stands personally.[11] It is clear that it is in this way that [the proposition] is disproved.

We may say that this difference results from the fact that the word 'necessarily' can either come to this composition after [the composition] has been terminated in relation to this subject (in which case it extends to that very subject and causes that very subject to stand simply in some way or

---

"I should say that the most usual reason for the choice of Antichrist as an example is that here we have a future individual who can be identified, and whose existence is epistemically certain (being guaranteed by revelation), but yet, like any unborn man's, is future contingent ontologically speaking. In your note 66 [*WSIL*, p. 42] you are I think right about the truth of '*anima Antichristi necessario erit*' taken *de re* (that any soul that will be will have no *potentia ad non esse* and will thus exist necessarily) but wrong about why the parallel *de dicto* reading is false." In this connection see Robert Grosseteste's (ca. 1175-1253) discussions of propositions about Antichrist in "On the Truth of Proposition" and "On God's Knowledge" (in McKeon, *Selections from Medieval Philosophers*, Vol. I, pp. 283-284, 285).

[8] '*Suppositum*' is a term common to medieval metaphysics and the doctrine of the properties of terms and here may be taken to mean a subject or substance considered as a basis for modifications of every and any sort.

[9] I.e., the subject has one or another sort of simple supposition, in which the word supposits the form immediately signified by it rather than suppositing for some individual or individuals bearing that form. See *Introductiones*, Chapter Five, Section 7, "A Note on the Three Modes of Simple Supposition" (*WSIL*, pp. 111-112).

[10] Reading '*alicui supposito subjecti*' for '*alicui supposito et subjecti*.'

[11] I.e., the subject has personal supposition, in which the word supposits for some individual or individuals bearing the form immediately signified by the word.

other) — this is the first case; or [the word 'necessarily'] can come to it before [the composition has been terminated in relation to this subject] (in which case it does not extend to the subject) — this will be the second case.[12]

The first case is signified by means of the composition [i.e., the compounded sense] of the sentence, the second by its division [i.e., divided sense];[13] for the composition signifies that the 'necessarily' falls over the whole, the division that it does not do so.

3. 'NECESSARILY' TOGETHER WITH THE EXCLUSIVE 'ONLY'

[Rule II:] *Sometimes there is an ambiguity in that the word 'necessarily' can include the word 'alone' or 'only,' or vice versa.*

On this basis the following sophisma is solved. Suppose that Socrates, Plato, and Cicero are running necessarily and that a fourth [man is running] contingently, and that there are no more [men]. Then only three men are running necessarily. Proof: Three men necessarily are running, [and no others necessarily are running;] therefore only three [men are running necessarily]. On the contrary, 'only three men are running' is contingent, because when the fourth is running it will be false and when he is not running it will be true; therefore it will be false when it has been modified by the mode of necessity.

It is clear that it is proved by means of the force of the exclusion and according as the 'only' includes [the 'necessarily'], while it is disproved in the other way.[14]

4. 'NECESSARILY' TOGETHER WITH THE EXCLUSIVE 'ALONE'

Sophisma: Necessaries alone necessarily are true. Proof: Necessaries necessarily are true, and no others [necessarily are true] (which is proved inductively); therefore necessaries alone necessarily [are true]. On the contrary, 'necessaries alone are true' is false; therefore it will be false when the mode of necessity has been added. Alternatively: on the contrary, con-

---

[12] On the analysis in terms of the arrival times of the components of the sentence see Chapter I, n. 43.
[13] On compounded and divided senses see Chapter I, n. 47.
[14] The sentence would most readily be interpreted in this second way if the modal adverb occurred as the first word in it: 'necessarily only three men are running.' See n. 5, this chapter.

tingents necessarily are true since 'contingents are true' is necessary; therefore not necessaries alone [necessarily are true].

It must be said [74] that the 'necessarily' can determinate the predicate either in respect of the thing belonging to it, in which case the whole 'are necessarily true' is one predicate, equipollent to 'are necessary,' and the locution is true absolutely; or it can determinate the predicate in respect of the composition belonging to it. It can do this in two ways: either by including the 'alone,' in which case the first "on the contrary" will apply and [the proposition] will be false, or by being included by [the 'alone'], and this in two ways — either by noting inherence or [by noting] coherence. In the first case '[necessarily] true' signifies that this predicate necessarily is in the supposited significata of 'necessaries'[15] and necessarily is in no other supposited significata, and in this case [the proposition] is true. In the second case ['necessarily true'] signifies that this predicate necessarily coheres with this subject and not with the opposite subject. In this case [the proposition] is false and the second "on the contrary" applies, since in this case 'contingents [necessarily are true]' is true, as was said before.[16]

5. 'NECESSARILY' TOGETHER WITH THE DISTRIBUTIVE SIGN 'EVERY'

[Rule III:] *Sometimes ambiguity occurs in that the word 'necessarily' can either include a division or be included by it.*

For example, suppose that all men who exist now are running necessarily as long as they exist, and similarly with respect to future men. Thus every man necessarily is running. Proof: 'Every man is running' is necessary; therefore it will be true when it has been modified with the mode of necessity. Then if Socrates is a man, Socrates necessarily is running.

It must be said that in the first [proposition] the 'necessarily' can either include the division, in which case it is proved and true, or be included by it, in which case it is disproved and false. The first sense signifies that 'every man is running' is necessary; the second signifies that any and every singular [proposition] belonging to it is necessary.[17] But if he wants always to take it in the first sense, there will be a fallacy of *figura dictionis*, [going]

---

[15] Reading *'necessaria'* for *'necessarium.'*
[16] Chapter XV, Section 2.
[17] I.e., that any and every singular proposition the subject of which is a proper name or definite description picking out an individual man and the predicate of which is 'is running' is necessary.

from immobile supposition to mobile, for the word ['every'] is immobilized by the force of the mode.[18]

6. 'OF NECESSITY' TOGETHER WITH THE DISTRIBUTIVE SIGN 'EVERY'

This distinction likewise applies to the following sophisma. Every man of necessity is an animal, but Socrates is a man; therefore Socrates of necessity is an animal.[19]

But in the first place one must draw the distinction that 'every' can divide either for numerical parts or for specific parts.[20] If it divides for numerical parts, it can, moreover, either include the mode or be included by it. If it includes the mode it signifies that this one necessarily is an animal, [and that one,] and so on with respect to the others. If it is included [by the mode] it signifies that 'every man is an animal' is necessary (and if we assume that there always are men, that will be true, while if we assume that it is possible that the 'every' be deficient,[21] it will be false). If, on the other hand, the 'every' divides for specific parts and includes [the mode], [the proposition] is true. And if it is included [by the mode], then likewise [it signifies that 'every man is an animal' is necessary]; and in the first case it signifies that 'man conditionally in every one of its supposita is animal' is necessary, in the second case that 'man conditionally in Socrates is animal' is necessary, and so on with respect to the others. But the 'is' there [22] indicates conditional being.[23]

Therefore if ['every'] is used [to divide] for numerical parts and includes [the mode], the argument holds but the first [proposition] is false; if ['every'] is included by [the mode] it is immobilized, and when he descends [to 'Socrates of necessity is an animal'] he produces a fallacy of *figura dictionis*. If, on the other hand, ['every'] is used [to divide] for specific parts, then when he descends to Socrates there will be either an equiv-

---

[18] Cf. *WSIL*, p. 47, n. 88.
[19] Peter of Spain also discusses this sophisma (*Tr. syn.*, tr. Mullally, p. 68). And cf. his fuller discussion of 'necessarily' and 'contingently' generally (pp. 65–73).
[20] See Chapter I, Section 2.
[21] I.e., that there be fewer than three men. See Chapter I, Section 5.
[22] Something like this is probably what is intended here, but this does not literally translate the Latin, which in O'Donnell's edition reads '*Sed si ibi est.*' I find P difficult to decipher at this point (I have not seen O). It is not at all clear that the first two words are to be read as '*Sed si.*' Indeed, it seems at least possible to read them as '*Sortes etsi,*' in which case the sentence might be translated as "Although [the discrete name] 'Socrates' occurs there, it indicates conditional being."
[23] See Chapter XIII, Section 3.

ocation (in that he is using that very sign ['every'] as if it stood for numerical parts) or a paralogism of accident (because although man [24] is the same as Socrates, it is not so in respect of the fact that it is animal of necessity; for [man] is the same as Socrates in respect of his actual being and thus not of necessity).[25]

---

[24] Reading '*homo*' for '*li homo*' (see *WSIL*, p. 117, n. 48).
[25] I.e., man is animal of necessity, but that there is a man named 'Socrates' is a contingent fact.

CHAPTER XVI. *'Begins' (Incipit) and 'Ceases' (Desinit)*

§ 1. 'BEGINS' AND 'CEASES' USED CATEGOREMATICALLY AND SYNCATEGOREMATICALLY

Next, as to the words 'begins' and 'ceases.'[1] And it must be known that in one way they are syncategorematic, in another way categorematic

---

[1] The discussion of these words may seem incongruous in a treatise devoted to discussing words of special interest to logicians. William Kneale, immediately after making some brief remarks on Sherwood's *Syncategoremata*, says, "The fact that medieval logicians found it worthwhile to write separate treatises about such words shows that they appreciated their importance for formal logic. But it is probably a mistake to suppose that these signs were universally recognized as formal in a very strict sense. For the words *incipit* and *desinit* (meaning 'begins' and 'stops') were sometimes included among *dictiones syncategorematicae*, although they are concerned with temporal distinctions." (*Development*, pp. 233–234, followed by a reference to the *De puritate artis logicae tractatus longior* of Walter Burleigh, fl. 1325). But, as the rules given by Sherwood in Sections 4 and 5 of this chapter show, these words are of interest here because they affect distribution and supposition as do the other syncategorematic words considered in the treatise. Sophismata centering around these two words occur in twelfth-century texts (see De Rijk, *Logica modernorum*, Vol. I, Index C, "*desino*" and "*incipit*"), but I know of no attempts to consider the logico-semantic character of the words earlier than those made by Sherwood and by Peter of Spain (*Sum. log.*, ed. Mullally, pp. 114–118; *Tr. syn.*, tr. Mullally, pp. 58–65). Mullally suggests that "the exposition of 'beginning' and 'ending' in the *Summulae* is based to some extent upon Aristotle," in particular, *Metaphysics* V, 1 and 17, and *Physics* IV, 11 (219a22–23, 219b11) ("Introduction" to his edition of *Sum. log.*, pp. lxxv–lxxvi). It certainly is true that the discussions of these words by Peter of Spain and by William of Sherwood are based to some extent upon Aristotle, but the passages Mullally refers to are of so general a nature that they are unlikely to have been the direct inspiration for these discussions. Later logicians frequently discussed 'begins' and 'ceases.' References may be found in Prantl, *Geschichte der Logik im Abendlande*, to such discussions by Duns Scotus, William Ockham, John Buridan, Albert of Saxony, William Heytesbury, Marsilius of Inghen, Peter of Ailly,

words. For example, the word 'begins' signifies the beginning of some act in the subject and for that reason always requires (*vult*) that an infinitive designating that act be attached to it. Sometimes, however, it relates (*respicit*) to that act either in respect of a thing belonging to it or insofar as it is predicable [of the subject].² In the first way it relates to it [75] in some particular belonging to it; in the second way [it relates to it] simply and in general. And in the first way it has the nature of a categorematic word; in the second way, of a syncategorematic word.³

For example, suppose that Socrates sees one man from morning until evening and begins to see another at the third hour.⁴ At that time one will be able to say truly in the first way that Socrates begins to see a man, or one man, but not in the second way. For that specific seeing-a-man (*videre hominem*) has its beginning at that same [time],⁵ and so 'begins' relates⁶ to the act of seeing a man in respect of a thing belonging to it as in respect of some particular seeing—viz., in this particular seeing-a-man-at-the-third-hour, since this seeing is now in Socrates for the first time. And yet simply seeing-a-man is not now in Socrates for the first time. Therefore, when one says truly at the third hour 'Socrates begins to see a man,' the 'begins' does not relate to the act of seeing a man insofar as it is predicable of Socrates, for seeing-a-man considered simply is not now predicated of Socrates for the first time. But seeing-a-man itself, considered simply, does not have its beginning at that same [time] but was in him earlier.

Paul of Venice, Peter of Mantua, Peter Tartaret, and Faventinus Menghus. See also Curtis Wilson, *Heytesbury*, Ch. 2, "*De incipit et desinit.*" Wilson suggests that "the starting point of this discussion is to be sought in the Physica of Aristotle," in particular Books VI and VIII (p. 29), and he is almost certainly right.
² Cf. the parallel description of the different sorts of occurrences of 'necessarily' in Chapter XV, Section 1, especially the fourth paragraph.
³ Thus 'begins' (or 'ceases') occurs syncategorematically when it relates to the act designated by its accompanying infinitive insofar as that act is predicable of the subject of 'begins,' in which case 'begins' relates to that act "simply and in general" rather than in respect of some particular occurrence of it.
⁴ The "third hour" is the third hour after sunrise, and "morning" may be taken here to be sunrise.
⁵ From this point through the penultimate sentence of this paragraph the material translated is found only in O, which usually gives the appearance of being an uncorrected copy of P (or, more probably, of the source from which P was copied). Since the line of the discussion is clear enough without this material it may be a gloss incorporated into the text.
⁶ Reading '*respicit*' for '*respicere*.'

2. 'BEGINS' A SYNCATEGOREMATIC WORD DESPITE GRAMMATICAL APPEARANCES

It seems, however, that ['begins'] is in no way a syncategorematic word, since what is predicated is in the indicative mood,[7] but in the aforesaid example there is no indicative other than the verb 'begins.' Therefore it is predicated. Therefore it is not a syncategorematic word, for no syncategorematic word is a subject or a predicate but is rather a disposition of a subject or a predicate.

In response to this it must be said that there are two ways in which to say that something is a predicate: either as regards the form of the sentence and the manner of construing it, or as regards the corresponding reality (*aut secundum rem*). In the first way an indicative alone is predicated. In the second way an infinitive is correctly predicated, as in the aforesaid example; for it is the same as if one were to say 'Socrates sees a man now for the first time,' and so 'to see' is predicated as regards the corresponding reality and 'begins' indicates in what way it is predicated. Thus ['begins'] does have the nature of a syncategorematic word in a way, although not absolutely and properly, since as regards the manner of construing [the sentence] it is the predicate and not a disposition of the predicate.

3. THE EXPOSITIONS OF 'BEGINS' AND 'CEASES'

Let us inquire next regarding the expositions [8] of these words ['begins' and 'ceases']. Some say that [these words] sometimes indicate existence at an end [of a process] and at other times the process (*viam*) toward an end. For example, if one were to say 'Socrates begins to be white,' in the first case it signifies that Socrates is in the first instant (*in principio*) of whiteness; in the second case, that he is in [a state of] motion and process toward whiteness.[9] And [they say] also [that these words] are conjoined sometimes with fixed (*permanentibus*) [states] and at other times with

---

[7] Reading '*quia quod praedicatur est modus indicativus*' for '*sic quod praedicatur. Est modus indicativus.*'
[8] This suggests the medieval treatment of 'begins' and 'ceases' (along with several other syncategorematic words) as words around which "exponible" propositions are centered. Cf. Peter of Spain, *Sum. log.*, ed. Mullally, p. 104: "An exponible proposition is a proposition having an obscure sense and a need for exposition because of something syncategorematic located in it, implicitly or explicitly, or in some word, as in 'only man is animal,' 'Socrates begins to be white,' 'a line is infinite,' and so on."
[9] Cf. Aristotle, *Physics* V, 1 (224b10ff).

successive [states]. (Those [states] are fixed the parts of which are at one and the same time; [being] white is of this sort. Those [states] are successive the parts of which are not at one and the same time; running is of this sort.[10])

And it is said that [when 'begins' or 'ceases' is conjoined] with fixed [states] in the first way it is expounded by means of the positing of the present [indicative of the verb in the infinitive]; but the verb 'begins' eliminates (*privat*) the past while 'ceases' eliminates the future.[11]

But on the contrary, suppose that Socrates begins to be healthy and ceases to be sick. Then either the instant of beginning and the instant of ceasing will be one and the same, in which case he will be both healthy and sick at that instant, or they will be different, in which case a time will intervene at which he will be neither healthy nor sick.

It must be said, therefore, that every change is either into a successive or into a fixed state (*rem*). If it is into a fixed [state] — e.g., into health or whiteness — then at the same time as he is changed he has that into which the change is. For example, suppose that he is changed [from sickness] to health at t_2. Then at t_2 he will be healthy, and in the whole time before t_2 he is not healthy. Suppose, then, that there is an instant t_1, before t_2, at which he is unhealthy, or sick. Then one will say truly that at the end of t_1 — i.e., at t_2 — he is not sick, or he is not unhealthy.[12] Therefore, if I say 'he ceases to be sick, or unhealthy,' then 'to cease' indicates that the thing is at the end of the time in which it was such or such, since I am saying that at that end [of a period of time] he is not sick. I ought to say 'therefore he

---

[10] Peter of Spain employs the analysis of 'begins' and 'ceases' in terms of fixed and successive states and discusses them in some detail (*Tr. syn.*, tr. Mullally, pp. 59–60). Ockham, on the other hand, explicitly rejects this analysis in *Summa logicae* (ed. Boehner, Bk. II, Ch. 19; cf. Bk. I, Ch. 75, where he also discusses 'begins' and 'ceases'). See Wilson's remarks on Peter of Spain and William Ockham in this connection in *Heytesbury*, pp. 39–41.

[11] I.e., the expositions of 'Socrates begins to be white' and of 'Socrates ceases to be white' have a common first conjunct — 'Socrates is white now' — but different second conjuncts — 'it is not the case that Socrates was white just before now,' 'it is not the case that Socrates will be white just after now.' This exposition is less detailed than Sherwood's, which is presented in the last three paragraphs of this section.

[12] Sherwood's analysis is evidently based on a view of time as a sequence of discrete instants or periods — "at the end of t_1 — i.e., at t_2" — while a view of time as a continuum seems to underlie the "on the contrary," which claims that in case the instant of beginning and the instant of ceasing are not one and the same "a time will intervene at which he will be neither healthy nor sick." In other words, Sherwood seems to view time as if it were possible to identify an immediate successor (or predecessor) for any and every instant, while the objector seems to believe that for any two instants there is an instant between them. Cf. Chapter XVI, Section 7, last paragraph. Cf. Aristotle's discussion of time as a continuum in *Physics* VI, 2 (232a23ff).

is not sick,' and then at one and the same time he begins to be healthy and ceases to be sick; but the 'ceases' indicates not being. If, however, the change is into a successive state — e.g., into motion — then he does not have the motion at the instant of the change, but in the whole subsequent time.[13] And in that case 'ceases' has to be expounded by means of positing the present [indicative of the verb in the infinitive] and 'begins' does not; for at t_1 he ceases to be not moving and *is* not moving. Similarly, at t_1 he begins to be moving and *is not* [moving].

Therefore, since [76] every beginning and ceasing occurs together with a change, if that change is into a fixed [state] 'begins' has to be expounded by means of positing the present [indicative of the verb in the infinitive] but 'ceases' does not. For example, 'he begins to be healthy' — he is [healthy] and he was not [healthy] earlier; 'he ceases to be sick' — he is not sick [and he was sick earlier]. And this or that with which the verb 'ceases' is adjoined is either fixed or successive. If, however, the change is into a successive [state] — e.g., if one were to say 'he begins to be moving' — then 'begins' has to be expounded by means of the negation of the present [indicative of the verb in the infinitive] and 'ceases' by means of positing [it].

It can also happen, however, that that to which the word 'ceases' is adjoined cannot be at an end of its [period of] time — e.g., if one were to say 'he ceases to be at rest,' for there is no rest at that instant. In that case both ['begins' and 'ceases'] have to be expounded by means of the negation of the present [indicative of the verb in the infinitive].[14]

4. IMMOBILIZATION RESULTING FROM AN OCCURRENCE OF 'BEGINS' OR 'CEASES'

Rule [I]: [*'Begins' and 'ceases'*] *immobilize a following division.*

In connection with this [rule] one paralogizes as follows. Suppose that Socrates begins to know this stateable:[15] that you are running. Then Socrates begins to know everything he knows. Proof: He does know everything he knows, and he did not earlier know everything he knows; therefore he begins [to know everything he knows]. Then [someone may infer] 'therefore he begins to know that God exists,' which is false.[16]

---

[13] See Aristotle, *Physics* VI, 8 (239b1); and cf. VI, 5 (236a18).
[14] Cf. Wilson's discussion of this section in *Heytesbury*, pp. 38–39.
[15] See Chapter XIV, n. 10.
[16] At t_1 Socrates knows stateables $S1$–$S100$. At t_2 he begins to know $S101$ — that you are running. Thus at t_2 everything he knows consists of $S1$–$S101$, and therefore at t_1 he did not know everything he knows, and he began to know everything he

The 'everything [he knows]' is immobilized by the force of the negation belonging to 'begins.'[17] Thus when one descends [under the 'everything he knows'] one produces a fallacy of *figura dictionis*; or of the consequent, for the 'everything [he knows]' is less than 'that God exists,' and the negation in 'begins' precedes it, as in 'he begins to see Socrates; therefore [he begins to see] a man.'[18]

Understand, however, that if 'begins' is a categorematic word it does not relate to what follows it as such (*in se*) and in general, but rather in respect of a thing [belonging to what follows it]; and in that case such arguments do hold.[19]

5. CONFUSED SUPPOSITION RESULTING FROM AN OCCURRENCE OF 'BEGINS' OR 'CEASES'

Rule [II]: [*'Begins'* and *'ceases'*] confuse a following common term.

On this basis the following sophisma is solved. Suppose that Socrates is the whitest of the men who exist, but in the very next instant (*statim*) one whiter than he is born. Then Socrates ceases to be the whitest of men. Proof: He is the whitest of men, and he will not be (which is clear); there-

---

knows when he began to know $S101$. Thus at t_2 he begins to know everything he knows. If one attempts a logical descent under 'everything he knows' one may infer the false proposition 'at t_2 he begins to know that God exists' (where that God exists is, say, $S50$).

[17] The exposition of 'he begins to know everything he knows' results in the conjunction 'he knows everything he knows, and he did not earlier know everything he knows.' The second conjunct contains "the negation belonging to 'begins.'" Since this negation is part of what is meant by 'he begins to know everything he knows,' if the proposed descent is to succeed it must succeed under 'everything he knows' in the second conjunct as well as in the first; but of course it does not: 'he did not earlier know everything he knows; therefore he did not earlier know that God exists.'

[18] Calling the former inference a fallacy of the consequent should mean that the supposed *premiss* would follow from the supposed *conclusion*: 'he begins to know that God exists; therefore he begins to know everything he knows.' That does seem acceptable, since Sherwood evidently takes 'he begins to know everything he knows' as a correct description of any occasion on which he begins to know any stateable. As for the second inference, there is a perfectly natural reading of it under which it is acceptable. But if its conclusion is analyzed in the way provided for a syncategorematic occurrence of 'begins' the result is 'he does see a man, and he did not earlier see a man'; and since it is possible that the second conjunct be false although the conclusion is true, the inference is unacceptable. The analysis of 'begins' as a syncategorematic word requires reading 'he begins to see a man' as 'he begins to-see-a-man' — i.e., not just to see some man or other after not seeing that man but rather to see a man after not seeing any man. In the next paragraph Sherwood recognizes both readings as legitimate, but the first is the syncategorematic and the second the categorematic reading of 'begins.'

[19] See Chapter XVI, Section 10.

fore he ceases [to be the whitest of men]. Then [someone may infer] 'therefore [he ceases to be the whitest] either of the men who exist or of the men who do not exist.' If of the men who exist — on the contrary, he will always be the whitest of the men who exist; therefore he does not cease to be the whitest of them. If of the men who do not exist — on the contrary, he is not the whitest of them; therefore he does not cease [to be the whitest of the men who do not exist].

We accept this exposition of 'ceases' by means of positing the present [indicative of the verb in the infinitive], for,[20] as several [men] say — albeit more truly — it must be expounded by means of the negation of the present and the positing of the past [indicative of the verb in the infinitive], as has been said.[21] It must be said, therefore, that 'of men' stands [22] merely confusedly for both existent and nonexistent [men] in respect of the two times in the verb 'ceases.'[23] For that reason there will be a *figura dictionis* when one descends [under 'of men'].[24]

It seems, however, that there is an error in the proof, for 'of men' stood for present [men] in the first [proposition], for future [men] in the second.

It must be said that there is no [error], since in the conclusion ['of men'] is confused for all those [present and future men].

Again, it seems that the part 'ceases [to be the whitest] of the men who exist' can be granted (*dari*), for the predicate 'whitest of the men who exist' agrees with [Socrates] now and will presently not agree with him.

But this reasoning errs as a result of the different copulation of time in 'exist.'[25]

Again, it seems that the opposite can be proved, as follows: 'he will be the whitest of these [men]; therefore [he will be the whitest] of men.'

---

[20] The sense of this remark seems to call for 'although' here rather than 'for' (*quia*), since Sherwood, in order to proceed with the discussion, is allowing what he considers to be the mistaken analysis of 'ceases' provided in the first paragraph. The analysis provided is the one Sherwood has stipulated for successive-state contexts — viz., positing the present and negating the past — while the example presents a paradigm case of a fixed-state context, the stipulated analysis for which consists in negating the present and positing the past.

[21] In Section 3.

[22] O'Donnell's edition has '*state*'; '*stat*' in P.

[23] I.e., the present and the future on the successive-state analysis, the present and the past on the fixed-state analysis, the former analysis being the one accepted here. See the concluding paragraph of this section.

[24] The logical descent prohibited here is unusual in that 'of men' is not distributed explicitly (so as to suggest the possibility of such a descent) in any way noted thus far in the treatise. But see the third last and concluding paragraphs of this section.

[25] I.e., exist as of now or exist as of some stipulated time other than the present.

But this does not hold, since as a result of the force of the superlative the 'of men' stands universally.

It seems, however, [that the opposite can be proved] also as follows: [one may infer] 'he ceases to see a man; therefore [he ceases to see] a man who exists'; by analogy in the case before us (*in proposito*): 'he ceases to be the whitest [of men]; therefore [he ceases to be the whitest] of the men who exist.'

It must be said that this is not analogous, for 'ceases,' in virtue of the present and future [times] in it, confuses the 'of men' to both present and future [men], and at the same time 'whitest' makes it stand for all [men] conjointly, so that in the affirmative [aspect] of the verb 'ceases' [the 'of men' stands] for present [men] and in the negative [aspect] for future [men]. Thus 'whitest' and 'ceases' produce this defect at one and the same time.[26]

6. AMBIGUITY RESULTING FROM THE POSSIBILITY OF FIXED-STATE OR SUCCESSIVE-STATE EXPOSITIONS OF 'BEGINS' OR 'CEASES'

Sophisma: What begins to be ceases not to be. Proof: What begins to be takes being into itself, and what takes being into itself casts out not-being, and what casts out not-being ceases not to be; therefore, by the first [proposition], what begins to be ceases not to be. But what begins to be is, and what ceases not to be is not; therefore what is is not.[27]

It must be said [77] that if ['begins' and 'ceases'] indicate the process toward an end, 'begins' has to be expounded by means of the negation of that to which it is adjoined, while 'ceases' [has to be expounded] by means of the positing of that to which it is adjoined. Thus the sense is 'it begins to be; therefore it is not'; 'it ceases not to be; therefore it is not.'

If, however, they indicate existence at the end [of a process], then, in accordance with what was said at the outset,[28] 'begins' has to be expound-

---

[26] Cf. Peter of Spain's discussion of this sophisma (*Tr. syn.*, tr. Mullally, p. 62).
[27] The dubious metaphysics in the intermediate steps of the proof, which has action on X's part antedating X's existence, need not be taken seriously, since the heart of the sophisma is in the first and last sentences of this paragraph. The point of the sophisma is evidently directed against Sherwood's fixed-state expositions of 'begins' and 'ceases.' Being, like whiteness and health, seems to qualify as another paradigm case of a fixed state. If Sherwood's fixed-state analysis is applied to the original proposition, the result is 'everything that is existent and was not existent is not not existent and was not existent.' The 'not not' cancels out and we are left with a plain tautology. All that gives the sophisma its initial plausibility is its incomplete statement of the analysis.
[28] In Section 3.

ed by means of positing that to which it is adjoined when it is a fixed [state], while 'ceases' [has to be expounded] by means of the negation of that to which it is adjoined. Thus the sense is 'it begins to be; therefore it is being'; 'it ceases not to be; therefore it is not not-being,' for at the end of the ceasing is the last change from not-being to being, and then it has being. For that reason, at the end of the ceasing it is not not-being; and so 'what ceases not to be is not' is false.[29]

'What begins to be healthy ceases to be sick' (and the like) is similar to this.

7. AMBIGUITY RESULTING FROM THE COMPOUNDED/DIVIDED DISTINCTION IN CONNECTION WITH 'BEGINS' OR 'CEASES'

Suppose that Socrates is in the next to the last instant of his life. Then Socrates ceases to be not ceasing to be (*desinit esse non desinendo esse*). Proof: Socrates is not ceasing to be and will not be not ceasing [to be]; therefore he ceases to be not ceasing to be.[30] [But] therefore he ceases to be *while* he does not cease to be, or *if* he does not cease to be, or *because* [he does not cease to be].[31]

It must be said that 'to be' and 'not ceasing to be' can be either compounded or divided. If they are compounded, it signifies that the ceasing occurs in respect of the whole, and it is true, and in that case it is proved. If they are divided, it signifies, as such and divisively, that he ceases to be,[32] and it is implied that at the same time he does not cease to be, and in that case it is false.[33]

And if one accepts it in the sense in which it is true (*sicut vera est*) and

---

[29] Sherwood's reply thus leaves open the question of whether or not being qualifies as a fixed state and shows that both his fixed-state and his successive-state analyses when fully presented avoid the sophisma.

[30] This sophisma, too, seems directed against Sherwood's fixed-state analysis, and in this case with some special force, perhaps, since that exposition seems badly suited to a proposition involving the last instant of existence (adopting the change suggested in the concluding paragraph of this section). Peter of Spain discusses this sophisma (*Tr. syn.*, tr. Mullally, p. 64).

[31] These are standard readings for the ablative gerund construction. See Chapter VII, Section 3. Peter of Spain says "For a gerund ending in '-ing' ('-*ndo*') has to be resolved by 'while,' by 'if,' or by 'because,' just as a posited ablative absolute" (*Tr. syn.*, tr. Mullally, p. 64).

[32] Reading '*significat per se et divisim quod*' for '*significat quod per se et divisim quod.*'

[33] The difference between the compounded and divided senses here as in many other cases can be brought out in different intonation patterns. Compounded: 'Socrates ceases to-be-not-ceasing-to-be'; divided: 'Socrates ceases-to-be, *not* ceasing-to-be.' See Chapter I, n. 47.

wants to proceed further, then, according to some, 'he ceases to be while he does not cease to be' can be granted. But this is ambiguous as is the first.

According to others, however, it must be said that 'not ceasing [to be]' is not always equipollent to 'if [he does not cease to be]' or 'because [he does not cease to be]' or 'while [he does not cease to be],' but only when 'not ceasing [to be]' indicates only present time. But that is not the case here, for as a result of the force of the two times in 'ceases' [the 'not ceasing to be'] is confused to both present and future time. For when I say '[Socrates] is not ceasing [to be]' the 'ceasing' indicates present time; and when one says '[Socrates] will not be not ceasing [to be]' it indicates future [time]. But this can be properly granted: 'Socrates ceases to be and not to cease to be.'

It must be understood, however, that the following would be a better supposition: suppose that Socrates is in the last instant of his life; then as before. And this sophisma assumes that instants are immediately continuous with one another, which is false.[34]

8. A SECOND EXAMPLE OF SUCH AMBIGUITY

This is similar. Suppose that Socrates is in the next to the last instant before Plato's death. Then Socrates ceases to be before Plato's death. Proof: He is before Plato's death, and he will not be [before Plato's death]; therefore he ceases [to be before Plato's death]. On the contrary, he will be after Plato's death.

Solution: It is proved according as it is compounded, disproved according as it is divided. In the first case the ceasing occurs in respect of the whole 'to be before Plato's death'; in the second way in respect of 'to be' only.

9. A THIRD EXAMPLE OF SUCH AMBIGUITY

Let t_1 be the present instant. Then whatever ceases to be at t_1 will not be after t_1, but God ceases to be at t_1; therefore He will not be after t_1. The minor is proved in that He is at t_1 and He will not be at t_1.

It must be said that if 'to be' and 'at t_1' are compounded, the first [proposition] is false; if they are divided, the second is false.[35]

---

[34] See n. 12, this chapter.
[35] Sherwood discusses a version of this sophisma in his treatment of the fallacies of composition and division in *Introductiones*, Chapter Six, Section 3.1.3 (*WSIL*, pp. 143–144).

10. AN INFERENCE FROM AN INFERIOR TO A SUPERIOR ACCEPTABLE UNDER A CATEGOREMATIC USE OF 'BEGINS' OR 'CEASES'

It must be known that if ['begins' or 'ceases'] is taken categorematically an inference from an inferior to a superior holds — e.g., 'he begins to be white; therefore [he begins to be] colored' — since in that case it relates to 'colored' not as such and in common but for some one of the things belonging to it, and it signifies that some thing belonging to it — i.e., a color — has a beginning in Socrates. This is similar: 'he begins to see Socrates; therefore [he begins to see] a man.'[36]

---

[36] See Chapter XVI, Section 5.

CHAPTER XVII. *'If'* (*Si*)

1. CONJUNCTIONS AND PREPOSITIONS

Now that we have decided about the words whose functions pertain to the subject and also to the predicate in respect of the composition, and also about those that in one way are determinations of predicates but in another way are predicates, we must next decide about words that pertain to one subject in respect of another, or to one [78] predicate in respect of another, or to one composition in respect of another. Words of this sort are conjunctions.

A conjunction is an indeclinable part of a sentence conjunctive of other parts of a sentence.[1] I say 'parts [of a sentence]' because even though it conjoins sentences, it does so only insofar as they are parts of a compound sentence. Therefore, since a preposition is also conjunctive of parts of a sentence, we must ask what the difference between them is.[2]

In response it must be said that a preposition is devised to indicate def-

---

[1] This is Priscian's definition of a conjunction. O'Donnell supplies the reference to Book XVI, ed. Hertz, *Grammatici latini* (hereafter cited as *G.L.*), Vol. III, p. 93.

[2] Priscian discusses the difference between prepositions and conjunctions in Book XVI, *G.L.*, Vol. III, pp. 24–25. Cf. Otto Jespersen, *The Philosophy of Grammar* (London, 1924): "Nor is there any reason for making conjunctions a separate word-class [from prepositions]. . . . The only difference is that the complement in one case is a substantive, and in the other a sentence (or a clause). The so-called conjunction is really, therefore, a sentence preposition . . ." (p. 89).

initely a state by means of which [3] it signifies indefinitely something fortuitous (*praepositio inventa est ut dicat definite habitudinem quam significat casuale aliquod indefinite*); and therefore this state must not be indicated of two things, but rather of one thing — viz., of [something] fortuitous — in relation to another. A preposition, therefore, indicates a state of one thing in relation to another, as we say strictly,[4] and we derive its name from its proper function.[5] A conjunction, on the other hand, conjoins things neither of which has a state relative to the other, whether definitely or indefinitely signified or consignified, I maintain.[6] A preposition, therefore, conjoins things one of which in some way contains a principle [of a relation] in itself with the result that it is conjoined with the other. A conjunction, on the other hand, simply indicates a binding (*ligamentum*) of things, [a binding] that certainly is in neither thing.

2. THE DIFFERENCE BETWEEN 'IF' AND 'IT FOLLOWS'

Although there are many kinds of conjunctions, we intend [to deal] at present solely with consecutive, copulative, and disjunctive [conjunctions].

First, as to consecutive [conjunctions], and first among these the word 'if,' of which Priscian says that it indicates an order of things.[7] Similarly, we say that it signifies consequence. Then what is the difference between 'it follows' or 'it is ordered' and the word 'if'?

In response it must be said that the word 'if' notes a consequence as car-

---

[3] Reading '*qua*' for '*quam*.'
[4] Jespersen (see n. 2, this chapter) maintains that the only basis for the preposition/conjunction distinction is syntactical (and fairly unimportant syntactically) — viz., the difference between the two sorts of "complements." Sherwood, on the other hand, is attempting to base the distinction on (or is using a distinction based on) semantic differences. The preposition 'in,' for example, indicates definitely the state of containing (we might say), and it takes a grammatical object (more obvious in Latin where the prepositions govern distinguishable cases). The state of containing is indicated of the object of the preposition 'in,' as in the prepositional phrase '. . . in the house,' but this state is one that the object of the preposition has only in relation to something else.
[5] Evidently an allusion to the derivation of '*praepositio*' from '*praepono*,' 'to place before,' because the preposition is placed before its object.
[6] Conjunctions, on the other hand, do not indicate a state in one thing relative to another thing. The "I maintain" suggests that this is Sherwood's own view, and it is a view with important consequences for the treatment of 'if.' In Chapter XVII, Section 12, he seems to modify this view of the nature of conjunctions specifically for the case of certain occurrences of 'if.'
[7] In Book XVI Priscian describes 'if' as one of the "continuative" conjunctions, "which signify a continuation and consequence of things" or, more strictly, "which signify the order of the preceding thing relative to the following" (*G.L.*, Vol. III, p. 94, ll. 12–13 and 15–16).

117]

ried out by the mind of the speaker (*secundum quod exercetur ab anima proferentis*) while the others [note a consequence] as understood (*concipitur*). Thus 'if' indicates one thing under a condition relative to another, but 'it follows' does not do so; instead, it indicates that there is a consequence interrelating those things (*dicit harum rerum esse consequentiam*).[8]

3. WHY 'IF' IS NOT ATTACHED TO THE CONSEQUENT ALTHOUGH IT INDICATES CONSEQUENCE

Since it indicates consequence, why is it not added to the consequent?

It must be said that it does not indicate that something follows in the strict sense, but rather that a consequence — viz., that belonging to the consequent — is referred to something — viz., to the antecedent — and for that reason it is conjoined with the antecedent.

4. HOW 'ANTECEDENT' AND 'CONSEQUENT' ARE TO BE UNDERSTOOD IN CONNECTION WITH CONSEQUENCE

It seems also that *animal* has to be called an antecedent and *man* a consequent, for *animal* is by nature prior [to *man*] (and so on with respect to others).[9]

It must be said that when I say 'antecedent' or 'consequent' [these words] do not indicate the order of things considered as such but rather the order they have under the mind's interrelating (*comparatione*) [of them]. For when the mind orders these things it begins with the more specific, and in that respect *man* is antecedent [and *animal* consequent].

5. TRUTH AND FALSITY IN CONDITIONAL PROPOSITIONS

Now it must be asked, In a conditional, which composition is the one in

---

[8] The difference between 'if' and 'it follows' (*sequitur*) — leaving aside 'it is ordered' (*ordinatur*), which is ordinarily used in connection with syntactical arrangements within a sentence — is the difference between 'if p then q' and 'p; therefore q' (or 'from the fact that p it follows that q'). In order to draw the inference 'p; therefore q' one must already have grasped the consequence expressed in the conditional 'if p then q' or already be aware that there is a consequence interrelating 'p' and 'q' in that way.

[9] The standard medieval example of a consequence (*consequentia*) is expressed in the conditional 'if it is a man, it is an animal' (*si homo est, animal est*). The point of this remark is to suggest that there is something perverse in the terminology of consequences, according to which the man-description is the antecedent and the animal-description the consequent.

connection with which truth or falsity occurs?[10] Some say that [truth or falsity] occurs in connection with the composition belonging to 'if' in respect of the verb 'follows' supplied in thought (*subintellecti*).[11] But on the contrary, an utterance is a sign of a concept;[12] therefore an utterance [is a sign] of a principal concept. Therefore the utterance 'if Socrates is running, he is moving' is a proposition as far as the principal concept is concerned; therefore truth or falsity will occur in its principal concept; therefore not only in respect of something supplied in thought.[13]

Moreover, Boethius says[14] that when a conditional is negated the negation has to be referred to the verb belonging to the consequent but by including the condition under itself.[15] Therefore the composition belong-

---

[10] Truth or falsity occurs only in a proposition, the essence of which is the composition. In a conditional proposition there is the composition belonging to the antecedent, the composition belonging to the consequent, and perhaps also a composition belonging to the conditional considered as a whole, this last composition evidently identical with the consequence expressed in the conditional.

[11] This first suggestion is apparently unacceptable because of the distinction drawn between 'if' and 'it follows' in Section 2, if for no other reason. The suggestion seems to be that one interprets 'if it is a man, it is an animal' as 'from the fact that it is a man it follows that it is an animal,' thus uniting the (at least) two compositions belonging to the conditional within this single composition supplied in thought. Then the truth or falsity of the conditional is decided when the truth or falsity of this single composition is decided.

[12] See *Introductiones*, Chapter Five, Section 1: "Signification, then, is a presentation of the form of something to the understanding" (*WSIL*, p. 105).

[13] The "principal concept" signified by a conditional is evidently consequence (or implication). The claim in this "on the contrary" is that there is no need to *supply* anything in thought in order to read a conditional as a single proposition; its unity resides in its principal concept. But if this is all that is being claimed, it suffers from a crucial vagueness. Truth or falsity is supposed to be located in some *composition*, and it is by no means clear that consequence itself is such a composition. Both the first suggestion and this objection to it are alike in attempting to locate the truth or falsity of the conditional in the consequence-relation somehow. In this respect they bear a resemblance to twentieth-century interpretations of conditionals in terms of "strict implication," basing the truth or falsity of the conditional on something more than considerations of the truth or falsity of its antecedent and consequent.

[14] O'Donnell supplies what he himself considers a doubtful reference to *De differentiis topicis*, Bk. III (*P.L.*, 64.1198D), which is pretty obviously not the passage alluded to here. A passage of this sort is far more likely to be found in *De syllogismo hypothetico*, and there are passages in it that suggest this one — e.g., Bk. I (*P.L.*, 64.843C–D) (see Kneale, *Development*, p. 191) — but I have not found Boethius saying just what is attributed to him here. Cf. Bocheński, *A History of Formal Logic*, p. 139, where a different interpretation of the negation of a conditional is attributed to Boethius: ". . . he treats the negation of a conditional as the conjunction of the antecedent with the negation of the consequent, according to the law, *which is not expressly formulated*: . . . Not if *p*, then *q*, if and only if: *p* and not-*q*" (italics added).

[15] Consider the negation of the false conditional 'if it is an animal, it is a man.' Following out the prescribed interpretation of the negated conditional we obtain 'it

ing to that verb was the principal composition; therefore the truth or falsity occurred in connection with it—which will be granted.[16]

6. CONDITIONAL PROPOSITIONS AND CATEGORICAL PROPOSITIONS WITH CONDITIONED PREDICATES

Nevertheless it must be known that the word 'if' sometimes relates to (*respicit*) the whole consequent and at other times to the verb belonging to the consequent. In the first case it produces a conditional [proposition]; in the second case a categorical [17] [proposition] with a conditioned predicate.

On this basis the following sophisma is solved. Suppose that Socrates is white. Then a white thing is running if Socrates is running. Proof: To-run-if-Socrates-is-running is in a white thing since [it is in] Socrates [and Socrates is white]; therefore a white thing [is running if Socrates is running]. But on the contrary, the antecedent can be true without the consequent [being true]; therefore the conditional is false.[18]

---

is not a-man-if-it-is-an-animal.' But this seems to require treating the original as "a categorical proposition with a conditioned predicate" rather than as a genuine conditional (see the next section).

[16] O'Donnell's edition has '*quod conceditur*' ('which is granted'), which sounds as if Sherwood is accepting this preposterous suggestion that the truth or falsity of the consequent is the direct index to the truth or falsity of the condtiional. In P this phrase reads '*quod concedetur*' ('which will be granted'), which sounds like a mere rhetorical flourish at the end of the suggestion.

[17] O'Donnell's edition has '*categorematicam*' here and has it (or some other grammatical form of the word) also at the four subsequent points in this chapter where the translation has 'categorical' (outside of brackets) rather than 'categorematic.' The abbreviation used in P is identical with the abbreviation of '*categoricam*' used by the same scribe in the manuscript of *Introductiones*, which appears just before *Syncategoremata* in P (see, e.g., f. 3 ʳ).

[18] This is a stricter truth condition for conditionals than the one given by Sherwood in *Introductiones*: "In order that a conditional be true the truth of its parts is not required, but only that whenever the antecedent is [true], the consequent is [true]" (*WSIL*, pp. 34–35). (That is, in order to know that 'if it is raining, the streets are slippery' is true we need not know whether it is in fact raining or whether the streets are in fact slippery but only that it is never the case that it is raining while the streets are not slippery, that whenever the antecedent is true the consequent is true.) The stricter truth condition employed in this "on the contrary," and hence probably employed by some discussant other than Sherwood himself, is the one offered by Peter of Spain: "The truth of the conditional requires that the antecedent cannot be true without the consequent, as in 'if it is a man, it is an animal'; thus every true conditional is necessary and every false conditional is impossible. For the falsity of the conditional it is sufficient that the antecedent can be true without the consequent, as in 'if it is a man, it is white'" (*Sum. log.*, ed. Bocheński, p. 8, 1.23). Cf. Peter of Spain's discussion of 'if' in *Tr. syn.*, tr. Mullally, pp. 50–58; particularly pp. 50–51 and 55.

[120

And it must be said that if 'a white thing' and 'is running' are compounded, it signifies that the 'if' relates to the whole [consequent], in which case it is a conditional and [79] false.[19] If, however, they are divided, it signifies that the 'if' relates to the predicate alone, in which case it is a categorical with a conditioned predicate. In that case it is signified that the predicate 'to run,' considered not simply but under the condition 'if Socrates is running,' is in some white thing; and in that case it is true and proved.[20]

It is customarily said by some that the 'if' is taken as a consecutive [conjunction] in the first case but as an adjunctive [conjunction][21] in the second case. Others say, however, that the proposition is false and that there is a fallacy of accident in the proof. And this is true, if [the proposition] were proved in the sense in which it is a conditional and not in the sense in which it is a categorical.

But it seems that ['if'] could never produce a conditioned predicate in such [categorical propositions], for the complete expression[22] ['Socrates is running'] bears no grammatical relation (*non habet ordinationem*) to the predicate ['is running'], which is a single word ['*currit*'], and so will not be adjoined to it by means of the word 'if.'

And it must be said that a verb [such as 'is running'] has an infinite composition,[23] and in respect of that [infinite composition the verb] can in some way be dependent upon and bear a grammatical relation to a complete expression.

---

[19] Notice that for purposes of this solution Sherwood seems to have tacitly accepted the strict truth condition employed in the "on the contrary." But he does not maintain, as Peter of Spain does on the basis of this truth condition (see n. 18, this chapter), that every true conditional is necessary; see Chapter XVII, Section 11.

[20] Compounded: 'if Socrates is running, there is something that is white and is running'; divided: 'there is something such that it is white and if Socrates is running it is running.' The compounded sense, in which it is a conditional rather than a categorical, is false evidently because although it is supposed that Socrates is white it is nevertheless possible that he not be white, and thus possible that he be running and no white thing be running.

[21] Priscian, Book XVI: ". . . the adjunctive [conjunctions] are those that are adjoined to subjunctive verbs, such as '*si*,' '*cum*,' '*ut*,' '*dum*,' '*quatenus*' . . ." (*G.L.*, Vol. III, p. 95).

[22] On complete expressions see *Introductiones*, Chapter One, Section 9 (*WSIL*, p. 25).

[23] Perhaps this means only that the verb can by some grammatical means or other be combined in a sentence with any other linguistic entity whatever.

7. ANOTHER EXAMPLE INVOLVING THAT DISTINCTION

This sophisma is similar. What is true is false if Antichrist exists.[24] Proof: It is true that Antichrist does not exist, and this is false if Antichrist does exist; therefore what is true [is false if Antichrist exists]. Alternatively: To-be-false-if-Antichrist-exists is in something that is true — viz., that Antichrist is not; therefore what is true [is false if Antichrist exists]. On the contrary, the antecedent is contingent and what follows is impossible; therefore the conditional is false.

And it must be said that if 'what is true' and 'is false' are compounded it is a conditional sentence and false. If they are divided it is a categorical with a conditioned predicate and true.[25]

8. CONDITIONAL PROPOSITIONS DISTINGUISHED FROM CATEGORICAL PROPOSITIONS WITH CONDITIONED SUBJECTS

['If'] can sometimes conditionalize (*conditionare*) an antecedent either with one expression or with another. For example, suppose that t_n is some future instant. Then everything necessary will be true at t_n, that God is if t_n will not be is necessary; therefore that God is if t_n will not be will be true at t_n. On the contrary, if t_n will not be, nothing will be true at t_n.

And it must be said that the conclusion is ambiguous in that the determination 'if t_n will not be' can be referred to 'that God is,' in which case it is proved and it is a categorical with a conditioned subject; or ['if t_n will not be'] can be divided from ['that God is'], in which case the sense is 'that God is will be true at t_n if t_n will not be,' which is a conditional and false, and in that case it is disproved.

9. AMBIGUITY RESULTING FROM THE OCCURRENCE OF A RELATIVE CLAUSE IN THE ANTECEDENT

When there is a relative clause in the antecedent the locution is ambiguous in that [the relative clause] can either fall under the condition or not, as in 'if Socrates is running, who is white, something white is running.' In the first case it is true, in the second case false.[26]

---

[24] Cf. Chapter XV, Section 1; also *Introductiones*, Chapter One, Section 24 (*WSIL*, p. 42). Note the resemblance of this sophisma to one of the "paradoxes of material implication."
[25] Compounded: 'if Antichrist exists, then every proposition that is true is false'; divided: 'there is a proposition such that it is true, and if Antichrist exists it is false.'
[26] Cf. Chapter XVII, Section 6.

10. 'IF' NOTING CONSEQUENCES ABSOLUTELY AND UNDER THE PREVAILING CIRCUMSTANCES

['If'] sometimes notes a consequence absolutely, sometimes under the prevailing circumstances (*quandoque ut nunc, rebus se habentibus ut nunc*). For example, if everyone other than Socrates were running someone might say (*est dicere*) 'every man is running if Socrates is running.' It is false in the first case, true in the second case.

11. NECESSARY AND MERELY TRUE CONSEQUENCES

['If'] sometimes indicates that something follows from something else necessarily, as in 'if Socrates is a man, he is an animal.' And at other times [it indicates that it follows] merely truly, as in 'if you will come to me, I shall give you a hundred marks,' for it is the intention of the speaker that the giving follow the coming truly, but not necessarily.[27]

12. NATURAL AND NONNATURAL CONSEQUENCES

['If'] sometimes notes a natural consequence and at other times a nonnatural consequence. [It notes] a natural [consequence] when it notes that the consequent follows from the antecedent in respect of some state of the one relative to the other.[28] [It notes] a nonnatural [consequence] when it notes that the consequent follows from the antecedent not in respect of a state of the one relative to the other but solely because of the impossibility of the antecedent or the necessity of the consequent. In the first case it notes an ordering of things in reality (*secundum rem*); in the second case it notes an ordering of things in discourse (*secundum sermonem*).

In a nonnatural consequence ['if'] sometimes notes a consequence in respect of any and every time, as when the antecedent is absolutely impossible or the consequent [absolutely] necessary. But at other times [it notes a consequence] in respect of the present or the future only, as when the antecedent is impossible *per accidens* or the consequent necessary [*per accidens*].[29] [80]

---

[27] See n. 18, this chapter. In a parallel passage Peter of Spain, who elsewhere maintains that "every true conditional is necessary and every false conditional is impossible" (*Tr. syn.*, tr. Mullally, p. 55), distinguishes between necessary and "possible or probable" (rather than "merely true") conditionals (*ibid.*, p. 50; cf. pp. 83–84).
[28] See Chapter XVII, Section 1.
[29] *Introductiones*, Chapter One, Section 23: "Notice, however, that 'impossible' is used in two ways. It is used in one way of whatever cannot be true now or in the

13. AMBIGUITY RESULTING FROM MULTIPLE OCCURRENCES OF 'IF'

['If'] sometimes is put twice [in the same sentence] and the sentence is ambiguous as regards composition and division. For example, 'if Socrates exists if Plato is running a man is arguing.' Proof: The antecedent is impossible; therefore the conditional is necessary. On the contrary, a contingent [proposition] is the antecedent and an impossible [proposition] follows; therefore the conditional is false. For the antecedent is 'if Socrates exists' and the consequent is 'if Plato is running a man is arguing.'

And it must be said that 'if Plato is running' can be compounded with 'if Socrates exists' with the result that the whole is a single impossible antecedent — viz., 'if Socrates exists if Plato is running' — or the one can be divided from the other, in which case the consequent will be impossible.[30]

Similarly, ['if'] sometimes is put three or four times [in the same sentence], and the distinction is similar in all respects.

14. AMBIGUITY RESULTING FROM EXCLUSION OR NEGATION IN CONDITIONALS

Sometimes there is ambiguity in that an exclusion can include a condition or vice versa. For example, 'Socrates alone is running if Socrates is running.' Proof: Socrates is running [if Socrates is running] and no one else is running [if Socrates is running], for 'someone else is running [if Socrates is running]' is false; therefore Socrates alone is running [if Socrates is running]. On the contrary, the antecedent can be true without the consequent [being true]; therefore the conditional is false.

And it must be known that the 'alone' includes [the condition] in the proof and is included [by it] in the disproof.

Similarly, a negation can either include [a condition] or be included [by

---

future or in the past (*quod non potest nec poterit nec potuit esse verum*); and this is "impossible *per se*" [or "absolutely"] — e.g., 'a man is an ass.' It is used in the other way of whatever cannot be true now or in the future although it could have been true in the past, as if I were to say 'I have not walked'; and this is "impossible *per accidens*." Similarly, in case something cannot be false now or in the future or in the past it is said to be "necessary *per se*" [or "absolutely"] — e.g., 'God is.' But it is "necessary *per accidens*" in case something cannot be false now or in the future although it could have been [false] in the past — e.g., 'I have walked' " (*WSIL*, p. 41).

[30] The description of 'Socrates exists if Plato is running' and 'if Plato is running a man is arguing' as impossible, rather than merely false, seems to be an expression of the strict view of conditionals to be found in Peter of Spain. See nn. 18 and 27, this chapter.

[124

it], as in 'not another is running [if Socrates is running].' In the first case it is true, in the second case false.

15. AMBIGUITY RESULTING FROM MODES IN CONDITIONALS

There is ambiguity also when a mode [31] is posited [in a conditional], as in 'if Socrates is running necessarily he is moving.' If the 'necessarily' includes [the condition] the sense is that 'if Socrates is running, Socrates is moving' is necessary, which is true. If it is included [by the condition], then [the 'necessarily'] can be compounded with the 'is running,' in which case it signifies that 'if Socrates is running necessarily, Socrates is moving' is true, which is true. If [the 'necessarily'] is divided [from the 'is running'] it signifies that if Socrates is running he is moving necessarily, which is false.

In the first case [the mode] is a note of the consequence, in the second case it is a note of the antecedent, in the third case it is a note of the consequent.

16. IMMOBILIZATION IN THE ANTECEDENT BUT NOT IN THE CONSEQUENT

['If'] immobilizes a division in the antecedent and not in the consequent.[32] Thus this does not follow: 'if every man is running, every risible thing is running; therefore if Socrates is running, every risible thing is running.' But 'therefore [if every man is running], this risible thing is running' follows correctly.

17. ASCENT AND DESCENT IN UNDISTRIBUTED ANTECEDENTS AND CONSEQUENTS

In an undistributed antecedent one may not ascend, but one may descend. For example, this does not follow: 'if an animal is running, a sensible thing is running; therefore if a body is running, [a sensible thing is running].' But 'therefore if a man is running, [a sensible thing is running]' follows correctly. (The situation is reversed in the consequent.)

---

[31] O'Donnell's edition has '*motus*'; '*modus*' in P.
[32] This occurs as the second of six rules cited by Peter of Spain as governing descent under terms in the antecedent or the consequent (*Tr. syn.*, tr. Mullally, pp. 54–55).

18. A PARADOXICAL CHAIN OF CONSEQUENCES

Sophisma: If Socrates is necessarily mortal, Socrates is mortal; and if that is the case, he can die; and if that is the case, he can not be; and if that is the case, he can not be mortal; and if that is the case, he is not necessarily mortal. Therefore, by the first, if Socrates is necessarily mortal, he is not necessarily mortal.

Different men say different things about this; but we can say that opposites are implied (*implicantur*) in the antecedent. For by reason of the 'necessarily' the necessity of his existence is posited, while by reason of the 'mortal' the possibility of [his] not being is posited there. Nor is it the case that that from which opposites follow (or even its own opposite [follows]) is inconsistent.

19. A SECOND PARADOXICAL CHAIN OF CONSEQUENCES

The following is similar. If every proposition is true, then that God exists is true; and if that is the case, then its contradictory is false; and if that is the case, some [proposition] is false. Therefore if every proposition is true, some [proposition] is false.

And understand that since to posit that some proposition is true is to posit that its contradictory is false, to posit that every [proposition] is true is to posit that the contradictory of any and every [proposition] is false — i.e., that every [proposition] is false. Thus opposites are implied in the antecedent.[33]

But here is the kind of sophisma in which the inference from the first [antecedent] to the last [consequent] does hold: 'if no proposition is true, it is not true even that God exists (*tantum deum esse non est verum*); and if that is the case, its contradictory is true; and if that is the case, some [proposition] is true. Therefore, by the first, if no [proposition] is true, some [proposition] is true.'

And it must be known that the second argument [34] holds only if we suppose that there is some proposition. This is not supposed in the first [antecedent], however. Rather, its opposite is supposed, since for none to be true is for none to be, and for that reason [the inference] from the first [antecedent] to the last [consequent] does not hold.

---

[33] Peter of Spain discusses a variant of this sophisma (*Tr. syn.*, tr. Mullally, p. 53).

[34] 'Argument' (*argumentum*) here and even more strikingly in the similar passage in Section 20 is evidently used to refer to a conditional occurring as a premiss in the inference. See n. 39, this chapter.

▶ 20. A THIRD PARADOXICAL CHAIN OF CONSEQUENCES

The following is similar. If there is no time, it is not day;[35] and if that is the case, it is night; and if that is the case, [81] there is some time. Therefore, by the first, if there is no time, there is some time.

It must be said that the second argument is not necessary unless it is supposed that there is some time, and the opposite was supposed in the first [antecedent].

Some say [36] that such an inference does not hold because there is an argument from a quantitative whole [37] in the first [consequence] and an argument from contraries [38] in the second, and so the inference is not continuous.

But on the contrary, I ask whether the first antecedent could be true without the last consequent [being true]. If not, the inference from the first [antecedent] to the last [consequent] does hold. If it could, then I ask whether or not the first consequent is true. If not, the first argumentation [39] did not hold. If it is true and the last consequent is not, as you maintain, then the second reasoning did not hold.

It must be said, therefore, that if he infers solely from 'it is not day' in the second argumentation, there will be a fallacy of the consequent, for an affirmative never follows from a negative, but rather vice versa.[40] But if the affirmative 'there is some time' is understood along with ['it is not day'], then there is a fallacy of accident in the argument from the first [antecedent] to the last [consequent]. For although [the proposition] that it is not day is the same as [the proposition] that there is no time in the way in which a consequent [is the same as] an antecedent,[41] nevertheless [the

---

[35] O'Donnell's edition has '. . . *hic: nullum tempus est, et . . .*'; '. . . *hic: si nullum tempus est, dies non est, et . . .*' in P.

[36] Something like this line is suggested in Peter of Spain's discussion of this sophisma (*Tr. syn.*, tr. Mullally, pp. 52–53).

[37] See *Introductiones*, Chapter Four, Section 3.2.4 (*WSIL*, pp. 79–81).

[38] See *Introductiones*, Chapter Four, Section 4.2.1 (*WSIL*, p. 97).

[39] 'Argumentation' (*argumentatio*) here and in the next paragraph and 'reasoning' (*ratio*) in the next sentence are evidently used to refer to conditionals occurring as premisses in the inference. See n. 34, this chapter.

[40] I.e., in an "argument from contrary opposites." See *WSIL*, p. 97.

[41] The Latin for 'it is not day' — '*dies non est*' — can also be read as 'there is no day,' and Sherwood is evidently claiming that in the sense in which '*dies non est*' is implied by '*nullum tempus est*' it is just another way of saying that there is no time — i.e., that in the first conditional '*dies non est*' is equivalent to '*nullum tempus est*.' This interpretation is borne out in the next section, where Sherwood uses these words to describe an antecedent and consequent that are obviously formally equivalent to each other.

proposition that it is not day] differs from [the proposition that there is no time] insofar as it is considered from the standpoint of (*in quantum respicitur ab*) [the proposition] that it is night; for it is considered from the standpoint of that [proposition] in respect of a concept in respect of which it differed from the first [antecedent].[42] And the very same sort of observation applies to (*et ita penitus est in*) the preceding sophisma.

21. A FOURTH PARADOXICAL CHAIN OF CONSEQUENCES

Again, if every man is an animal, every non-animal is a non-man; and if that is the case, a stone is a non-man; and if that is the case, a stone is. Therefore, by the first, if every man is an animal, a stone is. But on the contrary, this antecedent can be true without the consequent [being true]; therefore it does not hold.

It must be said that the second argument holds only with the supposition that a stone is a non-animal. For that reason, although the first consequent is the same as the first antecedent, in the way in which a consequent [is the same as] an antecedent, still insofar as it is considered from the standpoint of the second consequent it is not the same. For it is considered from the standpoint of [the second consequent] in respect of a proposition supplied in thought, in respect of which it was not the same as the first, for [that proposition] is not supplied in thought in that [first consequent]. Thus in the argument from the first [antecedent] to the last [consequent] there is either a paralogism of accident or a begging of the original issue. For if he infers solely from 'every non-animal [is a non-man]' in the second argumentation, the argument will not hold; but if he supplies in thought [the proposition] 'a stone is a non-animal,' then he is supposing that a stone is, and thus is supposing that regarding which he had to show that it followed from the first [antecedent].

Some maintain, nevertheless, that this argument — 'a stone is a non-animal; therefore a stone is' — does not hold, just as this does not hold: 'a stone is inanimate; therefore it is.' In the treatise on the word 'is,' however, it has been said that in one way this does hold, in another way not.[43]

---

[42] The use of a past tense — '*fuit diversum*' — is awkward here, but the sense is plainly that while '*dies non est*' has to be read as 'there is no day' in order to be implied by 'there is no time,' it must be read as 'it is not day' in order to imply 'it is night.' And 'it is not day (now)' implies that there is some time.

[43] The relevant distinction — between its signification of being and its consignification of composition, or between taking it to indicate actual or taking it to indicate conditional being — is touched on in all three sections of Chapter XIII.

CHAPTER XVIII. *'Unless' (Nisi)*

1. THE LOGICAL AND GRAMMATICAL CHARACTER OF 'UNLESS'

Next, as to the word 'unless,' regarding which it must be known that it notes a consequent[1] in relation to a negated antecedent, for 'unless' is composed of 'if' and 'not.'[2]

Why then is it a conjunction rather than an adverb? The reason is that the consequential character (*consecutio*) [of 'unless'] falls over the negation [belonging to 'unless'] and is what completes its signification.

Why then is the negation touched on in the first syllable and the condition in the last? The reason is that the completion of its signification should be designated by means of the end of the word, as appears in the words 'white' and 'whiteness.'

It is customarily said, however, that one always concludes negatively from this [word 'unless']. This is plainly false, since one correctly says 'unless Socrates is healthy, he is sick,' assuming, I say, that the subject exists (*supposito dico subjecto*).

2. 'UNLESS' TAKEN AS A CONSECUTIVE CONJUNCTION

Rule: [*'Unless'*] *is taken sometimes as an exceptive and at other times as a consecutive* [*conjunction*].[3]

When it is taken as a consecutive the same distinctions can be assigned to it as were assigned to the word 'if.'

Here is one sophisma of this sort. No man lectures at Paris unless he is an ass.[4] Proof: 'Some man lectures at Paris unless he is an ass' is false, [82] for the antecedent[5] is necessary and what follows it is contingent; therefore 'no man [lectures at Paris unless he is an ass]' is true. On the contrary, therefore every man who lectures at Paris is an ass.

Some say that 'some man [lectures at Paris unless he is an ass]' is false but that its contradictory is 'not some man [lectures at Paris unless he is an ass],' which, however, is ambiguous in that the negation could fall under the condition or over it. If under, then it does not contradict the first [prop-

---

[1] Reading '*consequens*' for '*consequentiam.*'
[2] It is easier to see that '*nisi*' is composed of '*si*' and '*non.*'
[3] On consecutive conjunctions see Chapter XVII, n. 7. Peter of Spain discusses the dual nature of 'unless' at length (*Tr. syn.,* tr. Mullally, pp. 83–85) in his discussion of this word (pp. 83–90).
[4] See *WSIL,* p. 4, n. 5.
[5] I.e., 'he is not an ass.'

osition], since it does not fall over the whole first [proposition]. If over, then it does contradict the first [proposition], but then 'not some' and 'no' are not equipollent, since the negation belonging to 'no' falls under the condition [belonging to 'unless']. Proof: the division belonging to 'no' falls over the subject of the consequent and in respect of the same, and so it seems it does not extend to the antecedent; therefore neither does the negation [belonging to 'no' extend to the antecedent].

But it must be said, as has been said before,[6] that the antecedent is as it were a determination of the consequent. Therefore the negation belonging to 'no' can be referred to the composition in the consequent whether or not it is already disposed as a result of the condition.[7] And I say the same as regards the division belonging to 'no.' Therefore I maintain that the locution is true if these two[8] are compounded but false if they are divided. Composition [in this case] is a sign that the negation falls over the whole, division [a sign that it does] not.[9]

3. 'UNLESS' TAKEN AS AN EXCEPTIVE WORD

Again, it is sometimes taken as an exceptive,[10] as in 'no man unless Socrates is running.' But in that case there is a doubt as to which things the conjunction 'unless' conjoins, for it denotes consecution, and there is consecution only of complexes. Here, however, there are not two complexes.

He will perhaps say that the verb must be repeated with 'Socrates,' with the result that the sense is 'no man is running unless Socrates is running.' But on the contrary, when the verb is predicated[11] [in the original proposition] it signifies that Socrates is running, for it is equipollent to 'no man but Socrates, who is running, [is running]' (*nullus homo praeter Sortem qui currit*).[12] But when the verb is repeated it is not equipollent to

---

[6] He describes an antecedent as a determination of a consequent in Chapter XVII, Section 8.
[7] I.e., whether it is already a consequent as a result of having been appropriately ordered together with the consecutive conjunction 'unless' and some other proposition as antecedent, or is considered as occurring separately.
[8] Viz., 'no man lectures at Paris' and 'unless he is an ass.'
[9] Cf. Peter of Spain's discussion of this sophisma (*Tr. syn.*, tr. Mullally, pp. 89–90).
[10] On exceptive words see Chapter X, especially Sections 1–3.
[11] Reading '*praedicatur*' for '*subicietur*.'
[12] The scribe either omitted the second '*currit*' or mistakenly inserted the '*qui*.' In view of the facts that 'no man but Socrates is running' says all that is needed here and that in the next sentence another proposition is picked out as one in which "the

that. Therefore it does not signify the same [as does the original proposition].

Again, if ['unless'] has the function of a preposition, as does the word 'but' (*praeter*), it seems it must be a preposition.

And we can say that a certain act is carried out by means of the word 'man,' [the act] of suppositing. But acts carried out [by means of words] may be well understood although they are not expressly signified, and this act has to be understood along with 'Socrates,' with the result that the sense is 'if Socrates is not supposited in this plurality, then no man is running.' And let the 'if' be taken confirmatively, in which case it will confirm that Socrates is not supposited in that plurality in respect of the negated predicate.[13] And in this way ['unless'] secondarily means that the predicate goes together with ['Socrates'] (*Et sic ex consequenti vult praedicatum ei convenire*),[14] and it has the force of an exception. And so it is clear which things ['unless'] conjoins,[15] and that it has the force of an exception not primarily, but secondarily (*non primo, sed ex consequenti*). And from this it does not follow that it is a preposition.

4. AMBIGUITY RESULTING FROM TAKING 'UNLESS' AS A CONSECUTIVE OR AS AN EXCEPTIVE

Sophisma: Nothing is true unless at this instant. Proof: Whatever is true is true at this instant; therefore nothing [is true unless at this instant]. On the contrary, therefore that you are an ass is not [true unless at this instant]; therefore it is true at this instant.

Some say that this is proved according as the 'unless' is taken as a consecutive, disproved according as [it is taken] as an exceptive. Others say that 'nothing is true unless what is true (*nihil est verum nisi verum*) at this instant' must be supplied in order that an exception be made from the subject.[16] But on the contrary, let both be said as follows—'. . . unless it

---

verb is repeated," it seems likely that '*praeter Sortem qui currit*' is to be read not as '*praeter Sortem qui currit currit*' but as '*praeter Sortem currit*.'

[13] I know of no technical use of the notion of taking 'if' "confirmatively." The suggestion in this passage seems to be that the 'if' is taken confirmatively if the conditional occurs together with the separate assertion of the antecedent. (It may seem especially plausible to suggest that such a special use of 'if' is involved when the conditional is asserted immediately *after* the separate assertion of the antecedent.)

[14] I.e., it means that 'Socrates is running' is asserted. St. Thomas frequently employs the distinction between signifying primarily (*primo*) and signifying secondarily (*ex consequenti*). See Deferrari, *Lexicon*, art. "*Significo*."

[15] I.e., 'Socrates is supposited in this plurality' and 'no man is running.'

[16] When the 'unless' in 'nothing is true unless at this instant' is taken as a consecu-

131]

is at another instant besides (*praeter*) this one' — and the sophisma goes through.[17]

It must be said, therefore, that the locution is true whether ['unless'] is taken as an exceptive or as a consecutive.[18] But if [it is taken as] a consecutive, then [the proposition] that you are an ass is true at this instant does not follow, for it does not follow if [the proposition] 'if it is not true at this instant, it is not true' is true, which, moreover,[19] is true. If, on the other hand, [it is taken as] an exceptive, then one may not descend under (*en*) the 'nothing,' for although the exception is not made *from* it, nevertheless it is made *in respect of* it. Thus there is a *figura dictionis* or a fallacy of the consequent in the descent. This is clear if the affirmative is compared with the affirmative and the negative with the negative. (This is the affirmative belonging to it: 'something is true at this instant.'[20]) This is clearer in the treatise on the word 'but,' where it is said that an exception immobilizes not only the division from which the exception is made but also [a division] in respect of which [the exception is made].[21] [83]

---

tive the sense is 'nothing is true if it is not true at this instant.' When it is taken as an exceptive the sense can be, as the first "on the contrary" assumes it to be, 'nothing is true except at this instant.' This sentence reports an objection to that reading. If the exceptive sense must be 'nothing is true except what is true at this instant,' as is claimed here, then the descent attempted in the first "on the contrary" is impeded; for its result would be 'that you are an ass is not true except what is true at this instant,' which is nonsense. The first reading of the exceptive sense takes the 'unless' to be excepting *in respect of* the 'nothing'; the second takes it to be excepting *from* the 'nothing.'

[17] The point of this second "on the contrary" is not clear to me. The possibility of taking 'unless' as an exceptive seems to have been ruled out by the insertion of 'it is' after it (*nisi est in alio instanti praeter hoc*). The 'is' could be read either as an existential 'is' or as a copulative 'is' with 'true' understood, but neither reading seems obviously correct. Both the original proposition and the result of the attempted descent seem either grossly implausible or nonsensical when revised in accordance with this suggestion.

[18] This seems most clearly correct if the 'is' in the original proposition is taken not as a tenseless copula but as the 'is' of the present tense.

[19] Reading '*praeterea*' for '*propterea*.'

[20] The point seems to be that while the particular affirmative 'something is true at this instant' does follow from 'nothing is true except at this instant,' the singular affirmative 'that you are an ass is true at this instant' does not.

[21] See Chapter X, Section 12. Cf. Peter of Spain's discussion of this sophisma (*Tr. syn.*, tr. Mullally, pp. 88–89).

CHAPTER XIX. *'But That' (Quin)*

Next, as to the expression 'but that,' regarding which it must be known that it is a consecutive noting the consequence of something from a negated antecedent, for it has negation within itself. For example, 'he does not run but that he moves.' The sense is 'if he does not move, he does not run.'

Here is a sophisma of this sort. You cannot truly deny that you are not an ass (*negare te non esse asinum*). Proof: You cannot deny truly what is necessary, but this is necessary; therefore you cannot truly deny this. Then [someone may infer] 'therefore you cannot truly deny that you are not an ass (*negare quod non sis asinus*);[1] therefore you cannot truly deny but that you are an ass; therefore you are an ass.'

The first [proposition] is ambiguous, however, in that the 'truly' can be compounded either with the 'you can[not]' or with the 'deny.' In the first case it is false, for I have the true power of denying anything whatever. If ['truly' is compounded] with 'deny,' it can be so in two ways – in relation either to what it has before it (*in comparatione quam habet ad ante*) or [to what it has] after it (*ad post*). In the first case it is false, since it signifies that active negation does not truly stem from me, which is false. In the second case it is true, since it signifies that the negation received into the negated thing says what is false;[2] let it be taken in this sense.

And it must be said that 'you cannot truly deny that you are not an ass' (*negare quod non sis asinus*) is ambiguous in that the verb 'deny' can be taken transitively or absolutely. If transitively, it follows from the first [proposition], and the whole 'that you are not an ass' takes the place of a single accusative and is not conjoined with the preceding as an antecedent with a consequent. And in this case the word 'that' (*quod*) does not have the force of consecution, and so it is not equipollent to 'but that' when the former (*ulterius*) sophisma goes through. If [the verb 'deny' is taken] absolutely, then the sense is 'it cannot be denied in such a way that at that same time you are not an ass,' and it signifies that these two – that you deny, and that you are not an ass – cannot stand together. And in this case it is false, and [the word 'that'] is equipollent to 'but that' since it has the force of consecution, but it does not follow from what is prior to it.

---

[1] Note the difference in the Latin constructions of this and of the first proposition of the sophisma. The clause occurring here in P – '*ergo non potes vere negare quod non sis asinus*' – is omitted from O'Donnell's edition.

[2] I.e., that the denial of 'you are not an ass' is false.

[133]

And the ambiguity is the ambiguity of amphibology,³ for it indicates a different construction of 'deny' with that which follows [it].⁴

There are other general distinctions and specific difficulties in connection with this which we need not be concerned with here.⁵

---

³ Sherwood discusses amphibology in *Introductiones*, Chapter Six, Section 3.1.2 (*WSIL*, pp. 139-140).
⁴ Cf. Peter of Spain's discussion of this sophisma (*Tr. syn.*, tr. Mullally, pp. 100-104).
⁵ Peter of Spain is concerned with many "other general distinctions and specific difficulties" in his lengthy discussion of '*quin*' (*Tr. syn.*, tr. Mullally, pp. 93-104).

CHAPTER XX. *'And' (Et)*

1. THE SIGNIFICATION AND FUNCTION OF 'AND'

Next, as to copulative conjunctions, a sort to which 'and' belongs. Priscian says of it that it signifies being together (*simul esse*).¹ Therefore if 'being together' does not indicate a syncategorematic notion (*intentionem*), neither does 'and.'

In response to this it must be said that the being together that is indicated by 'and' is of two predicates in one subject, or of two subjects in one predicate, or of two predicates in two subjects or vice versa; and this relation is certainly syncategorematic. Moreover, it sometimes indicates two determinations in a single determined thing and at other times the reverse. And in connection with the aforesaid difference it copulates in different ways — i.e., sometimes between terms and at other times between propositions — since to copulate is nothing other than to signify being together. Thus the signification of this conjunction is clear.

2. COPULATING BETWEEN TERMS OR BETWEEN PROPOSITIONS IN A SINGLE SENTENCE INVOLVING EXCLUSION

It is customary to draw the distinction that it can sometimes copulate either between terms or between propositions in one and the same sen-

---

¹ O'Donnell supplies the reference to Book XVI (*G.L.*, Vol. III, p. 93, l. 4). Priscian lists as copulative conjunctions '*et*,' '*que*,' '*ac*,' '*atque*,' '*quidem*,' '*quoque*,' '*at*,' '*ast*,' '*sed*,' '*autem*,' and '*vero*.'

tence, as in 'of two alone a part is one and no number' (*solius binarii pars est unitas et nullus numerus*).² Proof: Of two a part is one [and no number], and of no other than two a part [is one and no number]; therefore of two alone [a part is one and no number]. On the contrary, this is a copulative [proposition] the first part of which is false; therefore the whole is false.

And some say that it is proved according as the 'and' copulates between terms, disproved according as [it copulates] between propositions. But on the contrary, there is actual copulation here; therefore actual copulata. There are not actual propositions here, however;³ therefore propositions are not the copulata here.

It must be said that 'and no number' can be either compounded with or divided from what precedes it. The composition signifies that the negation belonging to 'alone' falls over the whole. The division, on the other hand, [signifies] that it remains in the 'one.' It is true in the first case, false in the second case.⁴ And in the first case the exclusion includes [84] the copulation; in the second case it is the other way around.⁵ Although in both cases (*semper*) 'and' copulates between terms, still, since in the second case it is the same (as far as truth and falsity are concerned) as if it were copulating between propositions, it is said that it copulates between propositions.

3. A SECOND EXAMPLE OF SUCH COPULATING

But here is another inference. Of two alone [a part is one and no number]; therefore of two alone a part is one and no four.

It must be said, however, that this is a paralogism of the consequent, since 'no number' is in fewer things than is 'no four.'⁶ Thus he ascends in the term in respect of which the preceding exclusion is made.⁷

---

² The smallest *number* was considered to be two, not one, which was unity as distinct from number. And since unity has *no* parts, of two alone a part is one and no number.

³ I.e., there is no proposition that might serve as the second copulatum (conjunct) of 'and.'

⁴ Compounded: 'of two alone it is the case that one is a part of it and no number is a part of it'; divided: 'of two alone a part is one, and no number is a part of two.' In the divided sense although the second copulatum is true, the first is false.

⁵ See Chapter XI, Sections 11, 17 and 18.

⁶ It is true of only one and two that no number is a part, while it is true of one, two, three, and four that no four is a part. Thus what looks like logical descent under 'number' is actually ascent.

⁷ See Chapter XI, Sections 9 and 15.

4. A THIRD EXAMPLE OF SUCH COPULATING

Again — 'of two alone [a part is one and no number]' having been granted — on the contrary, of three a part is one and one, and the latter one is no number; therefore of three a part is one and no number.

It must be said that if 'no number' could be an infinite term [8] [the inference] would proceed correctly. As matters stand, however, it does not, just as this one does not: 'I see a man, but a man is no ass; therefore I see no ass.' And [in this inference] there is not even the semblance [of acceptability].[9]

5. A DISTINCTION GIVING RISE TO DIFFERENT ANALYSES IN THAT THIRD EXAMPLE

Some draw a distinction in this [inference], distinguishing on the basis of whether 'part' can be construed *ex parte ante* [10] or *ex parte post*.[11] If [it is construed] *ex parte ante*, then [the original proposition] is false and 'of three a part [is one and no number]' is true, and the sense is 'of three a part is one and of three a part is no number.' And the word 'part' can supposit for any part whatever, for it is not confused by the negation following it. They say also that if 'part' is construed *ex parte ante* the 'no' must be placed after it, as has just now been said. If ['part' is construed] *ex parte post*, the 'no' must be placed before it, with the result that the sense is 'of three one is a part and of three no number is a part,' and this is false. Similarly with respect to all higher numbers. And in this way 'of two alone [a part is one and no number]' is true.

But on the contrary, even when it is construed [*ex parte*] *post*, ['part'] can still be correctly ordered before the 'one.' Therefore [it can be correctly ordered] before the 'no,' which is copulated with the 'one.'

For this reason it must be said that when 'and' copulates the 'no' with the 'one,' 'one' is ordered either with 'is' only or with what precedes it as

---

[8] I.e., if 'no number' (*nullus numerus*) could be read as 'a non-number' (*non numerus*). See Chapter XIV, Section 2.

[9] 'Semblance' (*apparentia*) is one of two technical terms essential to Sherwood's discussion of sophistical reasoning in *Introductiones*, Chapter Six: "Thus in every sophistical ground there must be the *Semblance* of some condition of a genuine syllogism together with its *Nonexistence*" (*WSIL*, p. 134).

[10] A marginal gloss at this point in P says "i.e., when it is placed *ex parte ante*."

[11] As the remainder of the section indicates, the question has to do with the logico-semantic effect of the 'no' on 'part' in various available analyses of the proposition 'of two alone a part is one and no number.' On another use of the phrases '*ex parte ante*' and '*ex parte post*' see *WSIL*, p. 128, n. 94.

well. If with 'is' only, then the 'no' must fall over the 'is' alone, and [the proposition] is true. If ['one' is ordered] in the second way, then ['no'] must fall over the whole of what precedes ['is'], and [the proposition] is false. But if 'part' is construed either *ex parte ante* or *ex parte post*, amphibology [12] may result; and in either case 'of two alone [a part is one and no number]' is true, provided that it is compounded and the exclusion includes [the copulation].[13]

There is another distinction in that the 'and' can copulate the 'no' either to 'one' or to 'part.' It does not have much effect on the sophisma, however, and so may be omitted.

6. COPULATING BETWEEN AN AFFIRMATIVE TERM AND A TERM TOGETHER WITH A NON-INFINITATING NEGATION

It must be known that a term together with a non-infinitating negation [14] in one way can be copulated with an affirmative term and in another way cannot.

I say [that it can] after the affirmative term has been ordered together with something else in respect of which the copulation must occur, but that it cannot before [that ordering has taken place]. Thus one says correctly 'a man is running and no ass,' but incorrectly 'a man and no ass is running (or are running).' (The reason for this has been stated in [connection with] the sophisma 'nothing and the chimera [are brothers].' [15]

7. 'AND' TAKEN DIVISIVELY AND TAKEN CONJUNCTIVELY

When the word 'and' is put twice it is always taken divisively; but when it is put just once it is taken sometimes divisively and at other times conjunctively, as in 'two and three are five.' In the first case the 'two' and the 'three' must be divided,[16] in the second case compounded. The distinction would not hold, however, in this case: 'Socrates and Plato are running,' because the predicate cannot grammatically (*congrue*) be signified as being in this subject 'Socrates' or [in this subject] 'Plato' divisively.[17]

---

[12] Sherwood discusses amphibology in *Introductiones*, Chapter Six, Section 3.1.2 (*WSIL*, pp. 139–140).
[13] See Chapter XX, Section 2.
[14] See Chapter XIV, Section 2.
[15] See Chapter VIII, Section 3.
[16] In which case the sense is 'two are five, and three are five.'
[17] This second example seems to trivialize the distinction, for the claim is evidently that while the result of taking 'and' divisively in the first example yields a grammati-

8. COPULATING A WHOLE EXPRESSION IN INDIRECT DISCOURSE OR ONLY A PART THEREOF

When ['and'] is adjoined to a word, sometimes it copulates a whole dictum [18] to it and at other times a part of it. For example: 'if it is true that two are three and four are five, you are a goat.' Proof: The antecedent is impossible; [therefore the conditional is true]. But [on the contrary], it is true that two [are three and four are five], for it is true that the dictum 'that two are three' and another four [19] are five.

In the first case ['and'] copulates the whole 'four are five' with what precedes it, in the second case only the 'four.' And in the first case the 'four' and the 'are' must be compounded, in the second case [85] divided.

[This solution] coincides with another — viz., that in the first case the dictum 'that two are three' stands significatively, in the second way materially.[20]

9. A SECOND EXAMPLE OF SUCH COPULATING

This is similar: 'if it is true that you are running and [you] are not running, you are a goat.' For the antecedent — 'it is true that you are running and you are not running' — is impossible. But [on the contrary], the dictum 'that you are running and you are not running' is true, for [the dictum] 'that you are running' and you are not running.[21]

In the first case ['and'] copulates the whole 'you are not running' with

---

cal (though false) result, the result in this case is the ungrammatical 'Socrates are running, and Plato are running.' Thus 'the men and the asses are running' *would* admit of either interpretation. The distinction would be more interesting if it were not so closely bound to the grammar and showed the differences among 'Socrates and Plato are brothers' (conjunctively only), 'Socrates and Plato are carrying rocks' (conjunctively or divisively, where the latter would be read as 'Socrates is carrying rocks and Plato is carrying rocks'), and 'Socrates and Plato are dead' (divisively only). Cf. Peter of Spain's discussion of this case (*Tr. syn.*, tr. Mullally, pp. 80–81) in his brief discussion of 'and' (pp. 80–83).

[18] I.e., an expression in indirect discourse. Thus the whole dictum in the example in this section is 'that two are three and four are five.'

[19] A marginal gloss at this point in P says "i.e., dicta."

[20] I.e., that in the first way it is being *used*, in the second way only *mentioned*. Cf. *Introductiones*, Chapter Five, Section 2: "Supposition, then, is on the one hand material, on the other hand formal. It is called material when a word itself supposits either [A] for the very utterance itself or [B] for the word itself, composed of the utterance and the signification — as if we were to say [A] 'man is a monosyllable' or [B] 'man is a name.' It is formal when a word supposits what it signifies" (*WSIL*, p. 107).

[21] Reading *'curritis'* for *'curris.'* The point is that it is not the case that both you and the dictum 'that you are running' are running.

what precedes it, in the second case only the 'you.' Moreover, in the first case the 'you' and the 'are not running' must be compounded, in the second case divided.[22]

10. WHETHER A COPULATIVE PROPOSITION CAN BE NEGATED BY A SINGLE NEGATION

There is a doubt whether a copulative [proposition] such as 'Socrates is running and Plato is arguing' can be negated by a single negation. It seems it cannot be, since there are two actual compositions here, neither of which is a determination of the other; therefore they stand in need of twofold negation; therefore they cannot be negated by a single negation. But on the contrary, if I say 'not [23] Socrates is running and Plato is arguing,' the mind understands this sentence well in this sense, that these two [compositions] are signified not to be true together, and in that case it is clear that [the 'not'] negates the entire copulative [proposition].

Although there are many reasons on the other side, we may nevertheless grant this, for the first composition is asserted as copulated to the other and is thus in some respect disposed by it, as if the second were somehow a disposition of the first. Therefore if the negation arrives in the first composition before it is copulated with the other, it is included by the copulation. In that case there must be a division of the two propositions, and the negation remains in the first. If, on the other hand, [the negation arrives] afterward, there must be a composition [of the two propositions], and in that case [the 'not'] negates the whole in such a way that neither part [is negated] in itself.

In this way the distinction could have been granted in [connection with] the sophisma 'Socrates alone is white and Plato is whiter than he.' [24]

11. WHETHER A COPULATIVE PROPOSITION IS MORE THAN ONE PROPOSITION

There is a question whether a copulative [proposition] is more than one [proposition]. It seems it is not, for 'and' signifies being together. Therefore, just as a sentence that says that one is together with another is not

---

[22] An interlinear gloss at this point in P says "and in that case 'that you are running' is taken materially." See n. 20, this chapter.
[23] '*Non*' in this position would ordinarily be translated as 'it is not the case that,' but it seems best here to preserve the ambiguity of the single Latin word.
[24] See Chapter XI, Section 11.

more than one, so neither is a copulative more than one. Besides, if 'Socrates is running and Plato is arguing' were more than one, then 'not Socrates is running and Plato is arguing' would be more than one. But the latter is not more than one, since that which is more than one can be divided into two propositions equipollent to it, and this negative cannot be divided in that way, as is clear enough. Therefore [a copulative] is not more than one. But on the contrary, more than one thing is subjected in that case, and likewise more than one thing is predicated; therefore it is more than one, which is true.

It must be said in response to the first [claim] that 'and' signifies being together as it is actualized, not as it is conceived of. What is signified in a copulative, however, [is signified] as conceived of. Two propositions are copulated; nevertheless they are signified as being together (*simul entia*). And for that reason [the copulative] remains more than one.

It must be said in response to the other [claim] that not every [proposition] that is more than one can be divided in that way but [only a proposition] in which the force of some other word does not supervene over its more-than-oneness (*pluralitatem*). The example is not of that sort, since the 'not' falls over the whole.

This is similar: 'not if Socrates is running Plato is arguing.' For although it is a conditional, it cannot be divided into antecedent and consequent, because the 'not' does not go with the one or the other of them, and that is because it supervenes over the composition.

CHAPTER XXI. *'Or' (Vel)*

1. 'OR' TAKEN AS A DISJUNCTIVE AND AS A SUBDISJUNCTIVE

Next, as to the word 'or,' which is a disjunctive conjunction. But how can it disjoin, since what is a conjunction must conjoin?

It must be said that it conjoins utterances into a single sentence but disjoins [the corresponding] real things; for the sense of a disjunctive conjunction is (*sentit disjunctiva conjunctio*) that the things between which it disjoins cannot be together. Thus it indicates that one [utterance] is true and that the other is false.

The rule that if one or the other is true the disjunctive [proposition] is true runs counter to this, however.

But it must be said that 'or' is taken sometimes as a disjunctive and at other times as a subdisjunctive. In the first case it indicates that one is true and the other is false; in the second case it indicates solely that one is true while touching on nothing regarding the other part.[1] [86]

⚜ 2. VARIOUS WAYS IN WHICH 'OR' DISJOINS

Rule: [*'Or'*] *sometimes disjoins two predicates in respect of the same subject, sometimes two subjects in respect of the same predicate, and sometimes two subjects in respect of two predicates.*

In the first case [the proposition] is categorical[2] with a disjoined predicate, in the second case [categorical] with a disjoined subject, and in the third case [the proposition is] disjunctive.

Accordingly, ['or'] disjoins sometimes between terms and at other times between expressions.[3] It seems, however, that a conjunction has to conjoin between expressions, for one first propounds a certain expression in which are all the parts of the expression but the conjunction and says that if the conjunction is added it is necessary that another expression follow.

Understand, however, that Priscian understands it in the following way: If [a conjunction] is added to an expression speaking as such (*orationi per se loquendo*), another expression does follow.[4] When ['or'] disjoins be-

---

[1] Cf. Priscian, Book XVI (*G.L.*, Vol. III, p. 97, ll. 17–19 and p. 98, ll. 3–4): "Disjunctive [conjunctions] are those that, although they conjoin words, nevertheless signify in a disjoined sense, and, indeed, [signify] that the one thing is but the other is not — e.g., 've,' 'vel,' 'aut.' . . . Subdisjunctive [conjunctions] are those that, [although they occur] in the utterance of disjunctives, nevertheless signify that both things are, either together, as the copulatives do, or separately."

[2] O'Donnell's edition has '*categorematica*'; '*categorica*' in P. See Chapter XVII, n. 17.

[3] See *Introductiones*, Chapter One, Section 8, where Sherwood distinguishes between a word, the smallest significant linguistic entity, and an expression, "an utterance significant by convention, parts of which taken by themselves do signify" (*WSIL*, p. 25). In all probability the intention here is to contrast terms, which may be expressions and not just single words, with "complete" expressions. *Introductiones*, Chapter One, Section 9: "A complete expression is one that establishes a complete thought (*intellectum*) in the hearer's mind — e.g., 'the man is white' " (*WSIL*, p. 25).

[4] O'Donnell supplies a reference to Priscian, Book XVII (*G.L.*, Vol. III, p. 160, ll. 16ff). It seems more likely that Sherwood is referring to an earlier passage in Book XVII (*G.L.*, Vol. III, p. 116, ll. 11–13), where Priscian provides an example of an expression containing every part of speech "except a conjunction, which, if it is added, requires another expression."

tween terms, however, it is not added to an expression but to a term speaking as such.

3. AMBIGUITY RESULTING FROM A DISJUNCTION TOGETHER WITH A DIVISION

The following sophisma proceeds in accordance with the aforementioned distinction. Every proposition or its contradictory is true. (Let this be proved inductively.) Then [someone may infer] 'but not every proposition is true; therefore its — i.e., every proposition's — contradictory is true.' Alternatively: 'but "you are an ass" is either a proposition or its contradictory; therefore it is true.' Alternatively: '[but] every proposition or its contradictory is false; therefore something false is true.'

A distinction is drawn here to the effect that either a disjunction can include a division or vice versa. If it includes, it signifies that the predicate is in one of them — i.e., [in] every proposition or [in] every [proposition's] contradictory.[5] In that case it is the same as if one were to disjoin between propositions,[6] and in that case it is false and the first "on the contrary" goes through. If, on the other hand, the division includes [the disjunction], this can occur in two ways — in distributing either the whole disjoined term or the first part in respect of the other. In the first case it is false, since it signifies that everything that is contained under the term 'proposition or its contradictory' is true, and in that case the second "on the contrary" goes through. In the second case it is true, and it signifies that the term 'proposition' stands for any and every one of its supposita in respect of all that follows [that term in the sentence]. Thus in the third inference [7] the whole 'or its contradictory is true' must be the major extremity, and the whole 'or its contradictory is false' [must] be the minor, and it must conclude 'what is false or its contradictory is what is true or its contradictory.' Thus if the propositions are taken in the true sense [8] [the fallacy of using a locution] in a certain respect as well as absolutely [9] will occur in that inference as a result of the omission of the determinations.

It must be said, therefore, that the 'or its contradictory' can be com-

---

[5] Reading '*contradictoria*' for '*contradictoriae*.'
[6] Reading '*disjungeret*' for '*distingueret*.' The propositions in question are 'every proposition is true' and 'every proposition's contradictory is true.'
[7] I.e., in the third "on the contrary."
[8] I.e., in the senses in which they are true.
[9] Sherwood discusses the fallacy of using a locution in a certain respect as well as absolutely (*secundum quid et simpliciter*) in *Introductiones*, Chapter Six, Section 3.2.2 (*WSIL*, pp. 153–155).

pounded with 'proposition,' in which case it will be signified that that whole is distributed (this is the second sense); or it can be divided from it, in which case it is either compounded with the predicate or divided from it. If it is compounded with it, it will be signified that that whole is one predicate receiving the respect of the division, and if one must syllogize from that in the first figure, 'proposition' will be the middle term and all the rest will be the major. If, on the other hand, it is divided from the predicate, it will be the third sense, and it is thereby signified that it is divided from 'proposition,' which is not distributed, and in that case [the disjunction] in no way falls under the division, but rather vice versa; and in that case ['or'] has the force of a subdisjunctive [conjunction].[10]

4. A SECOND DIFFICULTY IN CONNECTION WITH SUCH AMBIGUITY

It seems, however, that the complete expression 'every proposition [or its contradictory is true]' must always be in the force of a disjunctive (*in virtute disjunctivae*), for the 'its' is relative, not reciprocal,[11] and so does not want to come into the same clause with [its] antecedent. Thus 'or its [contradictory is true]' will have the force of another clause.

We can say that 'one clause' (*aliqua una clausula*) is used in two ways — viz., either [in the sense of] one absolutely (as where there will be no conjunction, and in such a case such a relative [as 'its'] does not come together with its antecedent grammatically (*congrue*)), or [in the sense of] one by conjunction (and in such a case a relative can come with its antecedent in one and the same [clause]). Or we can say that the 'its' (*ejus*) is improperly put here in place of the relative [12] 'its' (*sui vel sua*).

5. A THIRD DIFFICULTY IN CONNECTION WITH SUCH AMBIGUITY

It seems, moreover, that it is false that the phrase 'or its contradictory' must be ordered with the predicate, for the 'its' is always referred to 'proposition' [as its antecedent].

---

[10] See Section 1, this chapter. Peter of Spain discusses this sophisma (*Tr. syn.*, tr. Mullally, p. 79) in his brief discussion of 'or' (pp. 77–79).

[11] Priscian seems to use the designation 'reciprocal' as modern Latin grammarians use 'reflexive,' and not as they use 'reciprocal.' See, e.g., Book XIII (*G.L.*, Vol. III, p. 14, l. 18), where '*sui*' is introduced as an example of a reciprocal pronoun, to be used where one and the same thing is both agent and patient. Cf. Sherwood's remark about '*sui*' at the end of this section.

[12] Perhaps '*reciproci*' should be read for '*relativi*' here. See n. 11, this chapter.

But it must be said that although ['its'] is always construed with 'proposition,' there is nevertheless a difference [87] resulting from the fact that ['or its contradictory'] is either compounded with the predicate or not.

6. A FOURTH DIFFICULTY IN CONNECTION WITH SUCH AMBIGUITY

It seems, however, that this makes no difference in the understanding, but in the utterance alone.

It must be said that this is by no means the case, for the composition of [the phrase 'or its contradictory'] with the predicate signifies that the division is made in respect of the whole.

This is similar: 'every man insofar as he is a man is an animal.' The reduplication [13] 'insofar as [he is a man]' must, according to Aristotle in the *Prior Analytics*,[14] be ordered with the predicate, and yet the 'he' is always construed with the subject.

7. A FIFTH DIFFICULTY IN CONNECTION WITH SUCH AMBIGUITY

It seems, moreover, that in the last inference [15] the conclusion must not be 'what is false or its contradictory is what is true [16] or its contradictory,' for the 'its' in the premises was referred to 'proposition' while in the conclusion [it is referred] to 'what is true' and to 'what is false.' Thus if [the inference] were concluded in that way the relation of ['its'] would be varied.

It must be said that that variation does not impede [the inference], for 'what is true' and 'what is false' stand for the same things for which 'proposition' stood.

This is similar: 'every man sees himself and every man touches himself; therefore whoever touches himself (*ergo tangens se*) is whoever sees himself.' This holds correctly, and yet the 'himself' was referred to 'man' in the premises and to 'whoever touches' and to 'whoever sees' in the conclusion.

---

[13] On reduplication see *WSIL*, p. 91, n. 103; p. 112, n. 31.
[14] O'Donnell supplies the reference to *Prior Analytics* I, 38 (49a25): ". . . in all instances of supplementary predication the reduplication must be attached to the extreme [i.e., major] term."
[15] I.e., the third "on the contrary" in Section 3, as analyzed in the second paragraph of that section.
[16] Reading '*verum*' for '*vera*.'

8. A SIXTH DIFFICULTY IN CONNECTION WITH SUCH AMBIGUITY

It seems, moreover, that ['every proposition or its contradictory is true'] could be proved by induction in the sense in which it is equipollent to a disjunctive just as in the other sense.

But it must be said that this is not true, since one performs an induction (*inducit*) neither in all the singulars belonging to 'every proposition is true' nor in all belonging to 'every proposition's contradictory is true.' Thus when one infers either the latter or the former one produces a paralogism of the consequent.

9. A SECOND EXAMPLE OF AMBIGUITY RESULTING FROM A DISJUNCTION TOGETHER WITH A DIVISION

This is similar. Suppose that every man owns an ass and that some [men] are running and their asses are not running, while other [men] are not running and their asses are running. Then every man or his ass is running. (Let this be proved inductively.) [Then someone may infer] 'but not every man is running; therefore his — i.e., every man's — ass is running.' Alternatively: 'but every man is either a man or his ass; therefore every man is running.' Alternatively: 'every man or his ass is running, but every man or his ass is a non-runner (*est non currens*); therefore some non-runner is running.' (Let the minor [in this last case] be proved inductively.) This is to be analyzed (*distinguendum*) exactly as was the one before.

10. A THIRD EXAMPLE OF SUCH AMBIGUITY

Every animal is rational or nonrational. (Let this be proved inductively.) But not every animal is rational; therefore every animal is nonrational. A distinction must be drawn here to the effect that 'or' can disjoin either between terms or between propositions; but this is objected to as before.[17]

It must be said, therefore, that the determination 'or nonrational' can be either compounded with or divided from what precedes it. The composition signifies that the whole 'rational or nonrational' is in every animal, in which case it is true and the division includes [the disjunction]. (Those who say that [the 'or'] disjoins [18] between terms understand this sense [of

---

[17] A marginal gloss at this point in P says "i.e., the beginning of the third folio before this one, in the sophisma 'of two alone a part is one [and no number]'" (Chapter XX, Section 2). Probably the gloss is mistaken and the reference is to Chapter XXI, Section 3.

[18] O'Donnell's edition has '*distinguit*'; '*disjungit*' in P.

the proposition].) The division [of 'nonrational' from what precedes it], on the other hand, signifies either that 'rational' is in every animal divisively [19] or that 'nonrational' is in every one. In this case the 'or' includes [the division], and it signifies the same as if it were said that it disjoined between propositions.

11. SPECIAL DIFFICULTIES FOR INDUCTIVE PROOFS IN CONNECTION WITH DISJUNCTION

Everything is everything or different from everything. Proof: Socrates is everything or different from everything, since Socrates is Socrates or different from Socrates, Socrates is Plato or different from Plato, and so on with respect to the others. Thus Socrates is everything or different from everything, and by the same reasoning Plato is everything or different from everything, and so on with respect to the others. Therefore everything is everything [or different from everything]. [But on the contrary,] therefore everything is everything or different from Plato, and therefore Plato is everything or different from Plato, which is false.

It must be said that 'Socrates is everything or different from everything' is false, as are the other singular [propositions]. Moreover, there is a fallacy of the consequent in its proof, for it is not sufficiently proved that Socrates is everything (for it is proved for one singular only), and it is not sufficiently proved that Socrates is different from everything (for it fails in one singular — viz., '[Socrates is] different from Socrates'). Thus one can infer one or the other of these divisions only as a result of having drawn upon singulars sufficiently [and that cannot be done in this case]. [88]

A disjoined term is equipollent to one common [term] — i.e., common to both [disjoined] parts. But a common [term] cannot actually be in something designated (*alicui signato*) unless it is so for some designated part. Therefore the disjoined term 'everything or different from everything' cannot be in Socrates unless it is so for 'everything' or for 'different from everything.' Each of these [parts], however, is insufficiently proved [of Socrates], as has been said.

If, however, we were to say 'Socrates is everything or different from that,' it would be ambiguous, for if the sentence is compounded it is true and the division includes the disjunction. In that case the sense is 'Soc-

---

[19] I.e., considered individually. See Chapter XX, Section 7.

rates is Socrates or different from that, Socrates is Plato or different from that, and so on with respect to the others.' If, on the other hand, it is divided it is false. In that case the sense is that 'to be everything' is in Socrates, or that 'to be different from that' [is in Socrates] if '[to be] everything'[20] is not in Socrates, both of which are false.

'Everything is everything [or different from that]' is likewise ambiguous. Thus if one infers 'but not everything is everything; therefore it is different from that,' [the inference] proceeds in the sense of division, which is false. If, on the other hand, one takes it in the true sense and says that the 'that' stands for everything and that therefore it is correct (*convenit*) to say 'everything is everything or different from everything,' there will be a paralogism of accident — as in 'every man sees himself, but the "himself" stands for every man; therefore every man sees every man.'[21]

12. AMBIGUITY RESULTING FROM THE OCCURRENCE OF A MODAL WORD TOGETHER WITH A DISJUNCTION

When a modal word is adjoined to a disjunction ambiguity occurs — as in 'that Socrates is running or not running is necessary.' If the 'not running' is compounded with what precedes it, it signifies that the necessity is in that whole, in which case the mode includes the disjunction. If [the 'not running'] is divided [from what precedes it], it signifies that the necessity is in one or the other part divisively, in which case the disjunction includes the mode, and it is the same as if [the 'or'] disjoined between propositions. In the first case [the sentence is] true, in the second case false.

But, it is asked, what does this necessity have to do with (*circa quod sistit haec necessitas*)? Perhaps he will say that it has to do with the disjunction itself. But on the contrary, every necessity is a truth, and every truth has to do with the composition belonging to a verb; therefore every necessity has to do with the composition belonging to a verb. (I mean complete truth and necessity.)

It must be said that both the truth and the necessity of [the proposition] have to do with the first composition, not absolutely but as disjoined from the other, for it is in that way that the first [composition] is asserted.

The same distinction applies to this: 'you know that the stars are even

---

[20] Reading '*quidlibet*' for '*quodlibet*.' The punctuation added to this passage in O'Donnell's edition obscures the sense.
[21] See Chapter I, Section 16.

or uneven [in number],' and to this as well: 'that the stars are even [in number] or that the stars are uneven [in number] is known to you.'

13. WHETHER A DISJUNCTIVE PROPOSITION IS MORE THAN ONE PROPOSITION

Is a disjunctive [proposition] one or more than one?[22] It seems it is not more than one; neither part of a disjunctive is affirmed assertively. It seems it is not one, for there is not one subject in it or one predicate, since by the same reasoning by which the subject of the first part is called the subject [of the proposition], the subject of the second [part may also be called the subject of the proposition].

And it must be said that in a disjunctive [proposition] the first composition is asserted,[23] not absolutely, but under disjunction in relation to the other. Thus one thing alone is asserted and [it is asserted] of one thing — not absolutely, however, but under a disjunction.[24] Nor is it like a copulative [proposition], although in it the first part is asserted as being together with or copulated with the second, for in that case to assert the first is to assert both. (This is spoken of in other ways for plausible reasons (*probabilibus rationibus*), however.)

---

[22] See Chapter XX, Section 11.
[23] Reading '*asseritur*' for '*non asseritur*.'
[24] O'Donnell's edition has '*distinctione*'; '*disjunctione*' in P.

CHAPTER XXII. *'Whether' or 'Or' (An)*

1. THE SIGNIFICATION AND FUNCTION OF 'AN'

Next, as to the word 'whether' or 'or,' regarding which Priscian says that it signifies doubt.[1] It must be understood that this is so when we are in doubt which of two things we are asking about should be agreed to, and those two things have to be conjoined by means of 'or.' For example, 'should I speak or (*an*) remain silent?'

But then there is a doubt how it is being used here — 'you know whether

---

[1] O'Donnell supplies the reference to Book XVI (*G.L.* Vol. III, p. 101, l. 9): "Dubitative [conjunctions] are those that signify doubt, such as '*an*' and '*ne*.'"

(*an*) Socrates is running' — and what it conjoins between; for if it signifies doubt it is incorrectly adjoined to the verb 'you know.'

It must be said, however, that just as something is first a question and subsequently is drawn into knowledge, so 'whether' is correctly ordered with the verb 'you know.' Thus one correctly says 'you know who is running' [although the interrogative pronoun 'who' (*quis*)] has to do with doubt in this way. And thus although ['whether'] does indicate doubt, [89] it is nevertheless correctly ordered with the verb 'you know.'

In response to the other point it must be known that when one [of a pair] of opposites is doubted the other is doubted too. The 'whether' indicates doubt of that sort [with respect to] 'Socrates is running,' and so both it and its opposite are adequately understood [in the sentence]. Thus ['whether'] conjoins between this [proposition] and its opposite. And since to know this doubt whether Socrates is running is to know one or the other contradictory part, 'whether' has the force of a disjunction.

Similarly, [it has the force of a disjunction] when it is used in an interrogation, since an interrogation asks regarding two things whether (*utrum*) this one or (*vel*) that one. And ['whether' or 'or' (*an*)] is sometimes used in that way in an interrogation, as when it is a question of [two] doubtful things;[2] and at other times it is used after a verb falling over the doubt. Example of the first: 'should I speak out [or remain silent]?'; example of the second: 'you know whether Socrates is running.'

2. THE DIFFERENCE BETWEEN 'AN' AND 'VEL'

But, it is asked, what is the difference between 'whether' or 'or' (*an*) on the one hand and 'or' (*vel*) on the other?

[The difference is] that whoever knows whether (*an*) Socrates is running knows determinately one or the other [contradictory] part, while whoever knows that Socrates is running or (*vel*) not running does not necessarily know determinately one or the other. And for that reason 'whether' or 'or' is called an elective conjunction, because it indicates the election of one or the other part determinately.[3]

---

[2] O'Donnell's edition has '*et cum quaeritur dubitativa*' followed by this note: "MSS. not clear." P, at least, is quite legible at this point and obviously has '*ut*' where the edition has '*et*.' The last word in the phrase appears in P as '*dub*' followed by an abbreviation regularly used for '*-orum*' or '*-arum*' endings and thus seems better read as '*dubitativorum*' here.

[3] O'Donnell's edition has '*determinatae*,' interpreting it as an adjectival form modifying '*partis*.' But in P both this form and the adverbial form '*determinate*' have the

3. 'AN' DISJOINING DIFFERENTLY DEPENDING ON ITS OCCURRING ONCE ONLY OR TWICE

It is a rule that the word *'an'* used once disjoins between opposites, but used twice [it disjoins] between theses (*proposita*).[4] Thus [an inference] from [a proposition in which] it is used once to [a proposition in which] it is used twice (or vice versa) does not follow. For example, if you know that Socrates is not running you know whether (*an*) Socrates is running, but you do not know whether (*an*) Socrates or (*an*) Plato [is running]. Likewise, if you know nothing about Socrates but you know that Plato is running, then you know whether (*an*) Socrates or (*an*) Plato is running but you do not know whether (*an*) Socrates is running.

4. THE EFFECT OF 'AN' ON INFERENCES INVOLVING CONTRARIES, PRIVATIVES, RELATIVES, OR CONTRADICTORIES

[An inference] from a contrary to a contrary does not hold when [*'an'*] is used. For [although] you know whether (*an*) Coriscus is white as regards the negated [proposition] (*pro parte negata*), nevertheless there is doubt whether he is black, since there is doubt whether he is.[5] Likewise in the case of privatives. For example, [although] you know of some blindman whether (*an*) he is sighted, nevertheless there is doubt whether (*an*) he is blind.[6]

In the case of relatives and contradictories, however, [the inference] does hold. For example, 'you know whether (*an*) there is a father; therefore you know whether (*an*) there is a child,' 'you know whether (*an*) Socrates is running; therefore you know whether (*an*) he is not running.'

---

same spelling, and it seems better read here as the adverbial form. On "elective" conjunctions O'Donnell supplies a reference to Priscian, Book XVI (*G.L.*, Vol. III, p. 98, ll. 25ff), where '*quam*' (but not '*an*') is described as a "disertive or elective" conjunction.

[4] Cf. the corresponding rule in Peter of Spain's discussion of '*an*' (*Tr. syn.*, tr. Mullally, pp. 73–77): "As often as 'or' (*an*) is posited once in a proposition, it disjoins the opposites of a contradiction; but whenever it is posited twice, it disjoins immediate contraries" (p. 75).

[5] The point seems to be that you know regarding Coriscus only that it is not the case that he is white. Thus you know whether Coriscus is white. But although it is (evidently) taken for granted that a man must be either white or black, you do not know whether Coriscus is black, since you do not know whether he is at all.

[6] Evidently this example is meant to be completed in the same way — 'since there is doubt whether he is.'

5. THE EFFECT ON INFERENCES OF THE LOCATION OF 'AN' RELATIVE TO A UNIVERSAL SIGN

[An inference] from [a proposition in which] ['*an*'] is used before a universal sign to [one in which] it is used after [a universal sign] does not hold. For example, you know whether (*an*) every man is Socrates. Proof: You know this or (*vel*) its opposite; therefore you know whether [every man is Socrates]. Then [someone may infer] 'therefore you know of every man whether he is Socrates (*ergo scis omnis homo an sit Sortes*); therefore you know that every man is Socrates or (*vel*) that every man is not Socrates.'

There is a paralogism of the consequent here, just as in 'you know that not everything [is so and so]; therefore you know that everything [is] not [so and so].'

It seems, however, that [the inference] could proceed in the following way. 'You know of Socrates whether (*an*) he is Socrates, you know of Plato whether (*an*) he is Socrates, and so on with respect to the individuals; therefore you know of every [7] [man] whether (*an*) [he is Socrates].' Then as before.

It must be said that there is a paralogism of the consequent in this induction, for 'you know of every man whether (*an*) he is Socrates' is equivalent (*valet*) to these two [propositions] under a disjunction: 'you know that every man is Socrates or (*vel*) that every [man] is not Socrates.'[8] For where the word 'whether' (*an*) is used the word 'not' must be used. Neither is sufficiently proved, however, since they accept only one singular [proposition] belonging to the first [universal proposition], while they accept all but one belonging to the second.

6. A SECOND EXAMPLE OF THAT EFFECT

If someone says 'you know whether (*an*) every man is Socrates or (*an*) differs from Socrates,' it will be false, for you know neither that every man is Socrates nor that every man differs from Socrates. But if someone says 'you know of every man whether (*an*) he is Socrates or (*an*) differs from Socrates,' it is true (supposing that you know everyone), and it signifies that regarding everyone you know that he is Socrates or that he differs from Socrates, determinately.

---

[7] Reading '*omnis*' for '*omnem*.'
[8] On the other hand, 'you know whether every man is Socrates' is equivalent to 'you know that every man is Socrates or you know that it is not the case that every man is Socrates.'

In the former case the whole 'every man is Socrates' in itself is one part of a disjunction. In the second case it is not, but the '*an*' disjoins between every singular belonging to that division and [the singular] that follows it, for the '*an*' is made virtually many (*multiplicatur enim virtualiter ly an*) in virtue of the preceding division.

But in addition it is ambiguous in the former case in that 'or (*an*) differs [from Socrates]' can be either compounded with or divided from what precedes it. If it is compounded, [the proposition] is true. If it is divided, [the proposition] is false and signifies the same as if [the '*an*'] were put before [the universal sign].

On this basis the following inference is solved. 'You know of every man whether (*an*) he is Socrates or (*an*) differs from Socrates; therefore you know whether every man [is Socrates or differs from Socrates],' for it goes through [90] in the sense of division. Therefore [an inference] from [a proposition containing] the word '*an*' put twice after [a universal sign] to the same [proposition containing the word '*an*'] put [once] before [the universal sign] does not follow.[9]

7. A THIRD EXAMPLE OF THAT EFFECT

This is similar. Suppose that every [man] owns an ass, and that some [men] are running and their asses are not while others are not running but their asses are, and that you know this. Then you know of every man whether he is running or his ass is running. (Let this be proved inductively.) But [on the contrary,] you do not know that every man is running; therefore you know that his — viz., everyone's — ass is running. Alternatively, you know of every man whether [he is running or his ass is running]; therefore [you know] whether every man or [his ass is running] — and then as in the preceding ["on the contrary"].[10]

It must be said that 'or his [ass is running]' can be either compounded with what precedes it or divided from it. If it is compounded, the distribution falls over the whole and each '*an*' has to be taken many times (*multotiens*) so that it disjoins between the singulars belonging to that division. In that case it is true and it is proved, and it is signified that of every single [man] [11] you know whether he is running or his ass [is running]. Or it

---

[9] Cf. Peter of Spain's discussion of this sophisma (*Tr. syn.*, tr. Mullally, pp. 76–77).
[10] Cf. Chapter XXI, Section 9.
[11] Reading '*singuli*' for '*singulari*.'

can be divided, and in that case it is signified that you know one or the other of these, divisively: 'every man is running or (*vel*) his ass is running.' In that case it is the same as if the '*an*' were put before [the universal sign], and each "on the contrary" goes through.

Some say, however, that this [proposition] is true [in the] divided [sense]. They grant [the proposition] 'you know that every man is running or (*vel*) you know that his ass is running,' and they say that the 'his' is referred [12] to 'man,' not under the same predicate but under its opposite, since if it were referred [13] under the same the sense would be 'you know that the ass belonging to him who is running is running.' In that way it would be implied (*implicetur*) that every man was running and that his ass [was running], and thus that each part of the disjunctive was false, which is counter to the nature of a disjunctive. If, however, ['his' is referred to 'man'] under the opposite predicate, it is implied that the parts of the disjunctive cannot stand together, which agrees with the nature of a disjunctive.

For the same reason they grant [the proposition] 'every proposition or (*vel*) its contradictory [is true]' [14] in the sense in which it is equipollent to a hypothetical.[15] But on the contrary [the proposition] 'that God is or its opposite is true' is true and not trivial (*nugatoria*). If, however, the 'its' were to be referred [16] under the opposite predicate, it would be a triviality (*nugatio*),[17] for [in that case] the sense is that the opposite of the expression 'that God is not true' is true. In that case the disjunctive would signify that God is true is true or (*sive*) that God is not true is not true, and in that case, it is clear, it would be trivial.

In the premiss [of the original inference] the 'his' is referred to 'every man,' and since you say [that it is referred] under the opposite predicate — i.e., 'not running' — it implies that every man is not running, and so it will be false.

---

[12] Reading '*refertur*' for '*refert.*'
[13] Reading '*referretur*' for '*referret.*'
[14] See Chapter XXI, Sections 3–8.
[15] 'Hypothetical' is not synonymous with 'conditional' here but is used in the broad sense in which it is used by Sherwood in *Introductiones*, Chapter One, Section 12: "A statement whose substance consists of two categorical statements conjoined [e.g., by 'or'] is called hypothetical" (*WSIL*, pp. 27–28). In the earlier discussion of this sophisma the question of whether it can be considered as a categorical rather than as a disjunctive (hypothetical) is raised (Chapter XXI, Sections 2–3).
[16] Reading '*referretur*' for '*referret.*'
[17] See *Introductiones*, Chapter Six, Section 2, where *nugatio* is defined as "pointless repetition of the same thing" (*WSIL*, p. 134).

It must be said, therefore, that [the 'his'] is referred to its antecedent for the same supposita for which it stood in the former [clause], regardless of (*non tangendo*) whether (*utrum*) under the same or (*vel*) the opposite predicate. Nor is it required that the disjoined parts be incompossible, except where disjunction is [taken] most strictly.

8. THE EFFECT OF 'AN' ON INFERENCES IN WHICH A RELATIVE PRONOUN IS PERMUTED FROM THE PREDICATE INTO THE SUBJECT

[An inference] involving the word '*an*' does not hold if a relative [pronoun] is permuted from the predicate into the subject.

For example, suppose that either Socrates or Plato is lying, but you do not know which one. Then you know whether (*an*) as regards the liar it is false that Socrates is he. Proof: If Socrates is lying, then as regards the liar it is not false but true that Socrates is he (and the 'he' is referred to 'the liar'). Again, if Plato is lying, then as regards the liar it is not false that Socrates is he, not because it is false of Plato lying that Socrates is he — i.e., the liar — but rather [because] it is false of Socrates not lying; for the expression 'Socrates is the liar' is neither true nor false of Plato. Thus whether (*sive*) Socrates is lying or (*sive*) Plato [is lying] it is not false as regards the liar that Socrates is he. And you know this; therefore you know whether (*an*) as regards the liar it is false that he is Socrates. On the contrary, if Socrates is lying, then as regards the liar it is not false but true that he is Socrates; if Plato is lying, then as regards the liar it is false [that he is Socrates]; and you do not know which case obtains; therefore you do not know whether (*an*) [as regards the liar it is false that Socrates is he].

It must be said that the first is true; [91] but, when the inference is drawn, there is a paralogism of the consequent, as follows: 'as regards the liar it is not false that Socrates is he; therefore as regards the liar it is not false that he is Socrates'; for the reverse does follow: 'it is not false that Socrates is the liar; therefore it is not false that the liar is Socrates.'

9. THE EFFECT OF 'AN' ON INFERENCES FROM AN INFERIOR TO A SUPERIOR

[An inference] from an inferior to a superior involving the word '*an*' does not hold.

For example, you know whether (*an*) as regards the liar it is false that Socrates is he; therefore you know whether (*an*) as regards the liar it is stateable that Socrates [is he]. On the contrary, if Socrates is lying, then as regards the liar it is stateable that Socrates is [he]; if Plato is lying, then that Socrates is he is not stateable as regards the liar, since it is not [stateable] as regards Plato. For there is a fallacy of the consequent by reason of the negation [in the inference] from the inferior to the superior, as follows: 'it is not false; therefore it is not stateable.'

10. A SECOND EXAMPLE OF THE EFFECT OF 'AN' ON INFERENCES INVOLVING CONTRARIES

As has been said,[18] [an inference involving the word *'an'*] from a contrary to a contrary does not hold.

For example, you know whether (*an*) as regards the liar it is false that Socrates is he;[19] therefore you know whether (*an*) as regards the liar it is true that Socrates is he.[20] On the contrary, if Socrates is lying, then as regards the liar it is true that Socrates is he; if Plato is lying then as regards the liar it is not true that Socrates is he; and you do not know which case obtains; therefore you do not know whether (*an*) as regards the liar it is true [that Socrates is he]. It is a paralogism of the consequent, as follows: 'as regards the liar it is not false; therefore it is true.'

But on the contrary, if we are speaking of a stateable, this does follow correctly — 'it is not false; therefore it is true' — and we are now speaking of the stateable 'and this is true.' Nevertheless, this does not follow — 'it is not false as regards this; therefore it is true as regards this.' For example, 'that you are an ass is not false as regards Plato; therefore it is true as regards Plato.'

---

[18] Chapter XXII, Section 4.
[19] A gloss at this point in the top margin of P says "this is true in every case, since as regards the liar it is not false that Socrates is he."
[20] A gloss at this point in the top margin of P says "but this is not true in every case, since if Socrates is lying then as regards the liar it is true that Socrates is he; but if Plato is lying then as regards the liar it is not true that Socrates is he."

CHAPTER XXIII. *The Particle 'Ne'*

Next, as to the word 'ne,' which is sometimes used interrogatively, as in 'is Socrates running?' (*curritne Sortes*). It is also used [interrogatively] in place of '*an*.'[1]

At other times '*ne*' is used prohibitively,[2] and that in two ways: [1] sometimes in such a way that the prohibition is effected by ['*ne*'] itself, and [2] sometimes in such a way that what is prohibited is itself ordered together with something preceding it. Example of [1]: 'do not run' (*ne curras*); example of [2]: 'I want you not to run' (*volo ne curras*).

And so a doubt regarding it occurs in the following sophisma. You want not to be confined, and you are wary lest you be confined (*tu vis ne tibi concludatur, et caves ne tibi concludatur*); therefore you want and are wary of one and the same thing.[3]

Some say that the '*ne*' in the first [clause] is equipollent to 'that not' (*ut non*) and in the second [clause] to 'that' (*ut*); and so it is not one and the same thing.[4] But against this is the fact that '*ne*' seems always to express negation (*semper videtur sonare in negationem*). Again, if one supposes that it is taken in place of 'that not,' the first is true as well as the second, for you are wary on this account, that you not be confined (*propter hoc ut non tibi concludatur*).

It must be said, therefore, that in the 'you are wary lest' [clause] the 'you are wary' can be taken either as transitive, in which case the sense is 'you are wary of this lest . . .' (*caves hoc ne etc.*), or as absolute, in which case the sense is 'you are wary on this account, lest . . .' (*caves propter hoc ne etc.*). In the first case it is false. In the second case it is true, and it must conclude 'therefore you want and are wary on account of one and the same thing' (*idem vis et propter hoc caves*).

---

[1] As in '*honestumne est an turpe?*' — 'is it honorable or base?' Cf. Ch. XXII, n. 1.

[2] The interrogative particle '*-ne*' has a short 'e'; the particle of negation '*nē*' has a long 'e.' Thus they may fairly be said to be two particles rather than two uses of one particle. But in either case it is only the second of the two that is of interest here.

[3] Notice that the different English expressions 'not to be confined' and 'lest you be confined' are translations of one and the same Latin expression, '*ne tibi concludatur.*'

[4] Cf. Priscian, Book XV (*G.L.*, Vol. III, p. 84, ll. 16–17), where he says of the "dehortative" adverb '*ne*' that it is used in place of '*neque*,' in place of '*ut non*,' and in place of '*valde*.'

[156

CHAPTER XXIV. *'Whether ... or ...' (Sive)*

1. THE COMBINATION OF A DISJUNCTION AND A CONDITION IN 'SIVE'

Next, as to the word 'whether,' regarding which it must be known that it signifies disjunction together with a condition.[1]

And then a doubt arises, as follows. If Socrates is running or (*vel*) Plato is running, Socrates is running. Proof: This is a disjunctive conditional the first part of which is true; therefore the whole is true. The first part is 'if Socrates is running, Socrates is running'; the second part is 'if Plato is running, Socrates is running.' But [on the contrary,] since this is a disjunction together with a condition, [92] it is equipollent to 'whether (*sive*) Socrates is running or (*sive*) Plato is running, Socrates is running.' But this is false; therefore the first [proposition is false].

It must be said that the disjunction belonging to '*sive*' has to fall in the antecedent and not in the consequent, and the 'if' [belonging to it] has to fall over the disjunction. But on this analysis the first was false, for the sense was 'if the disjunctive "Socrates[2] is running or (*vel*) Plato is running" is true, Socrates is running.' In the first case 'or Plato is running' must be divided from what precedes it, in the second case compounded with it.[3] Therefore [in the second case] it signifies a consequence of something in relation to a disjunctive[4] [proposition] and hence in relation to each part of it.

2. A SECOND EXAMPLE OF THAT COMBINATION

Let there be one more sophisma, as follows. Suppose that there is only a white ass. Then whether (*sive*) there is a man or (*sive*) a white thing, there is an animal. Proof: That there is an animal follows from the first part and likewise from the second. Proof: A white thing is the same as the ass, but animal follows from ass; therefore from white thing. But on the contrary, in case only a white stone exists 'there is a man or (*vel*) a white thing' is true, and it does not follow that there is an animal.

---

[1] This is more apparent in the Latin word '*sive*,' a combination of '*si*,' 'if,' and '*vel*,' 'or.'
[2] Reading '*Sortes*' for '*si Sortes.*'
[3] The first case is the reading on which the proof depends: 'if Socrates is running, or [if] Plato is running, Socrates is running.' The second case, the one just analyzed by Sherwood, is the reading on which the "on the contrary" depends.
[4] Reading '*disjunctivam*' for '*disjunctam*.'

It must be said that the first [proposition] is false and that there is a paralogism of accident in its proof, since although 'white thing' is in this case the same as 'ass' as regards the [corresponding] real thing, nevertheless it is so divisively in respect of the condition, for [the condition] has to do (*respicitur*) not only with what is white in this case but indifferently with anything [that is white]. In accordance with the rule regarding a term placed under a condition [the term 'a white thing'] stands not determinately but simply.[5] (This is not truly a difficulty regarding the word '*sive*.')[6] [93]

---

[5] It seems that the distinction here should be not between suppositing (standing) determinately and suppositing simply, but between suppositing determinately and suppositing confusedly. I have not found such a rule in the treatise.

[6] The two manuscripts have the following closing formulas. P: "*Tolle peripsema, post pete pulinam, spernis arulam. Expliciunt syncategoremata.*" O: "*Expliciunt syncategoremata magistri Willelmi de Sirewode.*"

BIBLIOGRAPHY AND INDEX

Bibliography

A fuller bibliography of works relevant to the study of thirteenth-century logic and of Sherwood's logic in particular is available in *WSIL*, pp. 171–174. The present list includes only works cited in this book and some relevant works not included in the earlier list (indicated by a prefixed asterisk). The works of Aristotle and Boethius cited in the notes are sufficiently identified there and are not included in this bibliography.

Abelard, Peter. *Dialectica*, ed. L. M. De Rijk. Assen: Van Gorcum, 1956.
———. *Peter Abaelards Philosophische Schriften*, ed. B. Geyer, *Beiträge zur Geschichte der Philosophie und Theologie des Mittelalters*, XXI. Münster i.W.: Aschendorff, 1919–1933.
* Ackrill, J. L. *Aristotle's Categories and De interpretatione. Translated with Notes.* Oxford: Clarendon Press, 1963.
* Arnold, Erwin. "Zur Geschichte der Suppositionstheorie," *Symposion: Jahrbuch für Philosophie*, III (1952), 1–134.
Bacon, Roger. *Opus tertium*, ed. J. S. Brewer, *Fr. Rogeri Bacon opera quaedam hactenus inedita*, I. London: Longmans, 1859.
Bocheński, Innocentius M. *A History of Formal Logic*, tr. I. Thomas. Notre Dame, Ind.: University of Notre Dame Press, 1961.
Boehner, Philotheus. *Medieval Logic: An Outline of Its Development from 1250–c. 1400*. Manchester: University Press, 1952.
Burleigh, Walter. *De puritate artis logicae tractatus longior*, ed. P. Boehner, *Franciscan Institute Publications*, Text Series, No. 9. St. Bonaventure, N.Y.: Franciscan Institute, 1955.
Deferrari, Roy Joseph. *A Lexicon of St. Thomas Aquinas*. 5 vols. Washington, D.C.: Catholic University of America Press, 1948–1949.
De Rijk, Lambertus Maria. *Logica modernorum: A Contribution to the History of Early Terminist Logic*, Vol. I. *On the Twelfth Century Theories of Fallacy*. Assen: Van Gorcum, 1962.
*———. *Logica modernorum: A Contribution to the History of Early Terminist Logic*, Vol. II. *The Origin and Early Development of the Theory of Supposition*, Parts One and Two. Assen: Van Gorcum, 1967.
Geach, Peter. *Reference and Generality; An Examination of Some Medieval and Modern Theories*. Ithaca, N.Y., Cornell University Press, 1962.
Grabmann, Martin. "Bearbeitungen und Auslegungen der aristotelischen Logik aus der Zeit von Peter Abaelard bis Petrus Hispanus . . ." *Abhandlungen der Preussischen Akademie der Wissenschaften*, Jahrgang 1937, Philosophisch-historische Klasse, nr. 5. Berlin: Akademie der Wissenschaften, 1937.

———. "Die Entwicklung der mittelalterlichen Sprachlogik" in his *Mittelalterliches Geistesleben*, I, 104–146. Munich: Hueber, 1926.
* Henry, Desmond Paul. *The De grammatico of St. Anselm: The Theory of Paronymy*. Notre Dame, Ind.: University of Notre Dame Press, 1964.
* ———. *The Logic of St. Anselm*. Oxford: Clarendon Press, 1967.
* Isaac, J. *Le Péri Hermeneias en occident de Boèce à Saint Thomas: Histoire littéraire d'un traité d'Aristote*. Paris: Librairie Philosophique J. Vrin, 1953.
* Jespersen, Otto. *The Philosophy of Grammar*. London: Allen & Unwin, 1924.
Kneale, William, and Martha Kneale. *The Development of Logic*. Oxford: Clarendon Press, 1962.
* Kretzmann, Norman. "Peter of Spain," in Paul Edwards, ed., *The Encyclopedia of Philosophy*, VI, 125–126. New York: Macmillan and Free Press, 1967.
———. "Semantics, History of," in Paul Edwards, ed., *The Encyclopedia of Philosophy*, VII, 358–406. New York: Macmillan and Free Press, 1967.
* ———. "William of Sherwood," in Paul Edwards, ed., *The Encyclopedia of Philosophy*, VIII, 317–318. New York: Macmillan and Free Press, 1967.
* ———. *William of Sherwood's Introduction to Logic*. Translated with an Introduction and Notes. Minneapolis: University of Minnesota Press, 1966.
* McKeon, Richard. *Selections from Medieval Philosophers*, Vol. I. New York: Scribners, 1929.
Mullally, Joseph Patrick. *The Summulae Logicales of Peter of Spain* (a practical edition and a translation of Tractatus VII with an introduction and bibliographies). *Notre Dame Publications in Medieval Studies*, VIII. Notre Dame, Ind.: University of Notre Dame Press, 1945.
Paetow, Louis John. *The Arts Course at Medieval Universities with Special Reference to Grammar and Rhetoric*. Champaign, Ill.: University of Illinois Press, 1910.
Peter of Spain. *Summulae logicales*, ed. I. M. Bocheński. Turin: Marietti, 1947.
———. *Tractatus syncategorematum*, tr. J. P. Mullally (with an introduction by J. P. Mullally and R. Houde). Milwaukee, Wis.: Marquette University Press, 1964.
Prantl, Carl. *Geschichte der Logik im Abendlande*. 4 vols. in 2. Leipzig: Gustav Fock, 1927 ("Manualdruck der Originalausgabe, 1855").
Priscian. *Institutionum grammaticarum libri XVIII*, ed. M. Hertz., in *Grammatici latini*, Vol. III. Leipzig: Teubner, 1855.
* Scott, Theodore Kermit. *John Buridan: Sophisms on Meaning and Truth*. New York: Appleton-Century-Crofts, 1966.
* Siger of Courtrai. *Summa modorum significandi*, ed. G. Wallerand, in his *Les Oeuvres de Siger de Courtrai* (*Les Philosophes Belges*, Vol. VIII). Louvain: Institute supérieur de philosophie de l'Université, 1913.
* Thurot, Charles. *Notices et extraits de divers manuscrits latins pour servir à l'histoire des doctrines grammaticales au moyen âge*. (*Notices et extraits des manuscrits de la Bibliothèque Imperiale*, XXII). Paris: 1869; reprinted Frankfurt a.M.: Minerva, 1964.
William of Sherwood. *Introductiones in logicam*, ed. M. Grabmann. *Sitzungsberichte der Bayerischen Akademie der Wissenschaften*, Philosophisch-historische Abteilung, Jahrgang 1937, H. 10. Munich: Akademie der Wissenschaften, 1937.
———. *Syncategoremata*, ed. J. R. O'Donnell. *Mediaeval Studies*, III, 46–93. Toronto: Pontifical Institute of Mediaeval Studies, 1941.
* Wilson, Curtis. *William Heytesbury: Medieval Logic and the Rise of Mathematical Physics*. (*The University of Wisconsin Publications in Medieval Science*, III). Madison: University of Wisconsin Press, 1956.

Index

Listings for "William of Sherwood" are confined to the Translator's Introduction. Except in cases (very rare) of exceptional interest, words and names occurring in Sherwood's examples and sophismata are not indexed.

Abelard, Peter: 14 *n.4*, 90 *n.1*, 94 *n.2*
ablative absolute: 49 *n.4&6*, 114 *n.31*
accident: 44, 45 *n.6*, 48; fallacy of, 22, 22 *n.22*, 23, 35, 37 *n.75*, 57 *n.6*, 61, 106, 121, 127, 128, 147, 158
accidents, dividing/multiplying: 48
act: 100, 101, 101 *n.5*, 107, 107 *n.3*; thing belonging to, 107, 107 *n.3*, 111, 131
adjective: 5, 13 *n.2*, 16 *n.12*, 17 *n.6*, 44, 52, 54 *n.1*, 113. *See also* name, adjectival
adjoining: *see* conjoining
adjunct: 41, 92
adverb: 13, 16 *n.12*, 81, 100, 100 *n.2*, 100 *n.5*, 129; modal, 100 *n.2*, 101 *n.5&6*, 103 *n.14*; dehortative, 156 *n.4*. *See also* mode, adverbial
affirmation: 55, 65, 94, 94 *n.3*, 96, 98; assertive, 148. *See also* assertion; positing
Albert of Saxony: 106 *n.1*
Albert the Great: 3
'all': *see* 'every' or 'all'
'alone' (*solus*): 38–39, 58 *n.3*, Ch. XI *passim*, 82, 87, 88–89, 90 *n.34*, 95, 103, 103–104, 124, 135, 139
alternation: 24 *n.30*
ambiguity: 4, 22, 22 *n.21*, 28, 33, 46, 49, 49 *n.4*, 50, 51 *n.11*, 55, 56, 67, 71 *n.9*, 72, 75, 76, 82, 83, 86, 87, 88, 89, 93, 103, 104, 113, 114, 115, 122, 124, 125, 129, 133, 134, 139 *n.23*, 146, 147, 152
amphibology, fallacy of: 134, 134 *n.3*, 137, 137 *n.12*

analogy: 26 *n.37*, 113
analysis: 16 *n.3*, 18 *n.8*, 24 *n.30&32*, 33 *n.60*, 34 *n.62,63,&64*, 36 *n.69*, 38 *n.76*, 39, 48 *n.23*, 57 *n.2*, 80, 83 *n.10*, 101 *n.5*, 109 *n.10&12*, 111 *n.18*, 112 *n.20&23*, 113 *n.27*, 136 *n.11*, 145, 157. *See also* exposition
anastrophe: 31 *n.55*
'and' (*et*): 56, 56 *n.6*, 68, 76, 80, 89, Ch. XX *passim*
'and' (*et*) taken conjunctively/divisively: 137, 137 *n.17*
'another': 29–30, 29 *n.49*, 71, 71 *n.9*, 72, 72 *n.13*, 86 *n.21*
antecedent: 118, 118 *n.9*, 119 *n.10,13,&14*, 120, 120 *n.18*, 122, 123, 124, 125, 125 *n.32*, 126, 127, 127 *n.41*, 128, 129, 130, 130 *n.6&7*, 131 *n.13*, 133, 138, 140, 157; undistributed, 125; separate assertion of, 131 *n.13*
Antichrist: 101, 101 *n.7*, 122, 122 *n.25*
antiqui: 7 *n.12*, 51 *n.11*
'any and every': 15 *n.9*, 19, 19 *n.11*
appellation: 5, 13 *n.2*, 23 *n.26*, 52 *n.16*, 60, 98 *n.16*
appellatum: 23, 23 *n.26*, 24, 25 *n.34*, 26 *n.38*, 26–27, 43, 52, 52 *n.16*, 98 *n.16*
apposition: 29 *n.46*
Aquinas, Thomas: 3, 131 *n.14*
argument: 126, 126 *n.34*, 127, 128; dialectical, 53 *n.19&20*
argumentation: 127, 127 *n.30*, 128
Aristotle: 4, 5, 14 *n.4*, 17 *n.5&6*, 19, 19 *n.9,10,&11*, 20 *n.12*, 23, 23 *n.27*, 25

163]

n.35, 26, 26 n.36, 27, 27 n.41&42, 32 n.59, 71, 71 n.10, 79, 79 n.34, 90, 90 n.2&3, 106 n.1, 108 n.9, 109 n.12, 110 n.13, 144, 144 n.14
ascent, logical: 36, 36 n.69&70, 65, 65 n.33, 125, 135, 135 n.6
assertion: 94, 94 n.3, 131 n.13&14, 139, 147, 148; absolute, 147, 148. *See also* affirmation
Attleborough: 3
attribution, subject of: 33–34, 34 n.62
auctores: 56, 56 n.8
Aylesbury: 3

Bacon, Roger: 3–4
Barbara: 26
begging the original issue, fallacy of: 128
beginning: 107, 109, 109 n.12, 110, 116
'begins' (*incipit*): Ch. XVI *passim*; affirmative and negative aspects of, 113
being: 26, 91 n.9, 92 n.12&13, 113 n.27, 114 n.29, 128 n.43; actual, 92, 92 n.15, 93, 106, 128 n.43; conditional, 92, 92 n.15, 105, 105 n.22, 128 n.43; diminutional, 93, 93 n.17
being together: 134, 139, 148; as actualized/as conceived of, 140
binding: 117
Bocardo: 24 n.31&33
Bocheński, I. M.: 119 n.14
Boehner, Philotheus: 20 n.17
Boethius: 4, 19 n.9, 85 n.18, 94 n.2, 119, 119 n.14
'both' (*uterque*): 15 n.9, 23, Ch. V *passim*
Buridan, John: 21 n.18, 106 n.1
Burleigh, Walter: 4 n.5, 106 n.1
'but' (*praeter*): 16 n.12, Ch. X *passim*, 71 n.12, 131, 132
'but' (*praeter*) taken additively/exceptively: 58, 59
'but' (*praeter*) taken counter-instantively: 58–59, 59–60, 61, 66
'but' (*praeter*) taken diminutionally: 58, 59–60, 60 n.9, 65, 66
'but that' (*quin*): Ch. XIX *passim*

capacity: 57, 57 n.4
case: oblique, 33–34, 51 n.11; nominative, 33–34, 94
categorematic words: 5, 17 n.6, 40, 41, 42, 44, 45, 47, 60, 70, 70 n.2&6, 80, 100, 101, 106–107, 111, 111 n.18, 116
categories: 70, 70 n.2
category difference: 72
'ceases' (*desinit*): Ch. XVI *passim*; affirmative and negative aspects of, 113
ceasing: 109, 109 n.12, 110, 114, 115

change: 109–110, 114
characteristic: 17 n.3
characterization: 18 n.7
clause: 143; relative, 28 n.44, 29 n.46, 85 n.20, 122. *See also* term involving a clause or phrase
coherence of forms in suppositum: 102, 104
commonly, words taken: 20, 20 n.17, 21, 21 n.20, 27
complement: 116 n.2, 117 n.4
'complete': 17, 17 n.5
completion: 23, 61
complexes: 130
composition, fallacy of: 115 n.35. *See also* pronunciation, compounded/divided; sense, compounded/divided
composition (relation between subject and predicate): 27, 27 n.42, 28, 53, 53 n.23, 54, 90, 90 n.3&4, 91, 93–94, 94 n.2&3, 95, 100, 101, 101 n.5, 102, 104, 116, 118, 119, 119 n.10,11,&13, 128 n.43, 130, 139, 140, 147, 148; components of, 90, 90 n.3; negation of, 94–95; one in respect of another, 116; principal, 120; infinite, 121, 121 n.23
concept: 119, 128; principal, 119, 119 n.13
conclusion: 21 n.18&19, 23 n.25, 75 n.20, 111 n.18
condition: 118, 119, 124, 125, 129, 130, 156, 158
conditionalization: 122
confirmation: 131
conjoining (or adjoining) of words with states: 108, 110, 113, 114
conjunction: 18 n.8, 24 n.30&32, 111 n.17, 116, 117, 119 n.14, 140, 141, 143, 148, 149
conjunctions: 13, 16 n.12, 116, 116 n.1&2, 117, 117 n.4,6,&7, 129, 141, 141 n.4; copulative, 68, 117, 134, 134 n.1, 141 n.1; consecutive, 117, 121, 129, 129 n.3, 130, 130 n.7, 131 n.16, 132, 133; disjunctive, 117, 140–141, 141 n.1; continuative, 117 n.7; adjunctive, 121, 121 n.21; subdisjunctive, 141, 141 n.1, 143; dubitative, 148 n.1; elective, 149, 149 n.3; disertive, 149 n.3
conpredication: 16, 90, 90 n.5
consecution: 130, 133
consent: 94
consequence: 117, 117 n.7, 118, 118 n.-8&9, 119 n.10&13, 125, 127, 133, 157; natural/nonnatural, 123; absolute/un-

[164

der prevailing conditions, 123, 123 *n.27*;
necessary/merely true, 123, 123 *n.27*
consequent: 118, 118 *n.9*, 119 *n.10,11,&-
14*, 120, 120 *n.16&18*, 121, 123, 124,
125, 125 *n.32*, 126, 127, 127 *n.41*, 128,
129, 130, 130 *n.6&7*, 140, 157; fallacy
of, 36, 36 *n.72*, 37, 37 *n.75*, 40, 41, 47,
55, 56, 67, 73, 74, 74 *n.19*, 75, 75 *n.20*,
78, 88, 95, 96, 97, 98, 111, 111 *n.17*,
127, 132, 135, 145, 146, 151, 154, 155;
destruction of, 62
consequential character: 129
consignification: 13 *n.2&3*, 16, 31, 90, 90
n.4, 91, 94, 100, 101 *n.5*, 117, 128
n.43
construal: 108, 136–137, 144
contingency: 106 *n.25*, 122, 124, 129; future, 101 *n.7*
'contingently' (*contingenter*): 100, 100
n.2, 101, 105 *n.19*
continuum: 109 *n.12*, 115
contradiction: 24 *n.30*, 130
contradictories: 126, 129, 142–143, 149,
150, 150 *n.4*
contraries: 93, 94, 150, 150 *n.4*, 155; argument from, 127, 127 *n.40*
contrariety: 4, 27 *n.41*
conversion: 91, 97, 97–98
copula: 90 *n.4*, 92 *n.14*
copulation (function of copulative conjunction): 56, 56 *n.6*, 68, 76, 80, 135,
136, 137, 138, 139, 140, 148; between
terms, 68, 80, 134, 134–135; between
propositions, 68, 134, 134–135. *See also*
term, copulated
copulation (property of terms): 5, 13
n.2, 29, 29 *n.49*, 30, 44 *n.2*, 57; merely
confused, 30, 31, 46; determinate, 31,
46; distributive confused, 45 *n.6*. *See
also* time, copulation of
copulatum (conjunct): 135, 135 *n.3&4*
copulatum (instance under property of
terms): 43 *n.1*, 44, 45 *n.6&7*, 57
counter-instantiation: 59, 64, 68, 89
counting: 59

Deferrari, R. J.: 131 *n.14*
definition: 71
demonstration: 26
denotation: 59, 81, 93, 94, 130
De Rijk, L. M.: 106 *n.1*
descent, logical: 24 *n.32*, 35 *n.66*, 36 *n.-
69&70*, 37 *n.75*, 45 *n.6*, 47, 47–48, 48
n.23, 62, 62 *n.17&18*, 65, 105, 110 *n.16*,
111, 111 *n.17*, 112, 112 *n.24*, 125, 125
n.32, 131 *n.16*, 132, 132 *n.17*, 135 *n.6*

description, definite: 35 *n.65*, 104 *n.17*
designation: 39, 48, 59, 64, 84, 84 *n.12*,
107, 129, 146
determination: 14, 14 *n.4*, 15, 15 *n.8*, 16,
16 *n.12*, 17 *n.3*, 51 *n.11*, 61, 61 *n.15*,
62 *n.17*, 81–82, 101, 101 *n.5*, 104, 122,
130, 130 *n.6*, 134, 139, 142, 145; syncategorematic/nonsyncategorematic, 14
n.4, 15 *n.8&10*, 81 *n.1*, 81–82, 100
dialectic: 16 *n.13*
'*dicendum quod*': 9, 16 *n.14*
dici de nullo: 48, 48 *n.2*
dici de omni: 25, 25 *n.35*, 26, 48 *n.2*, 71
dictum: 138, 138 *n.18&21*
difference, essential/numerical: 71, 72
diminution: 58
disassertion: 94, 94 *n.3*
discourse: 16, 16 *n.13*, 34, 34 *n.64*, 95; ordinary, 4, 5; universe of, 95 *n.5*; ordering of things in, 123; indirect, 138 *n.18*
disjunction: 140, 142, 143, 145, 146, 147,
148, 149, 150 *n.4*, 152, 154, 157; between propositions or expressions, 141–
142, 142, 145, 147; between terms, 141–
142, 145. *See also* term, disjoined
disjunction taken most strictly: 154
disposition: 13 *n.2*, 17, 17 *n.3&6*, 70, 71,
108, 139
disproof: 21 *n.19*, 29 *n.48*
disputation: 4, 16 *n.14*, 17 *n.2*, 19 *n.9*
dissent: 94
distribution: 6, 17 *n.4*, 21, 22, 23, 28, 29,
29 *n.49*, 30, 30 *n.50*, 31, 32, 35, 35
n.66, 36, 36 *n.67&69*, 37, 38, 39, 43, 43
n.1, 44, 45 *n.6*, 46, 46 *n.12*, 48 *n.22&23*,
50, 50 *n.10*, 51, 51 *n.11*, 54 *n.26&1*, 64
n.27, 65, 66, 71 *n.12*, 106 *n.1*, 112 *n.24*,
142, 152; respect of, 30, 30 *n.50*, 31, 32,
45, 45 *n.6*; mobile/immobile, 35 *n.66*,
47; multiple, 36 *n.69&70*, 37 *n.75*, 47;
force of, 38, 64. *See also* division (of a
term); term, distributed
division, fallacy of: 115 *n.35*. *See also*
pronunciation, compounded/divided;
sense, compounded/divided
division (of a term): 18, 18 *n.8*, 19, 19
n.11, 20, 24 *n.32*, 27, 43, 45, 46, 46
n.12, 47, 48, 49, 54, 54 *n.26*, 58, 61, 62,
63, 64, 64 *n.27*, 65, 65 *n.30*, 66, 71 *n.12*,
74, 79, 82, 93, 104, 105–106, 110, 125,
130, 132, 142, 143, 144, 145, 146, 152;
mobile/immobile, 61, 66, 74, 110; multiple, 66–67. *See also* distribution
division (relation between subject and
predicate): 93
doubt: 148, 148 *n.1*, 149, 150

165]

Duns Scotus, John: 106 *n.1*
'each and every': 15 *n.9*, 40, 44, 48
'each single': 19, 19 *n.11*
edition, Latin, corrections and revisions of: 20 *n.16*, 36 *n.73*, 39 *n.83*, 41 *n.1*, 42 *n.4*, 43 *n.1*, 44 *n.1&3*, 47 *n.13&18*, 48 *n.20*, 53 *n.21*, 54 *n.1*, 56 *n.11*, 57 *n.1*, 59 *n.6,7,&8*, 62 *n.17*, 64 *n.28*, 65 *n.29&33*, 68 *n.38*, 70 *n.3*, 72 *n.14*, 76 *n.23*, 79 *n.33*, 81 *n.2*, 83 *n.9*, 86 *n.23*, 88 *n.29*, 90 *n.2&5*, 97 *n.12*, 100 *n.3*, 101 *n.4*, 104 *n.15*, 105 *n.22*, 106 *n.24*, 107 *n.5&6*, 108 *n.7*, 112 *n.20&22*, 114 *n.32*, 117 *n.3*, 120 *n.16&17*, 125 *n.31*, 127 *n.35*, 129 *n.1*, 130 *n.11&12*, 132 *n.19*, 133 *n.1*, 138 *n.21*, 141 *n.2*, 142 *n.5&6*, 143 *n.12*, 144 *n.16*, 145 *n.18*, 147 *n.20*, 148 *n.23&24*, 149 *n.2&3*, 151 *n.7*, 152 *n.11*, 153 *n.12,13,&16*, 157 *n.2&4*
end: 108, 109, 110, 113, 114
English: 58 *n.1*, 74 *n.18*, 76 *n.22*, 96 *n.9*, 156 *n.3*
'entire': 40
enumeration, exhaustive: 29 *n.45*
equipollence: 17, 17 *n.4*, 40, 42, 44, 51, 51 *n.13*, 62, 62 *n.19*, 67, 74, 104, 115, 130, 133, 140, 145, 146, 153, 156, 157
equivalence: 127 *n.41*, 151, 151 *n.8*
equivocation: 45, 59, 85, 92, 93; fallacy of, 60, 60 *n.13*, 81, 105–106
'etc.': 24 *n.33*
'every' or 'all' (*omnis*): 15, 15 *n.9*, Ch. I passim, 43 *n.3*, 44, 44 *n.4*, 51 *n.13*, 51–52, 58, 63, 64–65, 65 *n.30*, 66, 67, 69, 70 *n.8*, 71 *n.12*, 93, 104–106, 125, 126, 142, 143, 144, 145, 147, 151, 152–153; deficiency of, 105, 105 *n.21*
'every' or 'all' (*omnis*) taken collectively/distributively: 39 *n.82*, 39–40
'every' or 'all' (*omnis*) taken divisively: 146, 146 *n.19*
'every' or 'all' (*omnis*) taken properly: 20, 20 *n.17*, 21, 21 *n.20*, 27
'everything': 110–111, 146–147, 151
excepted: simply, 65, 65 *n.32*; divisively, 68
exception: 58, 59, 60, 61, 61 *n.16*, 62, 63, 64, 65, 65 *n.31&32*, 66, 67, 68, 68 *n.37*, 69 *n.1*, 71 *n.12*, 131, 132; pluralization of, 68
exception from/in respect of: 131 *n.16*, 132
exceptives: 58, 58 *n.4*, 69, 71 *n.12*, 129, 130, 130 *n.10*, 131 *n.16*, 132, 132 *n.17*
exclusion: 69 *n.1*, 70 *n.7*, 71 *n.12*, 71–72,

[166

73, 74, 74 *n.18*, 75, 76, 77, 79, 80, 89, 103, 124, 135, 137; numerical, 72, 72 *n.15*; general/specific, 72–73, 82; affirmative and negative aspects of, 75, 75 *n.20*, 79, 87, 88; multiple, 77–78
exclusion around/in respect of: 77, 77 *n.26*, 86–89
exclusion around various things: 82–83, 83 *n.7&10*, 86, 86 *n.24*, 87, 87 *n.27*, 88, 89
exclusion in respect of various things: 81 *n.39*, 84, 87, 87 *n.25*, 88, 89, 135
exclusives: 58, 58 *n.3&4*, 69 *n.1*, 70 *n.7*, 71, 71 *n.10&12*, 78–79, 81, 81 *n.39*, 90 *n.34*
existence: 23 *n.26*, 108, 112, 113, 113 *n.27*, 114 *n.30*
existent: *see* part, actually extant
existential implication: 20 *n.15&17*
exponibles: 6, 108 *n.8*
exposition: 48, 108, 108 *n.8*, 109, 109 *n.11*, 110, 111 *n.17*, 112, 113, 113 *n.27*, 114 *n.30*. *See also* analysis
expression: 34 *n.62*, 91, 91 *n.8*, 95, 122, 133, 141, 141 *n.3*; ingredients in, 91, 92 *n.14*, 93; complete, 121, 121 *n.22*, 141 *n.3*, 143
expression true and false by parts: 78
extremes or extremities: 23, 23 *n.25*, 142

fallacy: 4, 21 *n.18&19*, 22 *n.21*, 128. *See also* accident; amphibology; consequent; equivocation; *figura dictionis*; in a certain respect as well as absolutely; paralogism; sophistical reasoning
falling under or over: *see* function, one falling under or over another
falsification: 95, 97
falsity: 49, 63, 76, 78, 119, 119 *n.10,11,&13*, 120, 120 *n.16&18*, 122, 123, 123 *n.27&29*, 124, 124 *n.30*, 126, 135, 155; analytic, 21 *n.18*, 29 *n.49*; absolute, 24
falsity for certain instances: 68
falsity of a statement as a whole: 66
figura dictionis, fallacy of: 21, 22 *n.21&22*, 22–23, 30, 31, 32, 36, 38, 47, 51, 55, 57, 67, 74, 85, 104, 105, 111, 112, 132
'finitely many': 42–43
following logically: 117, 118, 118 *n.8*, 119, 119 *n.11*, 123
form: 17 *n.5*, 18 *n.7*, 27, 28, 96 *n.10*, 102, 102 *n.9&11*, 119 *n.12*
fortuitous, something: 116
function: 5, 17, 17 *n.1&4*, 18, 28 *n.43*, 29 *n.49*, 34, 34 *n.64*, 51, 90 *n.4*, 117; prop-

er/improper, 26, 26 *n.37*; one falling under or over another, 56, 58, 62, 64, 66, 67, 76, 79, 80, 129, 129–130, 130, 137, 143, 148, 149, 157; inclusion of one by another, 67, 68–69, 71 *n.12*, 71–72, 77–79, 80, 103, 104, 105, 124, 125, 135, 137, 139, 142, 145, 146, 147; elements falling under or outside a, 74, 75, 76, 77, 103, 122, 130, 135, 137, 140, 152. *See also* syncategorematic word, function of

Geach, Peter: 37 *n.75*, 59 *n.8*, 67 *n.34*, 79 *n.33*, 101 *n.7*
gender, grammatical: 71, 71 *n.9*
genus: 14 *n.4*, 21, 22, 39 *n.81*, 48, 62 *n.17*, 65, 72, 73, 93
gerund: 57 *n.2*, 114 *n.31*
Grabmann, Martin: 4 *n.3*, 94 *n.2*
grammar: 16 *n.13*, 17 *n.6*, 25 *n.34*, 56 *n.8*, 57 *n.2*, 78 *n.29*, 137 *n.17*, 143 *n.11*; speculative, 94 *n.2*. *See also* case; construal; gender, grammatical; gerund; locution, ungrammatical; mood (grammatical); sentence; speech, parts of
grammatical relation: 15 *n.8*, 121, 121 *n.23*
Green, Romuald: 4 *n.6*
Grosseteste, Robert: 101 *n.7*

Hamblin, C. L.: 4 *n.5*
Helias, Peter: 94 *n.2*
Heytesbury, William: 21 *n.18*, 106 *n.1*
'himself': 34–35, 63, 64, 144, 147
hoc aliquid: 32 *n.59*, 32–33, 33 *n.60*, 36, 46, 46 *n.11*
'however many': 15 *n.9*
'however much': 44
hypothesis: 21, 21 *n.18&19*, 22 *n.23*

identification: 28 *n.43*
'if' (*si*): Ch. XVII *passim*, 129, 157, 157 *n.1*
'if' (*si*) taken confirmatively: 131, 131 *n.13*
immobilization: 32, 35 *n.66*, 35–38, 36 *n.67*, 47, 55, 61, 65–66, 66–67, 67, 73, 74, 82, 99, 105, 110, 111, 125, 131 *n.16*, 144
impeding: *see* immobilization
implication: 114, 119 *n.13*, 126, 128 *n.42*, 153; strict, 119 *n.13*; material, 122 *n.24*
imposition: 14 *n.4*
impossibility: 120 *n.18*, 122, 123, 123 *n.27&29*, 124, 124 *n.30*, 138

impossible absolutely/*per accidens*: 123, 123 *n.29*
'impossibly': 100 *n.2*
in a certain respect as well as absolutely, fallacy of using a locution: 142, 142 *n.9*
inclusives: 71, 71 *n.12*
incompossibility: 154
inconsistency: 126
indeclinables: 13 *n.2*, 116
indication: 40, 41, 42, 58, 69, 70, 70 *n.2*, 71, 84, 93, 105, 108, 109, 110, 113, 115, 117, 118, 123, 134, 140, 141, 149
individuals: 14 *n.4&5*, 18 *n.8*, 19, 19 *n.11*, 20, *n.12*, 22, 27 *n.42*, 37, 44 *n.4*, 48, 48 *n.23*, 49, 62 *n.17*, 65 *n.31&32*, 102, 102 *n.9&11*, 104 *n.17*, 151
induction: multiple, 37 *n.75*, 38 *n.78*; insufficient, 39–40
inference: 21 *n.18&19*; rules of, 5, 24, 24 *n.31*, 31, 32 *n.56*, 33 *n.61*, 35, 35 *n.66*, 47–48, 61, 62, 64, 65, 66, 73, 74, 99, 110, 116, 125, 125 *n.32*, 151, 154, 155; generalization, 30 *n.52*; noncontinuous, 127
inferior: 20, 20 *n.12*, 24, 24 *n.31&32*, 36 *n.69&70*, 73, 93, 99 *n.19*, 99–100, 116, 154–155
infinitation: *see* negation, infinitating
'infinitely many' (*infinita in plurali*): Ch. IV *passim*, 97, 97 *n.11*, 98, 98 *n.15*
infinitive: 107, 107 *n.3*, 108, 109, 110, 112
inherence: 27, 27 *n.42*, 28, 84, 102, 104. *See also* predication
insolubilia: 4, 55, 55 *n.3*
instant: 108, 109, 109 *n.12*, 110, 111, 114, 115, 122
interemption: 27 *n.40*
interrogation: 149, 156; particle of, 156, 156 *n.2*
intonation-patterns: 29 *n.47*, 68 *n.37*, 76 *n.22*, 114 *n.33*. *See also* pronunciation, compounded/divided
invalidity: 22 *n.21*
'is' (*est*): 28 *n.43*, Ch. XIII *passim*, 93–94, 94 *n.3*, 128, 128 *n.43*, 136–137; copulative/existential, 132 *n.17*; present-tense/tenseless, 132 *n.18*
'it follows': *see* following logically
'it is ordered': 117, 118 *n.8*

Jespersen, Otto: 116*n.2*, 117 *n.4*

kind: 18 *n.8*. *See also* genus; sort; species
Kneale, William: 106 *n.1*, 119 *n.14*
knowledge: 149

167]

Lambert of Auxerre: 3, 5
languages: 58 *n.1*, 59
Latin: 15 *n.10*, 45 *n.7*, 49 *n.4*, 58 *n.1*, 74 *n.18*, 76 *n.22*, 81 *n.1*, 91 *n.11*, 96 *n.9*, 100 *n.20*, 105 *n.22*, 117 *n.4*, 127 *n.41*, 129 *n.2*, 133 *n.1*, 139 *n.23*, 143 *n.11*, 156 *n.3*, 157 *n.1*
Locke, John: 27 *n.39*
locution: judging a, 33–34, 34 *n.62&63*; subject of, 33–34, 34 *n.62&63*; ungrammatical, 63, 137, 137 *n.17*, 143
logic: medieval, 4–5, 21 *n.18*, 22 *n.21*; philosophical, 8; formal, 22 *n.21*, 106 *n.1*
logica antiqua/moderna: 5, 5 *n.8*
logica vetus/nova: 4
logicians: modernist, 5; terminist, 5; medieval, 101 *n.7*, 106 *n.1*
Lombard, Peter: 4
'ly' (or '*li*'): 15 *n.6*, 70 *n.3*

magnitude: 23 *n.27*
manuscripts of *Syncategoremata*: 8, 9, 9 *n.18*, 13 *n.3*, 41 *n.1*, 43 *n.6*, 44 *n.1*, 45 *n.5*, 47 *n.13,14,16,&19*, 50 *n.10*, 51 *n.12*, 53 *n.17,20,&21*, 54 *n.1*, 55 *n.2,3,&4*, 56 *n.9,10,&11*, 57 *n.1*, 59 *n.6&7*, 60 *n.11&12*, 61 *n.16*, 62 *n.17,18,&21*, 65 *n.33*, 67 *n.35*, 76 *n.23*, 77 *n.26*, 81 *n.2*, 84 *n.13*, 88 *n.29*, 90 *n.2*, 97 *n.12*, 98 *n. 13&14*, 100 *n.2*, 101 *n.4*, 105 *n.22*, 107 *n.5*, 112 *n.22*, 120 *n.16&17*, 125 *n.31*, 127 *n.35*, 136 *n.10*, 138 *n.19*, 139 *n.22*, 141 *n.2*, 145 *n.17&18*, 149 *n.2&3*, 155 *n.19&20*, 158 *n.6*
Marsilius of Inghen: 106 *n.1*
matter: 17 *n.5*; determinate, 95
meaning: 24 *n.29*
measure: 81
Menghus, Faventinus: 106 *n.1*
metaphor: 26 *n.37*
metaphysics: 113 *n.27*
mind: 118, 139, 141 *n.3*
mnemonics: 6
modal word: 147; position of, 101 *n.6*, 103 *n.14*. See also adverb, modal
mode: 105, 125, 147; adverbial, 14 *n.4*, 15 *n.8*. See also adverb, modal
modifier: 29 *n.46*, 42 *n.3*
modus significandi: see signifying, modes of
mood (grammatical): indicative, 108, 109, 110, 112; subjunctive, 121 *n.21*
more-than-oneness: 140
motion: 110
Mullally, Joseph Patrick: 96 *n.10*, 106 *n.1*

name: 91; substantival, 13, 13 *n.3*, 14 *n.4&5*, 16 *n.12*, 18 *n.7*, 92 *n.14*; adjectival, 13, 18 *n.7*, 92 *n.14*; proper, 25 *n.34*, 35 *n.65*, 104 *n.17*; common, 35 *n.65*, 86 *n.21*; finite/infinite, 56, 56 *n.7*, 74. See also adjective; noun; term
'*ne*': 16 *n.12*, Ch. XXIII *passim*
'necessarily' (*necessario*): Ch. XV *passim*, 107 *n.2*, 125, 126. See also 'of necessity'
necessary absolutely/*per accidens*: 123, 123 *n.20*
necessity: 101, 102, 103, 104, 105, 106, 106 *n.25*, 120 *n.18*, 121 *n.19*, 122, 123, 123 *n.27&29*, 124, 126, 127, 129, 147
negation: 24, 26, 51, 51 *n.4*, 62, 62 *n.19*, 65, 66, 71, 73, 74, 78, 93, 94, 94 *n.3*, 95, 98, 99, 99 *n.19*, 100 *n.20*, 110, 111, 111 *n.17*, 112, 112 *n.20*, 119 *n.14&15*, 124–125, 129, 130, 131, 133, 135, 136, 136 *n.5*, 139, 150, 155, 156; scope of, 49–52, 53–55, 57; multiple, 55, 96, 113 *n.27*, 139; absolute, 73; infinitating/non-infinitating, 74, 94, 95 *n.4*, 137; referring of, 87, 88, 95, 119, 130; negating, 95 *n.4*; express/virtual, 96; active/received, 133; particle of, 156, 156 *n.2&4*
negation within a genus: 73, 95
'neither' (*neutrum*): Ch. IX *passim*
'no' (*nullus*): 15 *n.9*, 17 *n.4*, Ch. VII *passim*, 54 *n.1*, 66, 130, 135–137, 136 *n.8&11*
nonexistence: 136 *n.9*
nonexistents: 24, 24 *n.29&32*, 52, 53 *n.17*, 98–99, 112
nonsense: 131 *n.16*, 132 *n.17*
'not' (*non*): 17 *n.4*, 51, 51 *n.13*, 62, Ch. XIV *passim*, 125, 129, 139, 140, 151
'not' (*non*) taken extinctively: 95
not being: 110
note: 91, 125
'nothing' (*nihil*): 53 *n.21*, Ch. VIII *passim*, 62, 85, 85 *n.20*, 137
noting: 123, 129, 133
noun: 5, 13 *n.3*, 16 *n.12*. See also name, substantival
number words: Ch. III *passim*, 41–42, 60, 60 *n.14*, 65, 66, 78–79, 82
number words taken collectively: 60. See also term taken conjunctively/divisively
numbers: 135 *n.2&6*
numerical limit: 42

O (Oxford manuscript): 9 *n.18*. See also manuscripts of *Syncategoremata*

[168

Ockham, William: 106 *n.1*, 109 *n.10*
O'Donnell, J. R.: 4 *n.2*, 8, 9, 19 *n.10*, 20 *n.12*, 23 *n.27*, 26 *n.36*, 27 *n.41&42*, 71 *n.10*, 79 *n.34*, 90 *n.1&3*, 94 *n.2*, 116 *n.1*, 119 *n.14*, 134 *n.1*, 141 *n.4*, 144 *n.14*, 148 *n.1*, 149 *n.3*. See also edition, Latin, corrections and revisions of
'of every sort' (*qualelibet*): 43 *n.1*, Ch. VI *passim*
'of necessity': 105–106
'on the contrary': 21 *n.19*, 22 *n.23*, 29 *n.48*
'one': 85–86, 86 *n.21&23*
one-not-with-another: 69, 71 *n.10*, 73
one-with-another: 69
'only' (*tantum*): 58 *n.3*, 70 *n.7*, 73, 81 *n.39*, Ch. XII *passim*, 103
opposites: 126, 150; argument from, 99, 99 *n.18*. See also contradictories; contraries
'or' (*vel*): Ch. XXI *passim*, 149, 157, 157 *n.1*. See also 'whether . . . or . . .' (*sive*)
order: 117, 117 *n.7*
'other': see 'another'
Oxford: 3, 8

P (Paris manuscript): 9 *n.18*. See also manuscripts of *Syncategoremata*
Paetow, L. J.: 56 *n.8*
paralogism: 21 *n.18&19*, 22, 22 *n.21&22*. See also fallacy
paralogizing: 63, 110
Paris, University of: 3, 8, 129
part: 13, 58, 60, 61, 62, 82; specific/numerical, 18 *n.8*, 18–20, 19 *n.11*, 20 *n.15*, 21, 22, 23, 24 *n.32*, 43, 48, 49, 93, 105, 106; actually extant, 20, 21, 23, 24, 49; conditionally extant; 20, 21, 23, 27, 105; proximate/remote, 22–23, 48 *n.22*, 49, 65, 65 *n.30*
participle: 5, 49, 50, 50 *n.10*, 51, 51 *n.11*, 91, 91 *n.11*, 92 *n.14*, 95
particle: 156, 156 *n.2&4*
particulars: 17 *n.6*, 27 *n.42*, 71 *n.10*; corresponding, 44, 44 *n.4*. See also individuals; single things
Paul of Venice: 106 *n.1*
Peter of Ailly: 106 *n.1*
Peter of Mantua: 106 *n.1*
Peter of Spain: 3, 5, 6–8, 7 *n.12&13*, 26 *n.38*, 30 *n.51*, 33 *n.60*, 37 *n.74*, 38 *n.76*, 41 *n.3*, 43 *n.8&3*, 47 *n.13&19*, 49 *n.6*, 51 *n.11*, 53 *n.23*, 54 *n.28&1*, 55 *n.5*, 57 *n.2&6*, 58 *n.4*, 63 *n.24*, 69 *n.39*, 70 *n.7*, 72 *n.15*, 81 *n.39*, 83 *n.8*, 85 *n.15*, 90

n.34, 94 *n.2&3*, 95 *n.4*, 96 *n.10*, 101 *n.7*, 105 *n.19*, 106 *n.1*, 108 *n.8*, 109 *n.10*, 113 *n.26*, 114 *n.30&31*, 120 *n.18*, 121 *n.19*, 123 *n.27*, 124 *n.30*, 125 *n.32*, 126 *n.33*, 127 *n.36*, 129 *n.3*, 130 *n.9*, 132 *n.21*, 134 *n.4&5*, 137 *n.11*, 143 *n.10*, 150 *n.4*, 152 *n.9*
philosophia communis: 4
Plato: 13 *n.3*
plurality: 23, 26, 33, 35, 41, 42, 43, 45, 46, 58, 63, 84, 131
plurality taken once/more than once: 63, 63 *n.23*, 64
pluralization: 68, 69, 71
Porphyry: 4
positing: 109, 110, 112, 112 *n.20*, 113, 114, 125, 126, 150 *n.4*
possibility: 101, 105, 121 *n.20*, 123 *n.27*, 126
possible entity: 27 *n.39*
'possibly': 100 *n.2*
Prantl, Carl: 106 *n.1*
predicamental line: 20 *n.12*, 36 *n.69&70*, 99 *n.19*. See also inferior; superior
predicate: 5, 14 *n.5*, 15, 15 *n.7,8,&11*, 16, 16 *n.12*, 17, 17 *n.6*, 18, 18 *n.7&8*, 24 *n.29* 27–28, 28 *n.43*, 30, 31, 32 *n.56*, 37, 38, 39, 40, 41, 43, 46, 51 *n.13*, 52, 54, 55, 58, 59, 61, 66, 73, 74, 75, 77, 80, 81, 82, 85, 85 *n.19*, 86, 86 *n.23*, 90, 90 *n.4*, 91, 92, 92 *n.14*, 100, 101, 101 *n.5*, 102, 104, 104 *n.17*, 108, 116, 121, 131, 134, 141, 142, 143, 144, 148, 153, 154; affirmation of, 25, 25 *n.35*, 48 *n.2*; relating to the, 41, 43; receiving the, 44, 73; sharing the, 70, 72; one in respect of another, 116; conditioned, 119 *n.15*, 120–122; disjoined, 141
predicate-character, destruction of: 28 *n.43*
predication: 14 *n.5*, 15 *n.8&11*, 16 *n.12*, 17 *n.5*, 22, 23, 24 *n.31*, 25 *n.35*, 28 *n.43*, 53 *n.23*, 91, 92, 92 *n.14*, 93, 108, 130, 140; necessary, 21; universal, 27, 27 *n.41*. See also composition; inherence
premiss: 4, 13 *n.1*, 21 *n.18&19*, 23 *n.25*, 24 *n.31&33*, 26 *n.36*, 45 *n.6*, 47 *n.15& 17*, 75 *n.20*, 88 *n.30*, 111 *n.18*, 126 *n.34*, 127 *n.39*, 144
preposition: 13, 16 *n.12*, 116, 116 *n.2*, 117, 117 *n.4&5*, 131; object of, 117 *n.4&5*
priority, natural: 118
Priscian: 13 *n.3*, 19 *n.9*, 116 *n.1&2*, 117, 117 *n.7*, 121 *n.21*, 134, 134 *n.1*, 141,

169]

141 n.1&4, 143 n.11, 148, 148 n.1, 149 n.3, 156 n.4
probability: 123 n.27
process: 108, 113
prohibition: 156
pronoun: 5, 16 n.12, 17 n.6, 42 n.3, 54 n.1; determinate, 25 n.34; antecedent of, 35 n.65, 143, 144, 153, 154; reflexive, 35 n.65, 143 n.11; reciprocal, 143, 143 n.11; relative, 143, 143 n.11, 154; interrogative, 149; permuting a, 154. *See also* 'himself'
pronunciation, compounded/divided: 29 n.47, 30, 68, 68 n.37, 76, 76 n.22, 77, 137, 137 n.16, 138, 139, 142–143, 144, 145, 146, 147, 152, 157. *See also* intonation-patterns; sense, compounded/divided
proof: 21 n.19, 23 n.27, 29 n.48; inductive, 29, 29 n.45&49, 37 n.75, 50 n.9, 63 n.26, 145, 146–147
properties of terms: 5, 6. *See also* appellation; copulation; signification; supposition
property: 24 n.29
proposition: 13 n.1, 91, 91 n.7, 94, 94 n.2&3, 119, 126; copulative, 29, 68, 76, 135, 139–140, 148; twentieth-century notion of, 96 n.10; conditional, 118 n.8, 118–122, 119 n.10,11,13,14,&15, 120, 120 n.16&18, 121, 121 n.19&20, 122, 123 n.27, 124, 124 n.30, 125, 126 n.34, 127 n.39&41, 131 n.13, 138, 140, 153 n.15; categorical, 119 n.15, 120–122, 121 n.20, 141, 153 n.15; one understood along with another, 127; one considered from the standpoint of another, 128; whole, 130; actual, 135, 135 n.3; disjunctive, 141, 143, 148, 153, 153 n.15, 157; trivial, 153, 153 n.17; hypothetical, 153 n.15; disjunctive conditional, 157. *See also* statement
Pythagoreans: 23 n.27

quale quid: 32 n.59, 32–33, 33 n.60, 36
qualification: 14 n.4
quality: 14 n.4, 18, 18 n.7, 44, 69, 70, 70 n.2, 71 n.10, 84
quantifier: 17 n.6, 30 n.50, 32 n.56
quantity: 60 n.10, 71 n.10; adverb of, 81
question: 149. *See also* interrogation
'*quicumque vel quiscumque*': 40
'*quilibet*': 40
'*quisque*': 40
'*quotlibet*': 59 n.8

real thing: 40, 42, 43, 58, 59, 70, 90 n.3. *See also* reality, corresponding
reality: 26; corresponding, 42 n.5, 108, 140, 158; ordering of things in, 123
reason: 26
reasoning: 127, 127 n.39
reduplication: 20, 20 n.12, 144, 144 n.13& 14
reference: 98
referential opacity: 35 n.65
referring of a word: 36–37
relation: 29, 29 n.49, 30, 70, 70 n.2, 71 n.10, 117, 117 n.4&6; principle of a, 117. *See also* word relating mediately or immediately to another
removal, specific/universal: 73
replacement: 35 n.65
rhetoric: 16 n.13, 31 n.55
rule: *see* inference, rules of; suppositions, rule of; three, rule of

scholasticism: 19 n.9
'*sciendum quod*': 17 n.2
scientia sermocinalis: 16 n.13
scope: 15 n.8, 30 n.50, 32 n.56, 45 n.7, 62 n.22. *See also* function, elements falling under or outside; function, inclusion of one by another; function, one falling over or under another; negation, scope of
Scott, Theodore Kermit: 21 n.18
secundum quod et simpliciter: *see* in a certain respect as well as absolutely
self-reference, paradoxes of: *see insolubilia*
semantics: 17 n.1, 34 n.64, 117 n.4
semblance: 136, 136 n.9
sense, compounded/divided: 29, 29 n.47, 31, 38, 38 n.79, 46, 46 n.10, 49, 49 n.6, 50, 50 n.8&9, 52, 54, 54 n.25, 55, 57, 57 n.3, 68, 68 n.37, 69, 75, 76, 76 n.24, 77, 79, 85 n.20, 89, 89 n.32, 95, 103, 103 n.13, 114, 114 n.23, 115, 121, 121 n.20, 122, 122 n.25, 124, 125, 130, 133, 135, 135 n.4, 137, 145, 146, 147, 152, 153, 157, 157 n.3. *See also* pronunciation, compounded/divided; statement, senses of
senses, interchangeability of: 49
sentence: 13 n.3, 24 n.29, 116, 116 n.2, 121 n.23, 140; compound, 116; parts of, 116
separation: 59, 70, 71
Siger of Courtrai: 94 n.2
Sign: 17 n.4, 90 n.3, 91, 119; universal, 15, 15 n.9, 17 n.6, 36 n.67, 40, 62 n.19, 152, 153; distributive, 16, 31–32, 34, 35 n.65,

43, 44, 46–47, 48 *n.20&23*, 57, 69, 71 *n.12*, 79; particular, 36 *n.67*, 62 *n.19*; negative, 48, 57, 62 *n.19*, 96 *n.8*; affirmative, 62 *n.19*, 96 *n.8*
significance, conventional: 91 *n.8*, 141 *n.3*
signification: 5, 13 *n.2*, 14 *n.4*, 15, 15 *n.7&9*, 17, 17 *n.1,4,&6*, 18 *n.7*, 24 *n.29*, 29, 30, 37, 38, 40 *n.2*, 41, 44 *n.2*, 45 *n.6*, 46, 46 *n.10*, 58, 67, 68, 69, 70, 70 *n.2&8*, 71, 72, 76, 78, 90, 90 *n.2&4*, 91, 91 *n.8*, 94 *n.2*, 101, 101 *n.5*, 102, 102 *n.9&11*, 103, 104, 105, 107, 108, 114, 116, 117, 117 *n.7*, 119 *n.12*, 121, 125, 128 *n.43*, 129, 130, 131, 133, 137, 138 *n.20*, 139, 140, 141 *n.1&3*, 142, 143, 144, 145, 146, 147, 151, 152, 153, 157; proper/improper, 26 *n.37*; first, 81, 81 *n.1*; indefinite, 117; completion of, 129; express, 131; primary/secondary, 131, 131 *n.14*. See *also* consignification; denotation; designation; indication; noting
significatum: 59, 91; supposited, 104
signifying, modes of: 94, 94 *n.2*
single things: 22, 26, 29, 37, 38, 48, 63, 65, 71, 71 *n.10*, 92. See *also* individuals; particulars
solution: 21 *n.19*, 33 *n.60*
'some': 17 *n.4*
'something': 62
sophismata: 4, 21 *n.18&19*, 22 *n.23*, and *passim*
sophistical reasoning: 6, 136 *n.9*
sort: 44 *n.4*, 45. See *also* genus; kind; species
speakers: intentions of, 34 *n.64*, 95, 123; mental acts of, 118
species: 14 *n.4*, 19, 19 *n.11*, 20 *n.12*, 21, 22, 39 *n.81*, 48, 62 *n.17*, 65 *n.32*, 72
species term: 19
specificant: 92, 92 *n.13*, 93 *n.17*
specificate: 92, 92 *n.13*
specification: 92, 92 *n.13*
speech, parts of: 13 *n.2*, 55, 94 *n.2*, 141 *n.4*
standing for: 23, 23 *n.24*, 24, 27, 30, 36, 39, 43, 46, 50, 52, 85, 86, 99, 112, 113, 142, 144, 147, 154. See *also* supposition
state: 117, 117 *n.4&6*, 123; fixed, 108–109, 109 *n.10*, 110, 112 *n.20&23*, 113 *n.27*, 114, 114 *n.29&30*; successive, 109, 109 *n.10*, 110, 112 *n.20&23*, 113
stateables: 96–97, 96 *n.10*, 98 *n.15*, 110, 110 *n.16*, 111 *n.18*, 155
statement: 5, 13, 13 *n.1*, 16 *n.12*, 96 *n.10*; principal and secondary parts of, 13, 13

n.2&3, 14, 15, 15 *n.7&8*, 16, 16 *n.12*; universal affirmative, 24 *n.30,31,&32*, 25 *n.35*, 30, 38 *n.78*, 45 *n.7*, 66; particular negative, 24 *n.31*; singular affirmative, 24 *n.32*, 25 *n.34*, 30, 71, 104 *n.17*, 132 *n.20*, 145, 146, 151, 152; corresponding, 24 *n.32*, 50, 51, 66; senses of, 29 *n.47*, 41, 42–43, 51, 53 *n.18*, 72, 77, 79, 83, 86, 86 *n.24*, 87, 88, 89, 104, 121, 127 *n.41*, 128 *n.42*, 130, 131, 131 *n.16*, 133, 136, 137 *n.16&17*, 142, 142 *n.8*, 143, 145, 146–147, 153; particular affirmative, 45 *n.7*, 46 *n.9*, 132 *n.20*; universal negative, 53 *n.17*; exceptive, 66, 67; original, 66, 72; plural, 71; negative, 71, 74, 95–98, 99, 127, 132, 140; affirmative, 74, 95, 99, 127, 132; modal, 100 *n.1*. See *also* proposition
subject: 5, 14 *n.4&5*, 15, 15 *n.7,8,&11*, 16, 16 *n.12*, 17, 17 *n.5&6*, 18, 18 *n.7&8*, 20 *n.12*, 22, 27 *n.42*, 30, 37, 38, 39, 40, 41, 46, 52, 61, 61 *n.15*, 62 *n.17*, 64 *n.27*, 66, 69, 71, 73, 74, 75, 77, 80, 81, 82, 85, 85 *n.19*, 90, 91, 94, 100, 101, 102, 102 *n.8*, 104, 104 *n.17*, 107, 107 *n.3*, 108, 116, 130, 131, 134, 141, 144, 148; parts of, 15 *n.9*, 17 *n.6*, 18, 18 *n.7*, 51 *n.13*; subsumed under, 25, 26, 48 *n.2*; instance of, 25 *n.35*; one in respect of another, 116; conditioned, 122; existence of, 129; disjoined, 141
subjection: 140
substance: 13 *n.2*, 14 *n.4*, 17–18, 18 *n.7*, 27 *n.42*, 41, 41 *n.2*, 42, 48, 84, 84 *n.12*, 101, 101 *n.5*; primary/secondary, 14 *n.4*, 18 *n.7*, 27 *n.42*; infinite or indefinite, 18, 18 *n.7*, 44; diversity in, 84
substantive: 45 *n.6*. See *also* name, substantival
subtracting: 58
superior: 20, 20 *n.12*, 24, 24 *n.31*, 36 *n.69&70*, 73, 93, 99, 99 *n.19*, 116, 154–155; argument from the, 53 *n.20*
superlative: 113
supervening: 140
suppositing, act of: 131
supposition: 5, 13 *n.2*, 15 *n.7*, 17 *n.6*, 23 *n.24*, 30, 30 *n.52*, 40, 40 *n.2*, 44 *n.2*, 52 *n.16*, 53, 63, 64, 98 *n.16*, 106 *n.1*, 136, 151; merely confused, 30, 30 *n.52*, 31, 31 *n.56*, 33 *n.60&61*, 35 *n.66*, 39, 45, 45 *n.6&7*, 51, 64 *n.27*, 86 *n.21*, 111–113, 136, 158 *n.5*; determinate, 30 *n.52*, 31, 31 *n.56*, 33 *n.60&61*, 35 *n.66*, 45, 45 *n.7*, 46, 50 *n.9*, 51, 86 *n.21*, 136, 158, 158 *n.5*; change of, 31–32, 33–34; distribu-

171]

tive confused, 33 *n.61*, 45 *n.7*, 61, 64 *n.27*, 64–65, 86 *n.21*, 113; mobile/immobile, 36, 105; simple, 65 *n.32*, 102, 102 *n.9*, 158, 158 *n.5*; virtual, 86, 86 *n.22*; personal, 102, 102 *n.11*; significative, 138; material, 138, 138 *n.20*, 139 *n.22*; formal, 138 *n.20*. *See also* standing for
suppositions, rule of: 52, 52 *n.16*, 98 *n.16*
suppositum: 23 *n.26*, 24 *n.29*, 26 *n.38*, 27 *n.40*, 28, 30, 33, 35, 37, 41, 43, 43 *n.1*, 44, 45, 45 *n.7*, 48 *n.23*, 57, 60, 63, 86, 102, 102 *n.8*, 104, 105, 142, 154; designated, 65
syllable: 129
syllogism: 13 *n.1*, 23 *n.25*, 24 *n.31*, 26, 26 *n.36*
syllogization: 143
syncategorematic notion: 134
syncategorematic relation: 134
syncategorematic words: 5, 5 *n.8*, 13 *n.3*, 14–16, 15 *n.8&10*, 16 *n.12&13*, 17, 17 *n.6*, 40, 41, 42, 44, 45, 47, 58, 60, 62 *n.22*, 69–70, 70 *n.2&6*, 80, 81, 90, 90 *n.1&5*, 100, 101, 106–107, 106 *n.1*, 107 *n.3*, 108, 108 *n.8*, 111 *n.18*; function of, 5, 17, 17 *n.1*, 18, 51, 56 *n.6*, 70, 70 *n.2*, 71 *n.12*, 100 *n.2*, 116, 131; signification of, 5, 17, 17 *n.1*, 42, 44, 59, 70 *n.2*, 93, 134, 140, 148, 148 *n.1*, 157; treatises on, 6–8, 7 *n.13*
synonymy: 17 *n.4*
syntax: 17 *n.1*, 117 *n.4*, 118 *n.8*

Tartaret, Peter: 106 *n.1*
tautology: 113
temporal distinctions: 106 *n.1*
temporal metaphor (of statement construction): 28, 28 *n.43*, 37 *n.75*, 54, 54 *n.24*, 62, 62 *n.20&22*, 66, 80, 81 *n.39*, 90, 102–103, 103 *n.12*, 137, 139
term: 5, 6, 19, 23, 23 *n.26*, 141, 141 *n.3*; common, 17 *n.6*, 25 *n.34*, 26 *n.38*, 26–27, 70, 70 *n.7*, 96 *n.10*, 111, 146; minor, 23 *n.25*, 142; major, 23 *n.25*, 142, 143, 144 *n.14*; middle, 23 *n.25*, 143; discrete or singular, 25 *n.34&35*, 25–26, 37, 70, 70 *n.7*, 71; distributed/undistributed, 36, 36 *n.69*, 37, 37 *n.75*, 143; community of, 43; prescinded, 79; copulated, 80, 82–83; whole of/part of, 82, 83, 142; disjoined, 83 *n.10*, 83–84, 142, 146; concrete, 84 *n.11*, 84–85; equivocal, 85; negation of, 94–95; infinite, 136, 136 *n.5*; affirmative, 137; privative, 150; relative, 150. *See also* predicate; subject.
term involving a clause or phrase: 28–29, 52, 75–76, 77, 85, 85 *n.20*
term taken conjunctively/divisively: 60, 78, 78 *n.31*, 80, 84, 84 *n.11*. *See also* 'every' or 'all' (*omnis*) taken collectively/distributively; 'every' or 'all' (*omnis*) taken divisively; number words taken collectively
terms, convertible: 85, 85 *n.16*
theses: 150
thing, categorical: 69, 70, 70 *n.2*
thing itself: *see* real thing
things belonging to names or verbs: 14, 14 *n.5*, 15, 15 *n.7*, 29, 92, 92 *n.12*, 100, 101, 101 *n.5*, 104, 116. *See also* act
'things of any and every sort': 44
thought, complete: 141 *n.3*; supplied in, 119, 119 *n.11&13*, 128
three, rule of: 23 *n.27*, 23–24, 24 *n.30&32*, 25 *n.34&35*, 26, 26 *n.38*, 27 *n.39*, 32 *n.58*, 43 *n.3*, 52 *n.16*, 105 *n.21*
Thurot, Charles: 94 *n.2*
time: 107, 109, 109 *n.12*, 110, 112, 127, 127 *n.41*, 128 *n.42*; present, 23 *n.26*, 52 *n.15&16*, 52–53, 98, 104, 109, 110, 112, 112 *n.20,23,&25*, 113, 115, 123, 123 *n.29*; consignified, 31; exception in cases involving more than one, 68–69; future, 101 *n.7*, 104, 109, 112, 112 *n.23*, 113, 115, 122, 123, 123 *n.29*; past, 109, 112, 112 *n.20&23*, 123 *n.29*, 128 *n.42*; copulation of, 112
totality: 23, 23 *n.27*, 58, 60, 60 *n.10*
transformation: 32–34
truth: 49, 66, 78, 83, 119, 119 *n.10,11,& 13*, 120, 120 *n.16&18*, 122, 123, 123 *n.27&29*, 124, 126, 127, 135, 147, 155; analytic, 21 *n.18*; causes of, 95–98; mode of, 96; absolute, 104
truth conditions: 29, 68, 76, 120 *n.18*, 121 *n.19*, 124 *n.30*, 135, 140–141, 153, 157. *See also* verification
truth-value, alteration of: 28 *n.43*

understanding: 13, 70, 70 *n.8*, 95, 119 *n.12*, 131, 139, 144, 145, 149
unity: 84
universality: 15 *n.11*, 17, 17 *n.6*, 18, 18 *n.7*
universals: 17 *n.6*, 20, 27, 27 *n.41&42*
'unless' (*nisi*): Ch. XVIII *passim*
use/mention distinction: 138 *n.20*

utterance: 59, 91 *n.8*, 119, 138 *n.20*, 140, 144
verb: 5, 13, 13 *n.3*, 14 *n.5*, 16 *n.12*, 51, *n.11*, 81–82, 90, 90 *n.4*, 92 *n.14*, 93, 98 *n.16*, 100, 101, 101 *n.5*, 119, 120, 121, 121 *n.23*, 130, 130 *n.12*, 147, 149; principal, 50, 50 *n.10*, 53, 53 *n.23*, 57 verb resolved into 'is' and participle: 91, 91 *n.11*
verb taken absolutely/transitively: 133, 156
verification: 95, 96

Wallerand, G.: 94 *n.2*
well-formedness: 19 *n.11*
'whatever': 74
'when': 30–31
'when' taken indefinitely/relatively: 31, 31 *n.54*
'whenever': 31
'whether ... or ...' (*sive*): 40, 153, 154, Ch. XXIV *passim*
'whether' or 'or' (*an*): Ch. XXII *passim*
whole: 58, 61, 61 *n.16*, 69, 74, 76, 82; universal, 39, 39 *n.81*; collective/integral, 39, 39 *n.82*, 60; quantitative, 39 *n.81*, 53, 53 *n.19*, 99, 99 *n.17*, 127; universally distributed, 60
'whole' (*totum*): 15 *n.10*, 17, 17 *n.5*, Ch. II *passim*, 60
'whole' (*totum*) taken collectively/distributively: 60
wholeness: 40
William of Sherwood: death, 3; rector of Attleborough, 3; rector of Aylesbury, 3; treasurer of Lincoln Cathedral, 3; influence on others, 3, 4; at Oxford, 3, 8; in Paris, 3, 8; as a logician, 5–7; relative dates of composition of works, 6; and Peter of Spain, 6–8
WORKS: *Conciones*, 4; *De insolubilibus*, 4, 55, 55 *n.3*; *Distinctiones theologicae*, 4; *Introductiones in logicam*, 3, 4, 5, 6, 9, 13 *n.1,2,&3*, 14 *n.4*, 15 *n.7*, 17 *n.3,4,&6*, 21 *n.18*, 22 *n.21*, 23 *n.24*, 24 *n.28&29*, 25 *n.34*, 28 *n.44*, 33 *n.61*, 34 *n.64*, 35 *n.66*, 39 *n.81*, 44 *n.2*, 45 *n.6*, 48 *n.2*, 51 *n.13*, 52 *n.16*, 56 *n.7*, 58 *n.5*, 63 *n.23*, 65 *n.32*, 85 *n.16*, 86 *n.22*, 90 *n.4*, 92 *n.14*, 96 *n.8*, 98 *n.16*, 100 *n.1*, 101 *n.5&7*, 115 *n.35*, 119 *n.12*, 120 *n.17&18*, 121 *n.22*, 122 *n.24*, 127 *n.37&38*, 134 *n.3*, 136 *n.9*, 138 *n.20*, 141 *n.3*, 142 *n.9*, 153 *n.15&17*; *Obligationes*, 4, 4 *n.5*; *Petitiones contrariorum*, 4; *Shirovodus super sententias*, 4; *Syncategoremata*, 4, 6–9, 7 *n.12*, 15 *n.8*, 16 *n.12*, 19 *n.9*, 21 *n.18*, 22 *n.21,22,&23*, 23 *n.24*, 106 *n.1*
Wilson, Curtis: 21 *n.18*, 106 *n.1*, 108 *n.10*
word: 5, 14 *n.4*, 28 *n.43*, 74, 91 *n.8*, 94 *n.2*, 141 *n.3*; ending of a, 129; what occurs before a, 133; what occurs after a, 133, 134, 142. *See also* categorematic words; commonly, words taken; conjoining (or adjoining) of words with states; syncategorematic words
word relating mediately or immediately to another: 81–82, 89
words, acts carried out by means of, 131

www.ingramcontent.com/pod-product-compliance
Lightning Source LLC
Chambersburg PA
CBHW061447300426
44114CB00014B/1876